The Palestinians in Israel

International Library of Sociology

Founded by Karl Mannheim
Editor: John Rex, University of Warwick

Arbor Scientiae
Arbor Vitae

A catalogue of the books available in the **International Library of Sociology** and other series of Social Science books published by Routledge & Kegan Paul will be found at the end of this volume.

The Palestinians in Israel

A study in internal colonialism

Elia T. Zureik
Queen's University, Canada

Routledge & Kegan Paul
London, Boston and Henley

First published in 1979
by Routledge & Kegan Paul Ltd
39 Store Street,
London WC1E 7DD,
Broadway House,
Newtown Road,
Henley-on-Thames,
Oxon RG9 1EN and
9 Park Street,
Boston, Mass. 02108, USA
Set in 10 on 11pt Times by
Kelly & Wright, Bradford-on-Avon, Wiltshire
and printed in Great Britain by
Redwood Burn Ltd
Trowbridge and Esher

British Library Cataloguing in Publication Data

Zureik, Elia T

The Palestinians in Israel. – (International library of sociology).
1. Palestinian Arabs – Israel
I. Title II. Series
301. 45'19'2705694 DS113.7 78–40860

ISBN 0 7100 0016 2

Palestine ceased to be the strip
of land from which our forefathers
had come. We filled it with the
frenzied passion of years of
statelessness till it ceased to be
a state and became a state of mind.

Fawaz Turki
A Palestinian Writer

Contents

Preface

The present study is the culmination of research carried out during the last four years into the sociology of the Arabs in Israel. When I started this study, the availability of published research in this area was minimal. I therefore intended, to some extent, to remedy this situation, although after I had embarked upon an extensive search of the literature it became apparent that there were other works in the making dealing with the Arabs in Israel. I thus found myself being constantly overtaken, not only by the daily events in the Middle East, but also by the output of research in this area, as evident in the publishers' lists of the last four years. Indeed, as I was preparing the final chapter, the date of the 1977 Israeli elections was set. I have decided not to incorporate the implications of the Likud victory, for I had anticipated some of these implications in my discussion in Chapter 6.

There are numerous political and historical studies of the Middle East and the Palestine conflict. What is lacking, in my view, is a sociological interpretation of the Arabs in Israel, looking at Israeli society from the vantage point of race and ethnic relations. Even here I do not claim a monopoly of interest, since others' interest is revealed in the quantity of unpublished PhD theses and other research reviewed in this study, all of which deals with the sociological-anthropological aspects of the Arabs in Israel.

Many institutions and individuals helped in making this study possible. Foremost to be thanked is the Institute for Palestine Studies in Beirut, Lebanon, which made its research facilities available to me during the summer of 1974, and on other occasions. Dr Elias Shoufani of the Institute's Hebrew division provided much-needed assistance in gaining access to Hebrew sources. Likewise the co-operation of researchers and library staff at the Institute is greatly appreciated. To the editor of the *Journal of Palestine Studies*,

Professor Hisham Sharabi of Georgetown University, who has encouraged me to test some of my ideas by publishing parts of this research in the *Journal*, I would like to express my appreciation. Queen's University and the Department of Sociology granted me leave of absence in 1975 to pursue this research, and the School of Graduate Studies provided a grant for the typing and editing of the final manuscript.

Various individuals have commented either on parts of the manuscript or on its entirety. I am grateful to all of them. In particular, I would like to record my gratitude to Professors Janet Abu-Lughod and Ibrahim Abu-Lughod of Northwestern University, Noam Chomsky of MIT, and Khalil Nakhleh of St John's University, Minnesota. My wife, Mary, must be credited with providing the home environment for numerous stimulating discussions on the Middle East. This book is in large measure also the product of her enthusiasm.

I owe special thanks to Donald Pike for editing the final manuscript before it was sent to press.

None of the above individuals or institutions is to be held responsible for any interpretations I have made throughout this study. The responsibility is solely mine.

Elia Zureik
Kingston, Ontario

Acknowledgments

Acknowledgments are due to the *Journal of Palestine Studies* for granting me permission to use some of my material which was previously published in the *Journal*, to Frank Cass publishers for their permission to quote from John Cooley's *Green March, Black September* and to Medina University Press for allowing me to quote from Naseer Aruri (ed.), *The Palestinian Resistance to Israeli Occupation*. I also acknowledge the co-operation of my colleagues K. Nakhleh, Rosemary Sayigh and Ian Lustick for allowing me to quote from their unpublished researches on the Palestinians.

1 The problem stated

The first obstacle facing a researcher interested in the sociology of the Arabs in Israel is the paucity of published and reliable research in this field. While Israeli sociologists have written extensively on their society, they have tended to ignore the indigenous Arab population. This absence of a significant academic interest in the sociology of the Arabs in Israel is highlighted by the following comment made by S. M. Lipset:[1]

> Almost none of the academic research and policy decisions about the problems of education, or social mobility, ever deal with Arab citizens of the country. . . . Articles about the Israeli situation which break down attainments and statuses by ethnic background are generally headed 'The Israeli —— System', but have no column for the over 400,000 Israeli Arabs who comprise 14 percent of the population of the State.

The sociological literature coming out of Israel is replete with examples of this sort. A clear case of what Lipset's comment implies emerges from a 1974 paper by an established Israeli sociologist, Chaim Adler, entitled 'Social stratification and education in Israel'. One looks in vain in Adler's study for a discussion of the Arabs' place in the Israeli stratification system. Instead, one comes across the following footnote explaining why the Arabs were excluded from the analysis:[2]

> It ought to be stated quite clearly that this analysis does not deal with another aspect of stratification within Israel, namely the Arab–Jewish division. This has, unfortunately, so far been first and foremost a political problem and only secondarily a social or educational one.

Throughout the first fifteen to twenty years of the Jewish State's existence, academic research by Israeli sociologists – except in a very few cases – avoided examining the social consequences of the apparent transformation of the Palestinian Arabs from a majority to a minority, the occupational changes accompanying this transformation, and the likely repercussions on the internal workings of Israeli society, including the place of the Palestinians in it, not to mention the Arab–Israeli conflict in which the Palestinian question plays a central role. It is accurate to say that it was not until the middle of the 1960s that the first piece of sizeable research on the Israeli Arabs was published. Even here, one must admit, the research was limited in scope and funded through a contract from the US Department of Health, Education and Welfare.[3] The post-1967 period, which saw a marked increase in Arab politicization, was also a period which witnessed an upsurge of policy-oriented research on the Arab minority.

What little Israeli research has been done on the Arabs in Israel is mainly socio-psychological as well as socio-anthropological and tends to be ahistorical and is often rooted in the tradition of microsociology. In certain cases, this literature focuses on patterns of prejudice and social contact between Arabs and Jews, and in others it follows traditional approaches to modernization and development as evolved by social and cultural anthropologists. To mention the few main researches in the area of Arab sociology in Israel, we note Raphael Patai's[4] work on Middle Eastern societies, including Israel; Emanuel Marx's[5] research on the Bedouins; Erik Cohen's[6] work on Arab youth; Yochanan Peres'[7] investigations of Jewish–Arab ethnic relations; the most recent work, at the Technion, by E. Yalan and his colleagues,[8] which concerned itself with modernization of Arab villages; and finally Henry Rosenfeld's[9] research, resulting from his long-standing interest in the proletarianization of the Palestinian Arab peasantry. In its attempt to examine the transformation of the Arab class structure, Rosenfeld's work could be singled out as the main exception to mainstream social science research on the Arabs in Israel, although, as will be shown in this study, his work is mostly carried out with little regard for the colonial-settler character of Israeli society.

Still, it is striking that out of close to 300 bibliographical references cited by L. Weller[10] in his *Sociology in Israel*, only one or two relate directly to the Arabs. To be precise, out of 270 pages of text in Weller's book, a sum total of one to two pages are devoted to summarizing research on the Israeli Arabs. A perusal of a bibliographical volume, edited by Haya Gratch,[11] outlining the research carried out in the last twenty-five years by the Israeli Institute of Applied Social Research, produces a similar picture. And, as Noam Chomsky[12] rightly points out, Eisenstadt's[13] lengthy book *Israeli Society* devotes no more than 16 out of its 450 or so pages to the

'Non-Jewish Minority Groups'. This curious omission is repeated in another anthology,[14] of around 700 pages, edited by three noted Israeli sociologists, including Eisenstadt. We are offered two samples of Israeli sociology dealing with the Arabs: the 'Sedentarization of the Bedouin in Israel' and 'The Status of Arab Village Women'.

To overcome this research problem posed by Lipset, one has to turn to primary sources in Arabic, Hebrew and English, as well as to the total corpus of writings about the Palestinians, including material written by others who are not bona fide academics or scholars and who have been critical either of the thrust of fashionable interpretations offered by Israeli social scientists, or of the lack of research to begin with. Likewise, writings by Palestinian Arabs under Israeli rule, taken in conjunction with the mounting critical research by a minority of Israeli and ex-Israeli researchers, are useful sources in remedying this deficiency. But, in our view, a shortage of authoritative research is not the whole problem. A crucial deficiency of research on the Palestinians lies in the theoretical perspectives which typify the writings of Israeli and Western academics. As mentioned earlier, most of this research is dedicated to singling out the cultural and psychological peculiarities of Arabs and Jews, thus anchoring the roots of the conflict in the mental and psychic configurations of the protagonists.

It is the task of the sociology of knowledge to attempt an explanation of the lack of research on the Arabs in Israel. It must be stated, in passing, that this under-representation in established sociological circles of research on minorities is not a phenomenon peculiar to Israel. Recent Black Studies courses in American universities, and similar programmes on Native Studies (Indian and Inuit peoples) in Canadian universities, are two examples of reaction against this state of affairs which come to mind; in both cases the impetus came from the minorities themselves in their attempt to remedy a deficient and often biased treatment of their social history in North American academia. Moreover, an increase in interest in the study of minorities and native peoples is usually generated by changes in the social climate of the time. In the case of North America – and more recently England – social protest and violence in the context of race and ethnic relations have been followed by social-problem-oriented research. One can safely make the same observation in regard to Israel. For example, interest in researching the Oriental Jews (Jewish immigrants from the Arab countries of the Middle East and North Africa) is becoming increasingly fashionable among Israeli social scientists; this could best be understood as a direct correlate of acts of protest emanating from Oriental Jews, be they large-scale riots such as those which took place in Haifa's slum district of Wadi Salib in the late 1950s or the more recent bloody encounters in Tel Aviv between the Israeli Black Panthers and the police. The government's exhaustive investigation into the economic status of, and social discrimination against, Oriental Jews should be seen, not in the sudden revelations of poverty among this group, but in the context of the adoption of violent tactics by the disadvantaged Jews in Israel.[15]

A similar argument could be advanced in the case of the Arabs in Israel. It is puzzling to many Israelis that a section of Arab youth, most of whom were raised in this society, participate in guerrilla activities and express publicly their hostility to Israel;[16] likewise, the increasing unrest among the intellectual strata of Arabs in Israel is posing serious problems to the authorities. It is in the context of these phenomena that one can grasp fully the mounting Israeli interest, in government and academic circles, concerning the situation of the Arab minority.[17]

We are not implying here that such research has addressed itself to the particular social problem from the vantage point of the minorities. Far from it. Until recently, the sociologist has not only adopted the 'official' labelling of what is problematic, but also has borrowed a world-view which is in agreement with the dominant ideology. In this sense it is the sociological locus of the problem which has become the problem itself; in other words, the formulation of the solution to a particular social problem is rooted within the problem itself, which in turn has been defined in terms of the minority at hand; in short, the minority is seen as the problem! Adler's remarks which we quoted earlier are an example of this type of reasoning.

While researchers in the past tended to adopt a passive view of whichever minority they happened to be studying, the last decade or so has seen a change in the perspectives used in examining the situation of the blacks in the United States, the North American Indians, blacks in South Africa, and so on; the tendency to consider the fate of subordinate groups as a matter to be decided solely by those in positions of superordination has been replaced by more dynamic approaches. Black militancy in the United States, politicization of the North American Indian, and guerrilla warfare in Africa have prompted many sociologists to seek alternative explanations of race and ethnic relations. Conflict rather than consensus over values, separatism rather than assimilation, are increasingly entertained as viable analytical approaches.[18]

In the light of what has been said above, our purpose in this study is twofold: first, to fill a gap in the literature on the sociology of the Arabs in Israel; second, to delineate the institutional and ideological bases which govern the relationship between the subordinate Palestinian Arab minority and the dominant Zionist regime.

Specifically, in Chapter 2 we present a theoretical discussion dealing with pluralism, dependency theory and internal colonialism. It is expected that such an exposition will provide us with the necessary theoretical and conceptual tools with which to highlight the sociological features of the Arabs in Israel.

No thorough understanding of the current social structure of the Arabs in Israel could be attained solely on the basis of what has ensued in the last twenty-nine years or so, since Israel came into being. The Jewish–Arab cleavage is the result of a historical relationship dating back to the earlier part of this century, when the first serious attempt at Jewish colonization of Palestine took place – though there had been previous, unsuccessful attempts in the latter part of the last century. To substantiate empirically our thesis that the Jewish settlement in Palestine resulted in the land expropriation and social class distortion of Arab peasantry – irrespective of the intentions of Zionist ideologists – the evidence we provide must demonstrate that the economic development of the Jewish sector was accompanied by a corresponding underdevelopment and stagnation of the Arab sector. Our principal concern in Chapter 3 is to be able to show that, contrary to popular belief, the two sectors, the Arab and the Jewish, *did not develop separately and independently under similar conditions*, but that they were interconnected in an *asymmetrical* relationship, mediated by the British presence. Any separate developments that may have taken place did so only in socio-cultural areas, although here too they provided the ideological basis for the politico-economic asymmetry that was developing at that time.

Therefore, our historical treatment of the British Mandate period in Chapter 3 will be carried out in such a way as to depict the nature of the transformation of the Palestinian class structure and its eventual distortion, the consequences of the incursion of a European-financed capitalist economy on the Palestinian non-capitalist mode of production, and the consequences of British political and economic policies in Palestine.

Our task in Chapter 4 is to assess the place of Israeli writings on the Arab minority in the context of the theoretical perspective discussed earlier. In doing so, our central concern is to examine critically the relevance of the 'culture' thesis, advanced so often in writings on the Middle East, in explaining the situation of the Arabs in Israel, and to suggest in the coming chapters a shifting of emphasis taking into account the primacy of political economy in explaining the workings of settler societies.

Chapter 5 provides a logical continuation of the historical discussion presented earlier. In terms of the experience of the Palestinian Arabs, we contend that the post-1948 period ushered in a third cycle of colonialism: the first took place during the Ottoman rule; the second consisted of a mixture of Anglo-Zionist dominations, each possessing characteristics of its own; the latest cycle under Israeli rule has its own specificity manifested in the further transformation of Palestinian class structure from a communally based, land owning peasantry to a 'declassed' stratum, the continuing process of dispossession of Arabs of their land, and the eventual emergence of succinct patterns of prejudice and discrimination. The result of this third cycle of internal colonialism is that, except for a thin stratum of Arab compradors, it prevented the emergence either of a genuinely organized working-class segment among the Arabs, or of a bourgeoisie, capable of playing their respective roles in Arab political and economic life.

One institutional indicator of domination which we discuss in Chapter 5 is the Israeli legal framework of colonization, in particular as it impinges on the dispossession of Palestinian Arabs of their land. If it is the case that the institutional framework fosters discriminatory practices, such practices should find support in the system of beliefs and attitudes which typify the orientation of the Jewish majority. Turning to various socio-psychological and attitudinal studies, we document in Chapter 6, among other things, the saliency of another indicator of domination: patterns of prejudice and their consequences for the Arab minority in Israel. In addition to prejudice, we examine the nature of educational recruitment in the Arab sector and the outcome of being a subordinate minority as reflected in the encounter with social control agencies.

No matter how ruthless colonialism is, it produces its own contradictions and unanticipated consequences. Whereas in Chapter 2 we deal with Palestinian Arab reaction to the British Mandate and Zionist settlers, in the case of post-1948 Palestine we focus on the politicization of Arabs and the role of the Arab intelligentsia of students and writers in the context of Palestinian protest movements and Israeli political culture. It has become obvious to many that, contrary to the popular expectation held by many Israeli policy-makers, the more educated the Arabs become the less likely it is that they will respond positively to their situation in Israel. However, the noticeable protest activities exhibited by educated young Arabs lack a corresponding link with the larger segment of the Arab rural proletariat. The marginal class position of the majority of Palestinian Arab workers in Israel explains, in part, why a working-class protest movement has failed to emerge. A complete explanation of this failure has also to take into account the extent of the system of control and the lack of any rapport or alliance with the Jewish working classes. This is due to the fact that the latter have been organized by a nationalist trade union, the Histadrut, whose institutional structure is predicated on Zionist doctrine even though Arab workers are now accepted as members of the Histadrut.

In conclusion, we expect that a sociological study of the Arabs in Israel will highlight a relatively unresearched aspect of the Arab–Israeli conflict and will stimulate further research, placing the study of the conflict into a proper perspective, that of race and ethnic relations, with internal colonialism as its main focus.

2 The theoretical framework

No other topic of discussion in recent times has generated so much polemic in political and academic circles as has commentary on the nature of Israeli society. Not too long ago, though to a lesser extent now, a critical assessment of Israeli policies would provoke emotional accusations, often loaded with charges of anti-Semitism, even when the critics were Jews or Israelis. The political pundit James Reston could thus declare:[1] 'You can put it down as a general rule that any criticism of Israel's policies will be attacked as anti-semitism.' In the light of this it is understandable that many academics should think carefully before uttering what might be construed as criticism of Israeli institutions and policies. Many a professional career has been jeopardized on the altar of intellectual discussion and debate when the issue at hand involved Zionism, Israel or the Israeli–Arab conflict.

This situation has created an unhealthy political, moral and intellectual immunity which, for a long time, put Israel beyond the limits of critical analysis. The result, as far as social science writings about Israel are concerned, has been to produce a nationalistic, inwardly oriented interpretation of Israeli society which reflected preoccupation with Jewish social problems as these problems were defined by the ideologists of Zionism and the Jewish State. It is natural to expect that under such circumstances the Arabs would be assigned a peripheral role in Israeli sociological investigations.

Until recently, the Western view of Israel – a view adhered to by the mass media, social scientists, and policy-makers alike – acknowledged the pioneering, spartan and socialist character of the state, best epitomized in the *kibbutz* and the Israeli fighting soldier. The Israeli experiment captured the imagination of many Western social scientists. Peter Worsley, a leading figure in the British sociological establishment, is swept away by the communal image of Israel to the extent of recommending it as a successful prototype for other developing nations:[2]

> Israel provides one set of lessons: a country which has had to fight for independence, and which has actually made the desert bloom, using 'communitarian' methods of organization and living together which might well be adapted to African and Asian conditions. . . . African independent peasants, working on their own patches, within the context of traditional community cultures, thus find the Israeli *moshav* a more relevant model than the more strictly *collectivist* forms of organization such as the Soviet *Kolkhoz* or the Cuban state farms (neither of which has been eminently successful).

This characterization augmented the basic definition of the state, which was to provide a refuge for the persecuted Jews of the world. These images of the Jewish State incorporated counter-images of the Arabs – images which depicted the Arabs as, at best, traditional and backward and, at worst, irrational, psychologically inept, and determined to prevent the progress of the Jewish venture.

The fact that some of the early Zionist ideologists embraced socialist ideals and looked upon the Zionist settlement in Palestine as fulfilling a revolutionary aim and solving the problems faced by persecuted European Jewry should not in any way distract the researcher from examining critically the *unintended consequences* of this process and how it actually materialized.

In following this line of investigation, I am adhering to Peter Berger's[3] notion of 'sociological consciousness'. The ability to distinguish between the 'manifest' (intended) and 'latent' (unintended) functions of social processes is an essential ingredient in the 'debunking tendency in sociological thought'. In the following lengthy quotation, Berger utilizes Max Weber's study of Protestantism and capitalism to demonstrate the importance of 'unintended, unforeseen consequences of human action in society':[4]

> Weber's most famous work, *The Protestant Ethic and the Spirit of Capitalism*, in which he demonstrated the relationship between certain consequences of Protestant values and the development of the capitalist ethos, has often been misunderstood by critics precisely because they missed this theme. Such critics have pointed out that the Protestant thinkers quoted by Weber (such as Calvin) never intended their teachings to be applied so as to produce the specific economic results in question. . . . But Weber never maintained that Calvinism *intended* to produce these economic action patterns. On the contrary, he knew very well that the intentions were

> drastically different. The consequences took place regardless of intentions. . . . This does not mean at all that ideas are not important. It does mean that the outcome of ideas is commonly very different from what those who had the ideas in the first place planned or hoped.

Maxime Rodinson expressed a similar point of view in his reference to Zionism as an ideology:[5]

> as with any ideological movement, one must differentiate between ideal principles and variants that crop up in internal tendencies and with the passage of time, the implicit or explicit motivations of the masses of followers, the strategies and tactical plans of the leaders, the fulfillment of these plans (which is always only partial and which always comes about in somewhat unforeseeable circumstances), the consequences of these plans, etc.

This sociological perspective necessitates a research approach which would allow us to examine critically the official interpretations of Israeli society as they affect the Arab minority, and in so doing to entertain other interpretations which deviate from most conventional research by Israeli and Western social scientists. It should be borne in mind that our main concern is not to carry out a comprehensive study of Israeli society, though wherever applicable we will allude to the basic characteristics and premises of this society. Our purpose in this study is to shed light on the place of the Arab minority in the context of a Zionist settler regime.

Essentially, we highlight in this chapter the theoretical bases of two central models of society – pluralism and internal (or domestic) colonialism. Each of these models has been used in one way or another to describe Israeli society. Yet a total explanation of the data bearing upon Arab–Jewish relations, which we will be advancing in future chapters, necessitates a further consideration of the role of values, inter-ethnic contact, and occupational and educational statuses.

Models of society

A simplified sociological model usually centres around the consensus–conflict dichotomy.[6] While there is some justification for presenting the reader with a summary perspective of this sort, the consensus–conflict typology obscures important variations of interpretation associated with each of the above approaches. The consensus model – until recently, popular and dominant in North American social science writings – assumes that social integration is the ultimate goal of society and, furthermore, that it is attained on the basis of widespread identification with a representative value-system. This sharing of values in society is made possible, according to the consensus model, through the creation of institutions whose structures are assumed to be 'functional' in terms of maintaining the needs and goals of society at large.

Such a 'structural-functional' paradigm, as it is known in sociology, has an equally influential corresponding perspective in political science – that of pluralism (although as we shall see below this is only one variant of the so-called pluralist model). Pluralism conceived in this fashion depicts society as decomposed into numerous groups, none of which has an overriding influence in shaping the decisions emanating from the political sphere. These groups, each possessing power resources of its own and characterized by criss-crossing memberships, act to countervail and even cancel each other out, thus preventing the rise of one dominant group which would then have monopoly over power distribution in society.

What characterizes the consensus-plural model is the assumption of voluntarism and the absence of coercion, be it on the level of values or of actions – the two are sometimes equated. Man's actions are thought to be carried out in a utilitarian fashion, with little cognizance of the constraints, societal or otherwise, which impinge on individuals. We are presented with a view of man which sees him as being capable of shaping his destiny through voluntary action. It is this underestimation of the coercive factor in the nation–state which has led critics of the pluralist-consensus persuasion to turn to more viable outlooks in the analysis of society – outlooks which take into account conflicting group interests.[7]

Now, the so-called conflict theorists are many, and in no way do we intend to deal with all the various strands of their respective theories in this chapter. Suffice it to say that the impetus for these perspectives originated from the Marxian school of thought which, rather than placing primary emphasis on common, as well as integrating, aspects of society, looks for group differentiation based on the relations of the groups to the means of production, which ultimately give rise to opposing interests. However, if 'integration' on the level of values appears to be taking place, in the context of capitalist society, this school of thought attributes such a phenomenon to coercion, false consciousness and manipulative socialization.[8] Another variant of the conflict model accepts the presence of conflict in society, but considers this conflict to have been absorbed and channelled through various bureaucratic structures exemplified in political parties, trade unions and modern organizations. Conflicts become localized and manageable. This perspective sees the major point of contention as centring around lines of authority and not around group interests in the Marxian sense· This is basically Dahrendorf's[9] position, which stresses the lack of congruence or correspondence between the status positions of group members in society. Thus, a member who is in a position of dominance in one sphere of life is not likely to occupy the same position of dominance in another. In a way, while this version recognizes the inevitability of conflict at the micro-level (that is to say, organizational and bureaucratic in essence), it nevertheless sees some form of pluralism on a societal level. It is the criss-crossing of lines of power which, according to Dahrendorf, prevents the ossification of power positions in society.

Of the various models used in the analysis of multi-ethnic and settler societies, pluralism and colonialism stand out as the most relevant.

As conceived in the literature of race and ethnic relations, pluralism departs drastically from the 'political' model of pluralism to which we alluded previously. Pluralism in this sense denotes differentiation and segmentation along cultural, social and racial lines. While it is true that in most of the literature on race relations the ethnic and cultural factors exemplified in linguistic, regional and religious components have been stressed, the model does take into account coercive factors and leaves the possibility open that conflict is not necessarily the outcome of 'culture contact' *per se*. It is not, as Robert Park's[10] race relations theory states, one passing phase of the race relations cycle culminating in assimilation; rather it could result from the relative power positions of the various groups in society *vis-à-vis* each other. According to M. G. Smith, who has done a great deal to refine the concept, both theoretically and empirically, pluralism implies the following: 'Given the fundamental differences of belief, value and organization that connote pluralism, the monopoly of power by one cultural section is the essential precondition for the maintenance of the total society in its current form.'[11]

Pluralism is not without its critics. Some are sympathetic, but others, such as Oliver Cox, question the entire theoretical viability of the concept. Essentially, because of the multiplicity of its dimensions – social, political, legal, and so forth – Cox[12] sees pluralism obscuring one overriding factor in colonial situations, which, in his view, could be best understood only in terms of the groups' relationships to the means of production in the classical Marxist sense. Lockwood, while admitting that the concepts of class and plural society may go some way in illuminating black–white relations, remarks[13] that 'the concept of plural society is less of a novel contribution to social theory, and, in several respects, it poses less fundamental issues of sociological analysis.' He goes on to suggest that millenarianism may provide a better model for examining race relations in a society such as the United States.

In summarizing the utility of the various perspectives discussed in this chapter so far, Rex makes the following relevant observation:[14]

> It will be noticed that, relatively speaking, pluralist theory seems to accept a certain looseness in the relationship of one segment to another while at the same time attaching a crucial significance to cultural differences. By contrast, structural functionalist and Marxist stratification theories seem to point to a much closer involvement of one group with another. Functionalism emphasizes the ultimate value system, Marxism the activity with the social relations of production as the central issue in men's lives. Pluralist theory seems to imply that involvement in the polity and in production is less important for men, as a central life interest, than is the culture which governs their relations outside of their working-lives.

Nevertheless, Rex concludes by stressing the point:[15] 'the emphasis of pluralist theory does draw attention to some central features of colonial social structures, which Marxism, for instance, does not.' These features are best described in the presence of specific market-place relationships not depicted either in classical Marxist class relations or in situations which typify capitalist systems with so-called free labour.

Rex goes on to make an analytical distinction between colonial and metropolitan societies. In the case of metropolitan societies with colonial migrants, the modes of contact between colonizer and colonized are characterized by[16]

> (a) Urban systems of stratification of a variety of different kinds in which the migrants add to the system at the bottom, forming some kind of a new 'underclass' element;
> (b) Situations in which a particular group of outsiders is called upon to perform a role which, although essential to the social and economic life of a society, is in conflict with its value system, or is thought of as being beneath the dignity of the society's well-being. This is the process known as scapegoating.

It must be stressed that in Rex's terms the definition of what constitutes a metropolitan society is not identical with what other students of race and ethnic relations designate as metropolitan. Banton,[17] for one, reserves the definition for the traditional centre in the mother country which regulates the setting up of a colonial society; London, for example, played such a role relative to the overseas colonies. For Rex, the concept is not strictly bound up by a geographical relationship, but rather by the 'structural features' which determine the role played by the immigrant in the colonial economy. Thus, when colonial and metropolitan societies exist in one nation-state, as is the case in the United States, South Africa, and, we might add, in Israel, the geographical distinction between metropolitan and colonial societies vanishes: 'Thus a migration from the Deep South to Chicago for a Black American is akin to a migration from Jamaica to London or Birmingham, while on the other hand the board-rooms of Johannesburg are much like those of London or New York, a metropolitan economy and society having been established in this latter case as close as possible to the production system.'[18]

Aware of the various shortcomings and pitfalls inherent in pluralism, P. L. van den Berghe[19] does not restrict his conception to one dimension of society at the expense of another. Neither does he conceive of pluralism in a binary fashion, that is to say, either societies are pluralistic or they are not. Although pluralistic societies have to manifest institutional duplication, such duplication 'is a matter of degree' only:[20]

> Clearly, pluralism is best conceived as a matter of degree rather than an all-or-none phenomenon. A society is pluralistic to the extent that it is structurally segmented and culturally diverse. In more operational terms, pluralism is characterized by the relative absence of value consensus; the relative rigidity and clarity of group definition; the relative presence of conflict, or, at least, of lack of integration and complementarity between various parts of the social system; the segmentary and specific character of relationships, and the relative existence of sheet institutional duplication (as opposed to functional differentiation or specialization) between the various segments of the society.

The South Africa of 1964 – at the time van den Berghe wrote those words – offered a plausible test-case. The dual political structure was clear-cut, the cultural and national apartheid was highly visible; so was the dual economy 'with a high-productivity money economy [among whites] and a subsistence one [among blacks]'.[21]

So far, the social mechanisms which ensured the workings of the South African system are varied. While naked coercion is an obvious feature of this system, it is only one aspect of it, and not the most important one. The basic feature of this system is the adoption on the part of the African of 'compliance' procedures which imply adherence to instrumental norms connected with occupational roles, rules of etiquette, styles of dress, and so forth, yet retaining a degree of 'dissension concerning fundamental values'. In this manner, van den Berghe points out, the African is able to cope with the dual society through 'shuttling' between the native culture of the reserve and the white culture of the metropolis. Thus African 'migrant workers can adjust to town life, so that while in town they appear quite westernized, only to become very traditional at home in rural areas.'[22]

Notwithstanding the ability to adjust, the African social structure exhibited all the symptoms of social disorganization typical of colonial regimes. In spite of a distorted class structure, van den Berghe sees a revolutionary potential among the oppressed African masses:[23]

> In erecting a rigid colour bar, the dominant whites succeeded in maintaining a monopoly of leading positions in government, commerce, industry, finance, farming, education, and religion. By the same token, they prevented the rise of a class of Africans with a stake in the status quo; for all practical purposes, there is no African landed peasantry or bourgeoisie (in the Marxian sense of owners of means of production). Conversely, the whites created an exploited urban proletariat, a 'middle class' of underpaid clerks and other petty white-collar workers, and a tiny elite of professionals who are strongly discriminated against. All these strata share a common interest in radical change. The African intelligentsia furnishes the leadership of the liberatory movements; the white-collar workers, many of the local organizers; and the proletariat, the mass support.

Such optimism, which is also shared by Fanon,[24] who believed in the revolutionary potential of the colonized lumpenproletariat, is not shared by H. Adam.[25] According to Adam, the demise of South Africa through internally inspired revolutions is not likely to come about in the near future; this is attributable to the following two reasons: (1) increasing economic interdependency between the Africans and whites, which has resulted in a movement of Africans into lower-status jobs usually occupied by whites – it is argued that the dual economic system will eventually lose its pluralistic character through increasing economic integration; (2) South Africa's position of strength depends also upon its external economic power *vis-à-vis* the rest of Africa, for 'nearly one-third of all commodities produced for the market in Africa stem from this area.'[26] Although any drastic change taking place in South Africa has to be initiated outside South Africa, this does not seem to be in the offing, owing to the superior military preparedness of South Africa. In Adam's view, changes in the class structure will necessitate 'deracialization' and incorporation of the Africans into the productive and consuming sectors of society. While such a process might bring the subordinates into a relatively improved position, their fragmentary nature and the absence of organized political parties or trade unions on behalf of the Africans will compel the politicized African to withdraw and re-organize under the umbrella of African nationalism.

It is for this reason that Adam rejects the application of a 'vulgar' Marxian framework as a useful construct for explaining racial domination in South Africa. The emerging class conflicts between the whites, that is, the Afrikaners and the English, create a need for political accommodation based on the differing economic interests of the white groups, or, as Adam would prefer to label it, the need for a 'pragmatic race oligarchy'.[27]

Adam distinguishes between 'colonies of exploitation' and 'settler colonies'. Such a distinction is useful for our purpose. The former typifies classical colonialism where the colonizing group has no plans to settle permanently in large numbers in the colony and continues to conduct its affairs in terms of an official mother country. The latter, the settler group, remains in the country in relatively sizeable members, cuts off its official ties with a sponsoring foreign entity, and assumes responsibility for conducting its own affairs. It is this type which most closely relates to the situation in Israel:[28]

> The colony of this type is neither exploited in the interests of a foreign power, nor degraded to a market for foreign surplus commodities, but is characterized rather by a domestic colonialism which at certain stages might exceed the metropolitan colonies in degree of exploitation. But it is questionable whether this holds generally true. For a ruling class, the settlers are also forced to maintain a degree of harmony in the system. They have more at stake than a foreign colonial power, their own survival.

While official *de jure* apartheid of the South African variety does not exist in Israel, national apartheid on the latent and informal levels – as manifested in segregation in housing, land ownership (although, as will be shown in the coming chapters, because of land regulation laws, which are strictly based on national criteria, a case could be put forward that this is an example of official apartheid), education, interpersonal contact, modes of political organization and occupational distribution, not to mention the area of marriage – is a characteristic feature of Israeli society. Likewise, a significant part of the Jewish majority's core values reflects a feeling of cultural superiority and rejection of the Arabs. Evidence in support of this will be advanced in the coming chapters.

If South Africa had to resort to 'pragmatic apartheid', to quote Adam, Israel had to incorporate a wider range of pragmatic policies and compromises affecting the Arab population. The judicial system on more than one occasion upheld the rights of the Arab minority in its fight against the discriminatory policies of the Israeli government. Unlike blacks in South Africa, the Arabs can, and do, partake in the political process by electing Members of Knesset as well as members of local councils, although this process takes place in a rigidly defined Zionist political culture where the national aspirations of the Arab population are subdued. On more than one occasion liberal Jewish public opinion rallied to the Arab minority's side to protest against blatant injustices perpetrated by the Israeli government. Yet, in almost all crucial cases, the Jewish national interest was invoked to justify the circumvention of existing laws in dealing with the Arab population. In such cases, the Jewish voices of protest succumbed to the official dictate of the authorities. As will be demonstrated in future chapters, the invocation of the British Emergency Regulation Laws of 1945 (which were described as unconstitutional by the Hebrew Lawyers' Union in Palestine at the time of their application by the British Mandate against Jews and Arabs) have been used more than once to impose house detention, arrest and imprisonment without trial of Arab – and, if the case calls for it, Jewish – citizens. However, it must be remarked in this context that, as in South Africa, the Israeli legal system is not to be perceived as a single reflection of the class interests of a certain stratum of society. Probably more than to South Africa, the following statement by Adam applies to Israel: 'Laws are created and bent to fit the *collective* goal of group protection and not to further the advancement of officials in power or lobbyists' (my italics).[29]

Critical of pluralism, Wolpe[30] turns to a more refined model of internal colonialism. He argues that although this theory suffers from weaknesses inherent in the pluralist model – as the following quotation testifies – it does draw attention to certain aspects of class relations. Yet this class analysis is carried out in a manner which keeps racial and ethnic factors separate from the element of social class:[31]

> The . . . discussion of internal colonialism suggests that this theory presents society as a composite of class relations and ethnic, race, cultural, or national relations. To this extent the theory may be distinguished from conventional analysis of race, ethnic and similar relations, since in the latter approach these relations are accorded sole salience. On the other hand, the theory of internal colonialism is unable to explain the relationship between class relations and race or ethnic, etc. relations. As a consequence, the latter relations are once more to be treated as autonomous and in isolation from the class

relations. To this extent there is a close convergence between internal colonialism and conventional race relations theory, more particularly when the latter is based on a plural model of society.

However, an important aspect of internal colonialism is the development of an imperialistic relationship between capitalist and non-capitalist economies within one nation-state. Using South Africa as an example, Wolpe argues that the capitalist mode of production proceeded at the expense of preserving non-capitalist modes of production in black South Africa. For this relationship to persist, Wolpe says:[32]

> In certain circumstances capitalism may, within the boundaries of a single state, develop predominantly by means of its relationship to non-capitalist modes of production. When that occurs, the mode of political domination and the contents of legitimating ideologies assume racial, ethnic, and cultural forms and for the same reason as in the case of imperialism. In this case, political domination takes on a colonial form the precise nature of which has to be related to the specific mode of exploitation of the non-capitalist society.

Yet the crux of the internal colonialism model, when applied to South Africa, is that it stresses the availability of cheap labour-power in the form of a non-capitalist commodity reproduced in African Reserves: 'The most important condition enabling capitalism to pay for labour-power below its cost of reproduction in this way is the availability of supply of labour-power which is produced and reproduced outside the capitalist mode of production.'[33]

It would be extremely difficult for this economic exchange to persist in the absence of a clearly articulated political doctrine:[34]

> The political expression of this imperialist-type relationship takes on a colonial form. This is so because, at one level, the conservation of the non-capitalist modes of production necessarily requires the development of ideologies and political policies which revolve around the segregation, and preservation and control of African 'tribal' societies. The ideological focus, it must be stressed, is always necessarily on the 'racial' or 'tribal' or 'national' elements, precisely because of the 'tribal' nature of what is being preserved and controlled.

The repercussions of this system in understanding stratification patterns are outlined by Johnson[35] in his discussion of oppressed classes in internal colonies as contrasted with what he calls 'homogeneous' urban societies. Essentially, Johnson tackles the same problem to which Rex addressed himself in the latter's delineation of central features of metropolitan societies. According to Johnson, what distinguishes mobility patterns among colonized people belonging to differing racial groups, in contrast to those belonging to the marginal-underclass stratum of urban homogeneous societies, is the following:[36]

> Individuals within the marginal underclass have opportunities for social mobility, depending upon opportunity structures, to the limited degree that they can shake off their class origins and become socialized into the skills, values, and attitudes of the mainstream society. The opportunities for social mobility for individuals within an internal colony are more sharply circumscribed. The colonized can be mobile within the stratification system of the colony or, with difficulty, pass one foot into the class structure of the dominant society while the other foot remains implanted in the colony. The individual is mobile under conditions strictly defined by the dominant society. He becomes stripped of his culture and values, losing his identity with the class of origin, but remaining uncomfortably 'marginal' (to use the concept in the way that American sociologists have used it) in the dominant society. This is the case of the black bourgeoisie in the United States or the cholo of Peru.

A common assumption underlying the colonial and plural models of society is the notion of dependency. Though originally dependency implied economic asymmetrical relationships between the colonizing and colonized regions (whether on the internal or international levels), in contemporary writings dependency extends to the cultural and political spheres as well, as Lall points out; 'dependence is meant to describe certain characteristics (economic as well as social and political) of the economy as a whole and is intended to trace certain processes which are expected to adversely affect its development in the future.'[37] Lall goes on to describe the socio-political aspects of dependency in the following words:[38]

> [the] political structure of foreign rule still exists today though the agents are set differently, and it still mirrors the profound penetration of the dependent areas by the outside centres. This asymmetrical penetration of the dominating centres took place . . . in all the essential social fields. This was done by controlling the socialization processes in the widest sense of the word (cultural imperialism); by controlling the media of communication (communication imperialism), as well as political, military and legal systems (political imperialism). . . .

> A history of the political and social structures of the third world can be seen as a function of this external penetration.

This notion, so crucial to writers critical of the integrationist and consensual approach to politics, has been subjected to constructive criticism by Lall. If the concept is to have any analytical utility it must fulfil two criteria: '(1) It must lay down certain characteristics of dependent economies which are not found in non-dependent ones. (2) These characteristics must be shown to affect adversely the course and pattern of development of the dependent countries.'[39]

Basically, Lall argues that many of the characteristics attributed to the conditions of dependency – such as penetration of foreign capital, use of capital-intensive technology in a small industrial sector, export of primary commodities, élite consumption determined by advanced regions, unequal exchange, and growing inequalities in income distribution – exist among developed and less developed countries. These characteristics fail to distinguish dependent from non-dependent countries in an analytical way, owing to the increasing interdependency in the international system. In Lall's view, dependency is not a dichotomous quality, but could be understood on the basis of a continuum, for there is dependency among so-called developed countries; likewise, the less developed countries are on varying levels of dependence and some are beginning to exert influence *vis-à-vis* other less developed countries. In the light of this, Lall suggests the following:[40]

> It seems to be much more sensible to think in terms of a pyramidal structure of socio-political dominance (a scale rather than a unique condition of dependence) in the capitalist world, with the top (hegemonic) position held by the most powerful capitalist country and the bottom by the smallest and poorest ones, and a more or less continuous range occupied by various developed and less developed countries, with relative positions changing, between the two.

Therefore, according to Lall, the criticism should be directed against the internal economic structures of the less developed societies which perpetuate their link to the international capitalist system. In order to minimize the cost of dependency on capitalism, attention should be concentrated on how to break away from the capitalist mould through internal restructuring.

Values

Equally relevant to any discussion of the notions of dependency, colonialism or pluralism is the extensive use which some social scientists have made of the role of values in either impeding or accelerating social change. According to this school, represented in the works of David McClelland[41] and Daniel Lerner[42] (to mention two of its leading proponents), in order for developing societies to overcome their problems of economic stagnation they must acquire a value-system which is characteristic of Western industrialized nations; it is a value-system which, to use the Parsonian language,[43] stresses achievement (rather than ascription), universalism (rather than particularism), and specificity (rather than diffuseness). This solution to economic development which rests upon emulation of the ideal-typical Western values has been effectively criticized by André Gunder Frank,[44] and there is no need to go over this often repeated criticism here.

We will, however, refer to the general problem concerning the relationship between values and social change in the context of colonial societies. Hutton and Cohen[45] argue that instead of attributing to values an independent status in the chain of causation leading to behaviour, values themselves have to be accounted for. Behaviour is to be understood in a political-economic context involving, in the case of colonized societies, the type of infrastructure and value-systems existing in pre-contact stage, the nature of the contact, the role of the dominating power, and the mechanisms of incorporation it uses to bring the colonized into the orbit of a new social order. In the words of Hutton and Cohen:[46]

> We are not likely to be helped by attitude surveys and cultural studies designed to test receptivity to modernization. Rather we need some understanding of the ways in which particular economies, social structures, and cultures are tied together, and the impact on these of the experience of colonization and incorporation into a wider economy. . . . We do not want to suggest that peasant attitudes and opinions are irrelevant to the process of economic development, nor to the success or failure of local projects, but we are arguing that such attitudes are unlikely as such to be important independent variables, and are themselves part of the development situations which require explanation. We should not then ask how we can change peasants' attitudes to more appropriately modern ones before we have answered the question, why do people hold the attitudes towards development which they do have?

While Hutton and Cohen's main concern is with the relationship between values and economic development, Harold Wolpe and John Rex address themselves more directly to the shortcomings of attitudinal approaches in current race and ethnic relations studies.

In stating the position of the attitudinal perspective characteristic of the socio-psychological approach, Wolpe says: 'In sum, a member of a racial group is treated unequally, it is asserted, because it is *defined* as a member of that group' (my italics).[47] In replying to this position, he says:[48]

> This would seem to give rise to questions concerning the conditions in which definitions or attitudes of hostility arise but, in fact, sociologists who adopt this approach take these simply as given and, as a consequence, race relations are removed from both an economic and political structural context and treated as an area *sui generis*. Since it *is* taken as given, the need to account for race prejudice in structural form does not arise and all that is then considered necessary is a description of its consequence.

Rex comes down more harshly on the phenomenologists who pursue a similar approach:[49]

> This approach recognizes that social and mental phenomena are meaningful and the approach to discriminating any kind of structural situation must depend upon a consideration of 'definitions of the situation' used by participant actors. Hence it would seem that the problem disappears. If men typify a situation as racial, racial it must be, and all that the sociologist can do is to concentrate on the careful analysis of the structure of belief systems from which the concept derives. He cannot be expected to distinguish between false and true consciousness or between actual and held beliefs.

As stated earlier, our approach to the study of race relations in a settler society is more encompassing. We address ourselves to the structural as well as to the attitudinal aspects, to the historical antecedents as well as to the consequences of colonial regimes. Questions relating to manipulative socialization involving definition and re-definition of salient symbols of culture and personal identity are important elements in understanding the interplay between class and racial consciousness, the efficacy of social control agencies, and the emergence of justificatory ideologies to explain away subordination of one group by another. In brief, by addressing ourselves to the role of ideology and belief systems in the analysis of colonial societies, we tap one significant aspect of the process of incorporation and legitimation to which Hutton and Cohen referred.

The work of Herbert Blumer,[50] an influential figure associated with the interactionist perspective, provides a promising theoretical approach in terms of linking the behavioural to the historical aspects of race and ethnic relations. He sees the problem as being related to the *definition of a group's* image in society by more powerful groups who have access to the mass media and exposure in the public eye. Race relations problems, as well as their solutions, do not stem from changing *individual* attitudes and experiences. Improving race relations through individualized personal contact, for example, will not lead to positive results, according to Blumer. The 'definition of the situation' of minority groups which is the outcome of a *historical* process, is what must be challenged and modified if a subordinate group is ever to reconstruct its identity and collective experience. Access to the mass media by spokesmen of minority groups becomes an essential mechanism in combatting prejudice.

While Blumer does share with the conflict theorists the 'group' and 'power' aspects of the problem, he does not address himself to the issues raised by Anthony Richmond,[51] who questions the ability of the symbolic-interactionist approach to explain why, when, and under what circumstances, certain race relations problems are articulated in the public eye, and others are not; does it have to be assumed that prejudice and discrimination exist only when the problem is exposed in the public eye? These are the sorts of problems which Wolpe, Rex, and others foresaw in certain socio-psychological approaches to race and ethnic relations, as their above-quoted statements testify.

The socialization process has been singled out by numerous writers on plural and colonial societies as an essential aspect of racial legitimation and domination. The educational system and mass media have received substantial attention in this respect. This process of legitimation is not exclusive to multi-ethnic or plural societies, but as I have shown elsewhere[52] it exists in Western industrial societies. Socialization into dominant social-class and political norms have been described as central features of domination in Western societies.

Concerning racial domination, it is here only possible to sketch the most salient findings. One of the well-known studies into the origins of prejudice among young people is a longitudinal research carried out first in 1949 and repeated in 1959, covering an age span of seven to sixteen years;[53] the researchers, in seeking to uncover the determinants of ethnic attitudes at an early age, applied the Ethnocentricism Scale developed by the authors of *The Authoritarian Personality*.[54] The major finding of the initial study was that cognitive ability, reasoning and intelligence were significantly related to tolerance. They found that prejudiced children tended to overgeneralize, and to be dogmatic and intolerant of ambiguity. The comparison between the 1949 and 1959 studies using the same subjects could be summarized in the following points:[55]

> Over time, a 'hard core' of ethnically more prejudiced subjects (reportedly so at age seven) are found to be so nine years later. . . . At the same time, another 'hard core' of ethnically less prejudiced subjects are found who retain views at age sixteen and are at the same time manifestly superior in cognitive ability over the nine year interval. . . .
>
> . . . When a shift in ethnic attitudes occurs, there is a corresponding shift, though of a moderate degree, in a cognitive performance.

The stress on cognitive ability as a predictor of prejudice was expounded more recently by H. Tajfel.[56] He suggests that prejudice be examined not in terms of motivation and instinctive behaviour, but in terms of rationalization. In other words, attitudes toward ethnic groups should be examined in terms of the functions these attitudes perform in the life of the attitude-holder. On the cognitive level, the process of categorization is particularly important. A vivid example of this is the creation in the person's mind of stereotype images of other ethnic groups.

In contrast to the psychological and cognitive aspects of learning, Tajfel refers to social learning as an equally relevant process in understanding the development of ethnic attitudes among children. He refers to Mary Goodman's[57] classic study of race awareness in children as an example of the early sensitivity of children to racial distinction. Working with 3½- to 5½-year-olds, Goodman shows that whereas 92 per cent of the white children in the sample express a preference for their in-group, the corresponding figure among black children is much lower. A study by Morland,[58] also cited by Tajfel, compares the self-acceptance of black children in two different social environments and gives further support to the view that the outside environment influences social learning. Among a sample of Southern black children from Virginia, a minority of 22 per cent identified with black children, compared to 68 per cent of black children in the Boston area who identified with their in-group.

This negative perception of the self among black children has been undergoing a change in recent times. Judith Porter[59] attributes the decline of the traditional negative image among black children from a working-class background to the internalization of the new concept of self revolving around the notion advocated by the Black Power movement, for example, 'Black is beautiful.'

Background characteristics and inter-ethnic contact

Of the various socio-economic background variables, educational attainment is, according to Prothro and Grigg,[60] the best predictor of tolerance. Irrespective of social class and regional differences, they find with their American respondents that the highest level of tolerance is among those with the highest level of education. But Kirscht and Dillehay remark in their review of the literature on authoritarianism that the effect of education on ethnic attitudes is more complicated than it is made out to be:[61]

> In fact, certain aspects of prejudice seemed enhanced among those with more education while other aspects were relatively related to education or showed no relationship at all. . . . The effects of education in reducing prejudice were strongest when education separated the individual from his previous sub-culture.

The major emphasis in the literature on prejudice has been the correlation between prejudice and status ranks. Bettelheim and Janowitz[62] found that the downwardly mobile group exhibited the highest level of intolerance, while the upwardly mobile group showed the lowest level, with the two congruent groups falling in between. Those results are in line with the findings reached by Greenblum and Pearling.[63] Although the findings of *The Authoritarian Personality* refuted most of the arguments for objective indicators' being reliable predictors of ethnic attitudes, they did single out subjective status identification, defined in terms of a desired income, as being a useful indicator for assessing prejudiced attitudes. Bettelheim and Janowitz, investigating a sample of American army veterans, discovered a significant association between a feeling of economic deprivation and prejudice. Those who experienced economic deprivation manifested the highest level of intolerance. Of those who claimed to have had opportunities for economic advancement, the majority were tolerant.[64]

A recent attack on the status inconsistency theory as an explanatory tool for understanding prejudice was made in a British study by Runciman and Bagley.[65] They offered the theory of relative deprivation as an alternative for explaining the attitudes of white Britons to black and Asian immigrants. Thus they note that hostility to immigrants could be explained more successfully in terms of the respondent's sense of relative deprivation *vis-à-vis* other occupational groups adjacent to his class position; the greater the sense of deprivation, the higher the level of intolerance.

In addition to the correlation between background variables and prejudiced attitudes, there is a discussion in the literature of the impact that personal contact has on ethnic attitudes. Gordon Allport claims that contact *per se* between ethnic groups does not directly lead to tolerance: casual contact 'does not dispel prejudice; it seems more likely to increase it'.[66] Encounters between different ethnic groups on the basis of personal acquaintance and *equal* social status enhance tolerance. Residential contact has two types of effect, according to Allport. First, contact between groups living in segregated zones does not lessen the amount of hostility; and second, contact within the context of integrated communities significantly increases the degree of tolerance. These findings are not too dissimilar from those reached by the authors of the British study *Colour and Citizenship*, who concurred that 'the people who were least prejudiced tended to live near to coloured people; getting to know a coloured man as an individual, as a human being, is associated with a reduction in prejudice.'[67] Considering the relationship between age, sex, social class, and level of education, the British study concluded:[68]

> The findings so far indicate that the lowest incidence of extreme prejudice will be found among middle-class women under 35 years of age who have received some full-time education beyond the minimum school leaving age, the highest incidence occurring among men in the skilled manual working-class who are aged between 35 and 54 and who left school at 14 or 15 years of age.

Co-option

Viewing it within the context of colonialism, rather than race and ethnic relations *per se* as treated in Western industrial societies, Fanon[69] describes the system of incorporation as involving several stages. The first of these is adoption by the colonized people via its strata of national bourgeoisie of a language of politics which is not only irrelevant but also detrimental to the experience of colonized people: the adoption of Western liberal-democratic political precepts, such as individualism, compromise, competition, political parties, and so forth, is an example of such ideological imposition:[70]

> The colonialist bourgeoisie, in its narcissistic dialogue, expounded by the members of its universities, had in fact deeply implanted in the minds of the colonized intellectual that the essential qualities remain eternal in spite of all the blunders men make: the essential qualities of the West, of course. The native intellectual accepted the cogency of these ideas, and deep down in his brain you could always find a vigilant sentinel ready to defend the Graeco-Latin Pedestal.
>
> Individualism is the first to disappear. The native intellectual had learnt from his masters that the individual ought to express himself fully. The colonialist bourgeoisie had hammered into the

native's mind the idea of a society of individuals where each person shuts himself up in his own subjectivity, and whose only wealth is individual thought. Now the native who has the opportunity to return to these people during the struggle for freedom will discover the falseness of this theory. The very forms of organization of the struggle will suggest to him a different vocabulary. Brother, sister, friend – these are words outlawed by the colonialist bourgeoisie because for them my brother is my purse, my friend is part of my scheme for getting on.

Further:[71]

> At the decisive moment, the colonialist bourgeoisie introduces that new idea which is in proper parlance a creation of the colonial situation: non-violence. . . . Non-violence is an attempt to settle the colonial problem around a green baize table. . . . The idea of compromise is very important in the phenomenon of decolonization. . . . Compromise involves the colonial system and the young nationalist bourgeoisie at one and the same time.

A second feature of this incorporation is the importation of a brand of cultural imperialism[72] under the guise of Western social science whose main purpose is to legitimate an inferior and subordinate image of the colonized: 'Technologists and sociologists shed their light on colonialist manoeuvres, and studies on the various "complexes" pour forth: the frustration complex, the belligerency complex, and the colonizability complex. The native is promoted; they try to disarm him with their psychology, and of course they throw in a few shillings too.'[73]

Finally, in the process of establishing itself, colonialism resorts to co-opting two types of natives: 'the first of these are the traditional collaborators – chiefs, *caids* and witch-doctors. . . . Colonialism secures for itself the services of these confidential agents by pensioning them off at a ransom price'; and 'the lumpen-proletariat'[74] who, if it is not mobilized, 'will find itself fighting as hired soldiers side by side with the colonial troops'.[75]

Writing in the same tradition, Albert Memmi rejects any possible distinction between a colonial and a colonizer:[76]

> A colonial is a European living in a colony but having no privileges, whose living conditions are not higher than those of a colonized person of equivalent economic and social status . . . a colonial so defined does not exist, for all Europeans in the colonies are privileged.

Memmi tackles two further aspects of colonialism: (1) the predicament of the so-called left-wing colonizer, and (2) the options open for the colonized. Concerning the first aspect, there are two avenues open to socialist colonizers: to leave the colony, or to identify with the colonized in their struggle against the colonizers. It is the former option which is more realistic for the left-wing colonizer to adopt, since the tactics of liberation are abhorred by the left-wing settler:[77]

> Take terrorism, one example among the methods used in the struggle. We know that leftist tradition condemns terrorism and political assassination. When the colonized uses them, the leftist colonizer becomes unbearably embarrassed. He makes an effort to separate them from the colonized's voluntary action; to make an epiphenomenon out of his struggle. They are spontaneous outbursts of masses too long oppressed, or better yet, acts of unstable, understanding elements which the leader of the movement has difficulty in controlling.

Assimilation or revolt are the two possible alternatives confronting the colonized. Assimilation through emulation and imitation of the colonizer will be unsuccessful in the long run for two reasons. First, no matter how hard the colonized tries, he will fail to 'pass', and second, the continual rejection of this assimilation by the colonizer ensures the eventual collapse of assimilation attempts. Thus, Memmi declares, 'The refusal of the colonized cannot be anything but absolute, that is, not only revolt, but a revolution.'[78]

Conclusions and implications

On the basis of the preceding discussion, it is possible to draw up a list of the main features of settler societies which apply to a historical study of the Arab minority in Israel. First and foremost to be noted is the transformation in the economic and social structure of the indigenous Arab population, which took place in the context of superimposing a capitalist economy upon a traditional peasant social order. While this feature typifies to a large extent the situation of pre-1948 Palestine, its remnants are present to this day, as evidenced by the striking contrast between contemporary Arab and Jewish sectors. The asymmetrical relationship through contact and exchange between the Arab population and Jewish settlers was governed and regulated by the gradual emergence of the latter group's political institutions, by the importation by the Jewish settlers of European technology and know-how, and by the influx of Jewish capital and the steady increase in the number of settlers. An integral part of this process is the acquisition of land by the settlers, the resulting displacement of the native Arab population, and the eventual distortion of its class structure best reflected in the emergence of the Palestinian migrant worker, which continues to be a feature of the economic life of Israel. The asymmetrical relationship between the two sectors was augmented by maintaining a complete closure in the educational, cultural and residential facilities of the settler group *vis-à-vis* the indigenous population.

A second feature of a settler society is that the transformation in the economic fabric creates identifiable pockets of hinterland in the midst of areas with native concentration, while metropolitan centres appear solely in regions populated by the settler group or its agents. This situation clearly persists in present-day Israel. Two repercussions ensue from this economic dependency. First, it enhances the sectional development of the hinterland economy, exploiting those resources which could be processed in the metropolitan centres and exported to the hinterland regions. Second, the economic underdevelopment of the native regions keeps the native labour force in subordinate occupations since technical and administrative positions are monopolized by the settler group. Economic dominance ensures political dominance. Important political decisions are usually taken in the metropolitan centre dominated by the settler group. Likewise, through a system of co-option and segmentation, the political infrastructure is kept under the direct control of the superordinate group, with a view to discouraging any form of genuine political participation which might enhance the position of the subordinate group.

A third aspect of a settler regime is that it creates a justificatory ideology based on the dehumanization of the culture and way of life of the indigenous population. Thus the native is masked by a negative stereotypical image which is utilized to justify his exploitation. Needless to say, this type of image – augmented with an inferior perception of the self – is, often enough, internalized at one stage of colonization by the native people. An important corollary of this is that the native, even when he assumes an impressive numerical superiority, becomes, in the eyes of spokesmen for settler regimes, invisible. The indigenous ethnic, religious, national, and linguistic institutions are either submerged or are redefined so as to reflect a value-system which is consonant with the hegemonic structure of the colonizers. There is a fair amount of research bearing upon the cultural state of the Arabs in Israel which depicts the consequences of their subordinate status in a system of internal colonialism. More will be said about this in the later chapters of this study.

It is important to stress in concluding this chapter that, when viewed in a historical context, there are two distinguishable and separate periods in twentieth-century Palestinian history (or three, if we are to include the brief period of Turkish rule during this century). Whereas the post-1948 position of the Arabs in Israel is best described as domestic colonialism, the pre-1948 period is more complex. It should be seen as a period when a system of dependency existed with an implicit, and at times explicit, alliance between, on the one hand, a sponsoring imperial power (Britain) and the Zionist settlers, and, on the other hand, between large Arab landowners and the Zionists. It is the interplay between these factors which ultimately led to the development of a dependent socio-economic status among the Palestinians.

It should also be pointed out in this context that the initial Zionist pattern of settlement did not rest on physical subjugation of the indigenous Palestinian population, as has occurred in other cases of classical colonialism. Rather, the implicit aim of the Zionist movement was to *displace* the Palestinians and occupy their land; it was colonialism of the land. As will be shown in the next chapter, the manifest goal of the Zionist movement produced other consequences such as Jewish exclusivity, a developed Jewish sector and an underdeveloped Arab region, sporadic Arab rebellions – one of which lasted from 1936 to 1939 and was in part directed against Jewish colonies – and cultural and political differentiation. It is this system of domination of pre-1948 Palestine which laid the foundation for a social order in contemporary Israel in which the Arab minority more explicitly exhibits all the features of an internally colonized population.

3 Arab social structure in pre-1948 Palestine

In order to be valid, any interpretation of Arab social structure in Mandatory Palestine has to be developed in the context of an interplay between three operating forces: the indigenous Palestinian Arabs, Zionist settlers and British occupiers.

Our purpose in this chapter is not to provide a diplomatic history of Mandatory Palestine, of which there are numerous studies available. Our objective is to document the basic sociological features of Arab society in Palestine which resulted from the incursion of Zionist settlers and British occupiers in the area. In particular, we will discuss the land and demographic issues, early Arab reaction to Zionism, and the arguments pertaining to the economic and social development of the Jewish and Arab sectors. Our overriding concern is to show that there existed patterns of uneven development in the two sectors, mediated by the British presence, whereby the development of the Jewish sector was associated with a corresponding decline and stagnation of the Arab region.

The Turkish legacy and Zionist colonization

Before the influx of European Jewish immigrants into Palestine in the latter part of the last century, there were approximately 24,000 Jews in Palestine, residing mainly in the four cities of Jerusalem, Hebron, Safed and Tiberias. The Palestinian Arab population at the time was estimated at around 300,000.[1]

Overall, the official Turkish attitude towards Jews in the Ottoman Empire during that period (that is, before the advent of Herzl's political Zionism) was characterized by tolerance. The Sephardic Jews of the Ottoman Empire, in contrast to the Ashkenazi Jews of Eastern Europe, played a significant role in the economic life of many urban centres in the empire. Culturally and religiously, they fitted into the mosaic of nationalities comprising the Ottoman regime.

In contrast to the official attitude of tolerance, Jews as individuals who knew little about Zionism and its ideological intentions in Palestine, were at times subjected by local Arabs to epithet-labelling and in other cases to outright physical attack.[2] It is important to stress, however, that although there was this form of non-institutionalized Arab hostility to Jews, 'it would be incorrect', according to a report prepared by a Zionist emissary to Palestine in 1914, 'to speak of anti-semitism in the sense in which we usually use the term.'[3] Though there were sporadic attacks against Jews in Palestine as early as the 1830s, the situation was far from being clear-cut. For example, during the Safed insurrection in 1838, in which Druze rebels rose against Turkish rule, and – in the course of the uprising – attacked Jews of Safed and even extorted money from them, it was another Palestinian Arab who came to their rescue: 'Fortunately for them, an Arab friendly to Jews by the name of Muhammed Mustafa, who had tried to protect them during the troubles, lent them money and was concerned to procure food and clothing for them.'[4] It could also be argued that this ethnic hostility toward Jews, prevalent at the time, and still existing today, typified the communal group identification in the Middle East, where sectarian conflicts involving only Muslim Arabs are not an uncommon phenomenon.

In the early part of this century, the attitude of the Turkish authorities toward Zionist colonization of Palestine was far from uniform. On the whole, Turkey attempted to restrict Jewish immigration – under the auspices of the Zionist movement in Palestine – for fear of nurturing another national problem in its midst; another reason for this reluctance to encourage Jewish settlements in Palestine had to do with the Porte's fear that Russian-educated immigrants might inspire a Russian nationalist movement, which would be difficult to contend with in the light of Russian–Turkish relations and the difficulties faced by Turkey in the Balkans. However, these stated aims failed, primarily because of objections by the Great Powers to what they saw as drastic Turkish measures, but also because of reluctance to enforce such measures on the part of local officials, who accepted bribes in return for allowing land sales to Jews.[5]

By 1917, the time of the collapse of the Turkish rule in Palestine, two waves of Jewish immigration had taken place. The year 1881 signalled the coming of 'Lovers of Zion' immigrants from Russia, in the wake of Tsarist pogroms against Russian Jews. The following year the Biluim, a small group of Zionist settlers from Russia, immigrated to Palestine. They spearheaded the first wave of settlers to Palestine – the First Aliyah – which lasted until 1904. By 1903 the 'Lovers of Zion' movement, and that of the Biluim after it, were declared total failures. The outlook of members of 'Lovers of Zion' was described as non-political, personalistic, and lacking a specific national scheme. The agricultural enterprise of the First Aliyah could not have sustained itself, even for the short period it did, without the financial assistance of the Baron de Rothschild. Lucas describes the experience of this group of colonizers thus:[6]

> The settlers themselves had a capitalistic and colonialistic approach to the land and the Arab population which was seen as a reservoir of extraordinarily cheap labour. Under the influence of the Baron the Jewish enterprise assumed the flavour of the French colonization then evolving in North Africa.

A similar observation was made in 1891 by Asher Ginsberg, the Hebrew essayist known as Achad Ha-Am, after a visit to Palestine. He drew attention to the alarming number of land agents, both Arab and Jewish, who had speculated in real estate in order to make profits from the Jews' appetite for land colonization. Specifically, in his letter 'The Truth from Eretz Israel', Achad Ha-Am derided political Zionists who upheld Israel Zangwill's slogan 'Land without people, for people without a land', the reference being to the 'emptiness' of Palestine, at a time when it was abundantly clear to any visitor that Palestine had its indigenous Arab population.[7]

By 1914, the end of the Second Aliyah period, the Jewish population in Palestine constituted 12 per cent of the total population. Between 1914 and 1917, the Turkish authorities compelled Zionist immigrants to leave Palestine, and their numbers dropped from 85,000 to 57,000.[8] An earlier depletion in numbers occurred between 1882 and 1913, when, Mandel estimates, out of 100,000 Jews living in Palestine half returned home after a short stay, mostly because of their failure to adapt.[9]

From the point of view of the Zionist movement, the Second Aliyah imported with it a new ideological fervour, with which it hoped to rectify the shattered efforts of earlier colonizers. The assumption was that pioneer and socialist doctrines, augmented with diluted Marxism, would have to be the guiding principles if the Zionist colonization of Palestine were to succeed. A central concern of this group of settlers was to avoid repeating the mistakes of 'Lovers of Zion' and to develop instead a non-colonialist orientation to Jewish settlement in Palestine. This meant a redefinition of the settlers' attitudes to the land, which in turn gave birth to the so-called labour Zionism. To own the land, one had to work and till the soil, even if this led to downward social mobility.[10] In the words of the first Jewish sociologist, Arthur Ruppin, who was to put his talents at the disposal of Zionist colonization efforts in Palestine, 'Agricultural work has been enobled and "sanctified" in Palestine: it has been accepted as one of the essentials for the building of a Jewish commonwealth.'[11]

In particular, a concern with the 'normalization' of Jewish life gave rise to socialist doctrines with ultra-nationalistic components: notions such as *Kibush Hakarka* (conquest of the land), *Kibush Ha'avoda* (conquest of labour) and *T'otzeret Ha'aretz* (produce of the land) became the rallying slogans of the second group of settlers. The arguments underlying labour Zionism rested on the premise that Jewish settlement in Palestine had to focus on colonization of the land, and not of its inhabitants. But how this process was to take place without displacing and expropriating the indigenous Palestinian peasantry was neither dealt with in a serious manner by key Zionist ideologists, nor faced in a realistic fashion by the settlers themselves. The neglect of the Arab question, the pronouncements of key Zionist leaders, and the attitude of the settlers (including members of the Second Aliyah) have led some writers to conclude that, with certain qualifications,[12] the process of Zionist colonization and the Arab reaction to it reflect the characteristics of colonialism. This perception, we hasten to add, is prevalent in spite of the unsuccessful efforts of a minority of Zionist intellectuals who in the 1930s headed the bi-nationalist movement and, in the face of Arab opposition, reconciled themselves to advocating closer links between the Arabs and Jews of Palestine within the context of one nation-state.[13]

In addition to the ideological naivety of the first group of settlers, their major failure, in the eyes of the Second Aliyah, was their inability to create Zionist institutions which would work in concert with other Zionist organs abroad in order to tackle in a more successful manner the task of land acquisition and immigration absorption.

In 1901 the fifth Zionist Congress resolved to establish the Jewish National Fund for land purchases. In 1908, a branch was opened in Jaffa headed by Arthur Ruppin. In 1920 the Histadrut (the Hebrew Workers' Union) was set up. Both these institutions played a central role in Arab–Jewish relations: the first in alienating the Arabs from the land; the second in barring the Arab workers from the Jewish-controlled labour market. On land acquisition the policy adopted was dictated by the Jewish National Fund Constitution, which stipulated that once the land was Jewish-owned it belonged inalienably to the Jews of the world in perpetuity. Likewise, the laws of 'Jewish Labour' guarded by the Histadrut meant that non-Jews could not be hired to work on Jewish-owned land. As we will show later on, though the manifest intention of these laws was to 'normalize' the inverted Jewish occupational structure of the Diaspora, on the latent level they caused hardship to the Palestinian Arabs, resulted in their displacement from the land, and in the long run contributed to a truncated Arab class structure which is present to this day:[14]

> To the Arab labourer who was replaced by the Jewish socialist it did not much matter that the place of work he was being driven from had been created originally by Jews. All he knew was that he was being pushed back to the low living standards of the Arab village or of the Hauran tribes. The Jewish leaders never considered this effect, just as they tried to ignore, as far as possible, the very existence of another people in the country.

The recent recollections of a party functionary concerning the earlier days of Zionist colonialization in the name of socialist and nationalist principles are instructive in this regard:[15]

> I had to fight my friends on the issue of Jewish socialism, to defend the fact that we stood guard at the orchards to prevent Arab workers from even getting jobs there. . . . To pour the kerosene on Arab tomatoes; to attack Jewish housewives in the markets and smash the Arab eggs they bought; to praise to the skies the Keren Kayemet (Jewish Fund) that sent Hankin to Beirut to buy land from absentee *Effendi*.

The repercussions of the exclusivist Zionist philosophy of the Histadrut concerning Arab–Jewish labour relations were described by Waschitz as follows:[16]

> The conception of work and conquest of work held by the majority of the Histadrut is equally an obstacle, since it is difficult to explain things convincingly to an Arab worker. The discrimination in salaries between Jewish and Arab workers exasperates the Arabs, particularly since working conditions and price levels tend to be equal. In these circumstances it was easy for Arab organizations to send us their members to ask 'naive questions' at the time of the May Day demonstrations – 'Is proletarian solidarity compatible with a call for the conquest of labour and for the creation of the Jewish State?'

It is a mistake to equate the Histadrut with other, secular and universalist, trade union movements of this century. While one of the aims was to improve the conditions of the Jewish working class in Palestine, its *raison d'être* was to ensure the creation of a Jewish State, with Arab–Jewish working-class solidarity a secondary factor. After all, it was under the auspices of the Histadrut that the underground Zionist military force, the Haganah, was established.[17] One of the earlier splits between Arab and Jewish workers in Palestine came in 1922, over the issue of Zionist settlement, when Arab workers submitted to the British government their demands for limiting Jewish immigration. Yago summarized the role of the Histadrut in these words:[18]

> Along with the (Jewish) national institutions, the Histadrut acted as the appropriator of surplus produced in publicly oriented enterprises. The inflow of capital enabled the Histadrut to set up its companies (e.g., public works construction through Solel Boneh) and its services (health funds, etc.). However, the evolving labour bureaucracy is not to be confused with those of Western Europe or the US. It was not the product of a mass workers movement; rather, it was always an integral part of an expressedly nationalist movement. Its task was not solely to divert working class struggles, but to eliminate part of the working class (the Palestinian Arabs) from labour market competition in order to accomplish the two-pronged state building programme of the Zionist movement – 'conquest of labour/conquest of land'.

Thus, while Zionist institutions forged ahead, and a settler state in embryo was beginning to crystallize in the form of various national exclusivist institutions, there was no doubt that the viability of the enterprise was precarious without the protection of, first, the Turkish authorities and later, in a more crucial and sustained manner, of imperial Britain. Every Zionist leader, from Ben-Gurion to Jabotinsky, from Herzl to Weizmann, sought the consent of the British and other imperial powers in return for favours to be rendered in the area.[19]

Herzl's unsuccessful overtures to the Turkish government were expressed in the following words:[20]

> If His Majesty the Sultan were to give us Palestine, we could undertake to regulate Turkey's finances. For Europe, we would constitute a bulwark against Asia. Down there we would be the advance post of civilization against barbarism. As a neutral state, we would remain in constant touch with all of Europe, which would guarantee our existence.

As the events unfolded in Palestine, Arab opposition to British occupation and Zionist immigration mounted; Jabotinsky, the leader of the Revisionist movement, appealed to the British to allow Zionist colonists to set up a settler defence force along lines similar to those organized by white settlers in Africa: 'In Kenya until recently every European was obliged to train for the Settlers' Defence Force. Why should the Jews in Palestine be forced to prepare for self-defence underhand, as though committing a legal offense?'[21]

It would be inaccurate to conclude that the Zionist movement was monolithic in character. Cultural Zionism, political Zionism, pragmatic Zionism and labour Zionism are essential ingredients in the historical delineation of the Zionist movement.[22] With regard to the Arab question, which, on the whole, was not dealt with in any serious Zionist writing, almost every one of the key Zionist figures uttered, at one time or another, a reconciliatory statement directed toward the Arabs. Invariably, such statements came either after bitter Arab protests or after British pressure in the wake of violent Arab reaction. The feeble stand of the bi-nationalist movement was no exception. More than one Zionist Congress after the Balfour Declaration issued statements proclaiming the common destiny of Arabs and Jews in Palestine, built on justice and equality.[23] In *Altneuland*, published in 1902, none other than Herzl himself depicted the fictitious future state of the New Society in Palestine as based on human solidarity between Arabs and Jews, devoid of exploitation and racial hatred. It is a far cry from Herzl's *Judenstaat* (published in 1896) and his other diaries, in which the Arabs are either ignored or treated with contempt.[24] There, the solution to European anti-Semitism was eventually articulated at the expense of the Palestinian Arabs, guided by a fundamental assumption – the original promulgator of which was anti-Semitic Europe – namely, 'that the Jews were unique in a metaphysical sense and could not be assimilated'.[25]

It is a useful exercise in diplomatic history to pit one document against another, usually emanating from the same source, and show the contradictory and irreconcilable nature of the statements made. Such an exercise will not take us very far. While we acknowledge the complex facets of the Palestinian problem, our intention is not to labour to reconcile opposing ideological statements. A saving device for us is to be able to look with hindsight at the *actual developments* in Palestine, from Zionist colonization up to the present time. Actions are the best indicators of intentions.

Early Arab reaction to Zionism

Although by the end of the nineteenth century the number of Jews in Palestine was relatively small, the Arab reaction to Jewish colonization was evident even before the advent of Jewish immigrants during the First Aliyah. As remarked earlier, Arab pressure to curtail the inflow of Jewish settlers was exerted with little success upon the Turkish authorities late in the 1800s.

Mandel's thesis is that relations between Arabs and Jews in the latter part of the last century and the early part of this century prior to World War I were neither ambivalent nor amicable as assumed by many. Arab awareness and resentment of the slow but steady influx of Zionist colonizers into Palestine was reflected in the attitude of displaced peasants whose land was possessed by Jewish settlers. By 1919 British and Zionist intelligence in Palestine was reporting that 'the peasants were more prone to action and to revolt entailing self-sacrifice than other groups of society.'[26] Violent Arab protest did not take place until 1921, the date of the first serious disturbance in Palestine. This was followed by another one in 1929, and by the Arab Rebellion, which lasted from 1936 to 1939. Even if one accepts Mandel's assertion that Arab embitterment was caused in part by land transactions in which Jewish buyers fell victim to unfamiliar land laws and to 'the obscurities of the language in which contracts were written',[27] this theory of misunderstanding does not account for the persistent efforts by the Zionists to acquire land, knowing that such dealings, even when they were written in the most explicit and comprehensible language, were bound to result in hardships for, and displacement of, peasants. The aims and goals of Zionism were, and continue to be, the 'in-gathering of the exiles'; the reaction of the indigenous Palestinian population to such efforts has always been of secondary importance to the settlers. According to Herzl, the poor, displaced peasants were to be 'spirited' quietly outside the borders. The capitalistic ethic of Herzl was reflected in his hope that Zionism could also be used as 'a dam against the involvement of Jews in the socialist current'.[28] The well-to-do Palestinian Arabs had a place in this scheme of colonization. When, in 1899, the former Arab President of the Municipal Council of Jerusalem complained about the consequences of Zionist efforts in Palestine, Herzl replied:[29]

> You see another difficulty, Excellency, in the existence of the non-Jewish population in Palestine. But who would think of sending them away? It is their well-being, their individual wealth which we will increase by bringing our own. Do you think that an Arab who owns land or a house in Palestine worth three or four thousand francs will be angry to see the price of his land rise in a short time, to see it rise five and ten times in value, perhaps in a few months? Moreover, that will necessarily happen with the arrival of the Jews.

Arab nationalism, Mandel argues, manifested itself in reaction to Zionist settlement in Palestine as early as 1905. In an open letter to the Turkish authorities written in 1905, the Kaymakam of Nazareth (who was hanged by the Turkish authorities in 1915 for his nationalist activities) complained that the Jews 'have striven and are striving to buy most of the villages, lands, and estates in our illustrious Empire. The Jews do not mix at all with the Ottomans; they also do not buy from them. They have a special bank, the Anglo-Palestine Bank, which lends them money at 1 per cent a year'.[30] The statement went on to deplore the fact that Jewish settlers flew their own flag, had their own separate schools, national anthem, and postal service, and handled all their complaints through foreign representatives in the country.

Equally significant is the vociferous response which the Christian Arab minority expressed in reaction to Zionist colonization efforts.[31] Mandel's thesis, which is a popular one among historians, is that the roots of Christian Arab hostility are basically economic, namely that Christians felt that their economic dominance was being threatened by the incoming Jewish settlers.[32] This theory does not totally explain the well-known phenomenon of Christian Arab participation in the leadership of Communist and worker-based movements in Palestine, as well as outside it in the Arab world.

To comprehend the mechanism underlying the process of land expropriation from the Palestinian peasantry, one has to deal with the land tenure system first. This will be followed by an examination of the Zionist argument regarding the impact upon the Arab peasantry of the land tenure system and colonization.

Land tenure[33]

It is possible to isolate four categories of land ownership in Palestine, all dating back to the Ottoman time when the Land Code reform was instituted between 1856 and 1858, and remaining in effect even after the attempted land reform of 1856–8. First there is *Mulk* land, which is private and of limited extent. It includes building plots in towns and villages, as well as land adjoining dwelling houses. *Mulk* land also includes agricultural land which is portioned out to non-Muslims. Such land can be willed to heirs. The second category is *Waqf* land, which is designed to serve religious purposes. Although it is estimated that three-quarters of the land in the whole Ottoman Empire in the sixteenth century was *Waqf* land, with increasing secularization only a small portion remained *Waqf* land in twentieth-century Palestine. The third is *Metruke* land, which includes the seas, lakes, rivers and springs, wadis, pastures, and public roads, and is land designated for general use by the community. The fourth category is *Miri* land, the most prevalent type in Palestine. It covers the lands of the plains and valleys, such as the Plain of

Sharon and the Valley of Jezreel. Essentially, *Miri* land is owned by the state, but the rights of use are given to peasants.[34] Moreover, the land is passed from generation to generation, with the stipulation that it be passed down according to Muslim law. If the land remains uncultivated for a period of five years, or if there are no heirs, the land can be declared *Mahlul*, meaning state-controlled, with the intention of redistributing it. This process has never occurred during the Turkish or the British occupation of Palestine. However, the definition of *Miri* land assumes a special importance in post-1948 Palestine, when the Israeli government invokes this categorization to justify confiscation of Arab land either when the occupant of the land is an absent refugee or when he has not taken the opportunity to register the land during the British Mandate. The 1858 attempts to get the peasants to register the land were unsuccessful because they were afraid of being drafted into the Turkish army and of becoming taxpayers. Many peasants, on the other hand, registered the land in the names of urban dwellers (in some cases the names were fictitious), but in doing so they discovered that when the time came to establish ownership of the land their claims were rejected. This is perhaps one of the basic causes of the post-1948 Palestinian peasants' failure to show records of land ownership under Israeli rule.

The most common form of land usage was the egalitarian *Musha'a* system; it was a communal form of land ownership: 'In order to assure to every landowner his due portion both in fertile land and in poor land, both in near and in distant land, both on level and sloping ground, all the properties of villages were divided into categories called *Mawqa*, that is, land situated in different plots.'[35]

Furthermore, land was recycled every two years in order to ensure proper distribution in the most equitable manner. It is estimated that up to 1860 most of the land in Palestine and Syria, excluding Lebanon, was held in *Musha'a* ownership. Granott estimates that by 1936, 50 per cent of the land in Palestine was held in communal ownership.[36]

The land issue

Depletion of land, an increase in the tax burden, and a decline in the proportion of male wage-earners due to the Turkish government's war involvement, forced many villagers to turn to urban money-lenders. Many turned over their land to the owners from the cities in exchange for tax relief. The peasants were allowed to remain on the land while the owners paid the taxes – until, of course, the land was sold to Zionist settlers. It was during this period that the Sursocks (Christians from Lebanon who were considered to be among the largest landowners) gained control of 230,000 *dunums* in the Plain of Jezreel, which in turn was mostly sold to the Zionists. The practice of money-lending was not exclusive to the Arabs. The Bergheims, a Jewish family from Jerusalem, gained control of 200,000 *dunums* in Abu Shusha in a similar manner to the Sursocks.[37]

Conventional interpretations of the significance of the communal and inheritance systems of ownership have focused on their contribution to the economic stagnation of the Arab sector. Granott and Patai went to great lengths to document the negative effect of the system. Patai probably expressed the sentiments of many Zionist officials who sought justification either for the expropriation of Arab land, seen by them as inefficiently used, or for the existence of economic backwardness itself in the Arab sector; he went one step further to suggest that the reason for the Palestine Arabs' inability to emulate the Jewish co-operatives was their negative attitude to agricultural co-operation which is rooted in the *Musha'a* system:[38]

> Yet through communal life and cooperative living anything like that of the *kibbutz* is unknown in *fellah* society, certain of their external manifestations, such as the common holding and working of the land, tended to be identified by the *fellahin* with an old traditional institution which, by the time of the expansion of the *kibbutzim*, was well on its way to being liquidated, largely by the *fellahin* themselves. This traditional institution, which in the eyes of the majority of the *fellahin* was the source of much of their misery and poverty, was the *Musha'a*.

It is interesting to note, with reference to Patai's remark, that he sees no connection between the expansion of Zionist colonies in Palestine, such as the *kibbutzim*, and the disintegration of the Arab communal land system.[39] By any account, the *Musha'a* system was economically ineffective by Western standards. The question, however, is what sustains such an institution which, on the face of it, expresses values that are not conducive to 'modernization', as the concept is construed in standard research on the sociology of development? Here is Sayigh:[40]

> To put the matter in broader perspective, we must look beyond the culturally-specific institution, and recognize that both *musha'a* and partible inheritance together form a choice, or strategy, in coping with land shortage, as a result of which resources *and* poverty are fairly equally distributed throughout a peasantry, *and it remains on its land*; the alternative strategy is impartible inheritance (usually associated with primogeniture) and individual ownership, which polarize peasantries into

classes, the inheritors and the disinherited, with the latter forming a pool of landless labour.

The privatization and expropriation of peasant land can best be demonstrated in the decline of average land holdings: in 1900 it was 148 *dunums*; in 1927, 78 *dunums*; in 1936, 42 *dunums* (a *dunum* is equivalent to 0.25 acres).[41] One report, prepared in 1946, revealed that the proportion of Arabs living on the land in 1946, compared with the proportion of Arabs living there before large-scale land transactions took place, reached 229 per cent.[42]

Zionist writers, of various shades, are quick to offer an interpretation of pre-Zionist Palestine describing it as desolate, empty and feudal. Aumann described Palestine towards the end of the nineteenth century as 'a social and economic order that had the earmarks of a medieval feudal society'.[43] Furthermore, 'The Palestinian peasant was indeed being dispossessed by his fellow-Arab, the local sheik and village elders, the Government tax-collector, the merchants and money-lenders, and only when he was a tenant farmer (as was usually the case), by the absentee owner.'[44] A. Granott expressed a similar point of view: 'The net result of Jewish land acquisition – at least to a considerable part – was that properties which had been in the hands of large and medium owners were converted into holdings of small peasants.'[45] Surely it is *Jewish* farm settlers that Granott has in mind. Aumann goes on to advance another popular Zionist interpretation of Palestinian history, namely that 'the advent of the Jewish pioneering enterprise . . . sounded the death-knell of this medieval feudal society.'[46]

No one would deny that latifundia and larger family landowners typify the situation in many colonized societies, Middle Eastern and otherwise. In Latin America, for example, the lingering legacy of Portuguese and Spanish colonialism in Brazil and Mexico was to give rise to the hacienda, and in spite of various land reforms the dominance of large land-holders is present to this day. In the Middle East, Egypt and Iraq in particular suffered from a similar system of latifundia. The revolutions in both countries aimed at re-allocating land to the majority of landless peasants. While the success of these revolutions has not led to the complete eradication of the feudal heritage, the situation is better than in either Mexico or Brazil. Palestine, on the other hand, did not manifest these feudal characteristics exhibited by other Middle Eastern societies. Warriner comments in this regard:[47]

> Palestine, by comparison with other Middle East countries, does not suffer from the evils of absenteeism on a large scale. It is important to stress this point, because some Zionist writers paint a picture of Arab village life as a feudal society

> disintegrating into capitalist exploitation of the labourers by landowners and that in a process which, in Palestine at least, is not present to any marked degree. It was the indifference of the Arab landowners rather than their exploitation of their tenants which permitted the purchase of land by the Jewish National Fund.

A detailed study by Firestone[48] into the economics of crop-sharing in Palestine in the 1930s lends further support to Warriner's claims that the system was not a classical feudal system. Analysing the accounts of a large landowner in the village of Arrabeh in Jezreel between the two World Wars, Firestone reaches the conclusion that the relationship between landlord and tenant farmers was not regulated by feudal ethics but by 'irrational economics'. It is a mistake, Firestone claims, to apply Western experience in feudalism – a mistake evident, for example, in the work of Granott on Palestine – to explain the conditions in Palestine, for the agrarian system in the latter was dictated in part by Muslim law, which embodied a different definition of economic relations: 'In the west the crop "follows the ground": it belongs to the landowner or to his leasee, even if they have not sown it. In Muslim law, the crop "follows the seed": in principle it belongs to the owner of the seed [which is not the landowner].'[49]

In addition to the fact that the introduction of large-scale ownership was a recent phenomenon of the latter part of the last century – when the Turkish tax-collector, money-lender and army recruiter came to dominate the life of Palestinian peasants,[50] – and not a classical endeavour in the Western sense of a feudal economy, there is the fact that, when an analysis is made of the actual extent of land owned by large operators, we find that this system involved only a small percentage of the *populated* area of Palestine.

The total area of Palestine – the area west of the Jordan River – is 26,000,000 *dunums*. Nearly half of this total area is the Negev Desert, which to this day is sparsely populated. Granott,[51] in his detailed analysis of the land tenure system, presents data showing that, of the total area, 3,130,000 *dunums* were owned by large owners. However, 2,000,000 *dunums* of these large tracts were in the Gaza and Beersheba districts, which were relatively poor agricultural areas. If we concern ourselves with the more populated area of the coastal plains in the northern portion of the country (where the early Jewish purchases were made) we find that, of the northern 13 million *dunums*, 1,130,000 *dunums* – or less than 10 per cent of the populated portion of Palestine – were under the control of large landowners.

In spite of the fact that large landowners did exist in Palestine, and a Jewish purchase agency, the Keren Kayemet Le Israel Company, was set up at the turn of the century specifically for the purpose of land acquisition, it is estimated that by the end of the Mandate not more than 6 to 7 per cent of the total area of Palestine was sold voluntarily to the agency,[52] and, more important, the sale was not initiated by Palestinian peasantry; rather it was primarily absentee landlords and local landowners, in addition to foreign interests, who co-operated with the settlers. Walter Lehn's estimates derived from the Statistical Report of the Jewish Agency show that, in 1936, of the total land purchased by the Jews, including the Keren Kayemet,[53]

> 52 per cent was purchased from 'large absentee landowners', 24.6 per cent from 'large landowners' and 13.4 per cent from 'various sources' such as the government, churches and foreign companies, making a total of 90.6 per cent. This leaves only 9.4 per cent acquired from small Palestinian Arab farmers, and 40 per cent . . . of this land had been acquired during 1891–1900, i.e., before the *Keren Kayemet* was established.

This outcome must have come as a great disappointment to those believing in Jewish 'redemption' of land, a belief clearly expressed by Herzl in 1895:[54]

> The private lands in the territories granted to us we must gradually take out of the hands of the owners. The poorer amongst the population we try to transfer quietly outside our borders by providing them with work in the transit countries, but in our country we deny them all work. Those with property will join us. The transfer of land and the displacement of the poor must be done gently and carefully. Let the landowners believe that they are exploiting us by getting overvalued prices. But no lands shall be sold back to their owners.

Concerning the alleged benefits reaped by the Palestinian Arab peasants as a result of Zionist agricultural technology, the evidence does not substantiate the claim of Jewish–Arab sharing in agricultural know-how. No doubt there were individual cases of Jewish farmers advising Arab peasants: the official attitude of the Zionist organizations was otherwise. For example, attempts in 1931 to establish a joint agricultural school for Arabs and Jews financed by Sir E. Kadourie – an Iraqi Jew – failed because of the refusal of the Zionist executive, the rationale being that Jewish parents should boycott the school because the school would be using Arabic and English as well as Hebrew as the media of instruction. The upshot of this attitude was that two separate agricultural schools were established, one for Jews and another for Arabs.[55]

Only to the extent that the Arabs were willing to move to intensive, rather than remain on extensive, agriculture, and hence to sell large proportions of their land to Jews, was there any promise of assistance forthcoming from the Jewish side. Summarizing the evidence presented by Zionist leaders to the Royal Commission of 1936, Barbour says:[56]

> So far as could be gathered from Jewish evidence before the Royal Commission, particularly that of Dr. Ruppin and Dr. Hexter, the Zionist claim is that the potentially irrigable land still in the possession of the Arabs should be provided with irrigation by government and Jewish funds. This will, it is alleged, enable the Arabs to live by intensive cultivation on one-fifth of the ground with which he lives on the whole today. The remaining four-fifths will be sold to the Jews. It appears, indeed that the [Jewish] Agency are opposed to any large-scale measure on the part of the government to intensify or develop fellahin farming unless this involves the transference of some of the land in question to Jews.

Even this qualified concern with the betterment of Arab peasants on the part of the Zionists is challenged by Kolton. He argues that regularization of land ownership, by which large landowners would hand back land to the peasants, runs against the interests of the Zionists. The latter could buy land only as long as the feudal system and the confusion in land registration continued to thrive. According to a Keren Kayemet statement, quoted by Kolton, once the land issue is settled 'the conditions of land purchases become more and more difficult.'[57] Kolton went on to say that 'even Ben-Gurion, the Secretary General of the Histadrut, opposed land reform.'[58] Likewise, according to Kolton, Ussishkin, an influential Zionist figure, saw, in the limited attempts of the British to help Palestinian peasants in agronomy and the use of artificial fertilizers, a hindrance to further land sales.

Implicit in the claims put forward by Zionist writers is the belief that Zionism was a revolutionary and not a colonialist venture, and that resentment toward Zionist settlers on the part of Arab inhabitants was essentially an upper-class phenomenon led by local élites and *Effendis*, whose economic position was being threatened by Zionist socialist settlers. While there is an element of truth in this claim – after all, the same Jewish settlers were also resented by previous *Jewish* colonizers who gravitated to Palestine under the umbrella of Rothschild's capitalistic venture – it is not all that convincing *in toto*. It would be naive to dismiss the resentment of Jewish colonization as being solely led by a few *Effendis* on behalf of the gullible, mindless Arab masses. This explanation overlooks two factors: first, as pointed out earlier, a Palestinian national movement did exist early this century, and it reflected a concern common to other anticolonialist, pan-Arab nationalist movements in the area at the time; second, the resentment of Jewish colonization had a strong peasant base to it. A detailed examination of the 1936–9 Palestinian Arab rebellion led Tom Bowden to conclude that it was a 'spontaneous' peasant rebellion similar to other noted peasant rebellions in history. If there is any pattern to be detected in this uprising, it is that it was the peasants and not the élites who had the upper hand in the conduct of the rebellion:[59]

> The Arab revolt was a peasant war of major proportions in duration, cost and casualties. For a time it ended Mandatory control in certain areas of Palestine and threatened it, and the *Yishuv*, everywhere. However, it was an unsystematic, unstable insurging prone to anarchic lapses. Above all, it was not the product of the Mufti's machination attempting, as some would have it, to establish a Caliphate with himself as the Caliph. The control which the Mufti exercised over the actual revolt and especially the guerrillas in the field was minimal.

Referring to the reasons behind this rebellion, Barbour remarks that 'the question of land sales has, however, caused a profound sense of grievance, and was certainly a principal cause of the revolt of the peasantry which was maintained in Palestine for over three years.'[60]

Data referred to by Warriner[61] from the 1931 census show that around 30,000 families – that is, 22 per cent of the peasants who depended on agriculture – were landless. As to the number of peasants displaced as a result of land sales to the Zionists, the estimates vary. Referring to a 1937 memorandum, Aumann[62] quotes a low figure of 664 families. It is very likely that many of those who were displaced in 1931 were absorbed in urban economies by 1937; also it is important to note that unspecified numbers of peasants did not register their land for fear of tax collection and army recruitment during the Turkish regime. Taking a similar line of argument, Porath,[63] who underestimates the Zionist impact on Arab landlessness, accepts a figure of 4,000 displaced families. While this figure is a rather low percentage of the rural Palestinian population, its true measure of impact must be considered in terms of whether or not it contributed to the uprooting of whole communities, which it did.

The demographic balance

A key feature differentiating the Jewish from the Arab community in Palestine throughout this century is the source of numerical increase in each. For the Arabs growth in numbers was due mainly to natural increase, while for the Jewish population it has been immigration, both legal and illegal. Writers sympathetic to the Zionist cause have attempted to attribute a significant portion of the Arab increase, at least from the early 1920s until the early 1930s, to Arab immigration from neighbouring Arab countries. We will deal with this point in greater detail below. First, let us set out the numerical contrast in terms of land and population as it existed in pre-1948 Palestine.

At the establishment of the British Mandate, and by the end of the Second Aliyah, there were close to 60,000 Jews residing in Palestine. There were three other consecutive main Aliyot, 1919–23, 1924–31, and 1932–48,[64] at the end of which time the Jewish population in Palestine amounted to around 600,000, comprising 35 per cent of the total population in Palestine. Table 3.1 gives a breakdown by population size and land ownership for Jews and Arabs for selected years. While the Arab population sustained a 2.3-fold increase between 1919 and 1946, the Jewish population multiplied, primarily through immigration, by ten. Thus, at the time of the Balfour Declaration in 1917, in which Britain promised a 'national home' to the Jews in Palestine, 2 per cent of the land was Jewish-owned in a country whose population was more than 90 per cent Arab.

TABLE 3.1 *Land ownership, Arabs and Jews (1919–46)*[65]

	1919	*1921*	*1931*	*1936*	*1946*
Jewish population	57,000	72,000	172,000	384,078	608,225
Arab population	533,000	551,000	784,891	916,061	1,237,334
Total population	590,000	623,000	957,191	1,300,139	1,835,559
Per cent Arab	90.3	88.4	82.0	70.5	64.9
Per cent Jewish	9.7	11.6	18.0	29.5	35.1
Total	100.0%	100.0%	100.0%	100.0%	100.0%
Total Jewish-owned land (*dunums*)	650,000	741,833	1,201,529	1,410,578	1,585,365
Per cent area of Palestine Jewish claimed	2.04	2.08	4.6	5.4	7.0

Population movements

Before we turn to an examination of the social and economic consequences of Zionist settlements in Palestine, let us assess the argument advanced by some writers regarding the impact of Zionist immigration into Palestine upon the Arab population. In a 1973 article which has received a wide circulation, Gottheil[66] argues that between 1922 and 1931 Arab immigration into pre-state Israel contributed 38.7 per cent of the total increase of the Arab population. He further says that this Arab immigration was stimulated by the industrial development in the Zionist sector.

It is important to underscore the political significance of the above demographic claim. If the claim concerning Arab immigration is substantiated and if it does appear to resemble other known patterns of immigration (such as Jewish immigration into Palestine), then two logical conclusions would follow. First, the claim to Jewish settlement in Palestine is no different, in terms of its historical antecedent, from the Arab one; both groups relied on immigration to build their national populations. Second, Jewish immigration contributed to Arab immigration into Palestine, which means that the claim of Zionist colonialism is untenable; it is not in the interest of any colonialist movement, according to this argument, to contribute to an increase in the size of the indigenous population and to improve its standard of living. This is clearly a standard argument advanced against those who seek to equate Zionism with colonialism.

In his calculations, Gottheil notes that 54,790 Arabs immigrated into pre-state Israel between 1922 and 1931. Using the available data from a British census of 1922, he applies on a yearly basis the recorded rates of natural increase for the above-mentioned period and concludes that his projected Arab population estimate for pre-state Israel is lower than that recorded by the census of 1931 – a difference of 54,790.

Three objections could be raised to Gottheil's study. First, he assumes that census registration in rural Palestine (where more than 80 per cent of the Arab population resided) is a reliable enumeration of the population, and he does not allow for possible inaccuracies in census reporting. It is a fact, however, that even in advanced Western societies, rural areas usually under-register the population. According to Janet Abu-Lughod:[67]

> It should be noted that practically all censuses, even those conducted in highly advanced countries such as the United States, undercount population by at least 5 per cent, with undercounts most likely in rural areas. Official figures are usually adjusted upward to compensate for this. There was apparently no such adjustment in the 1922 census of Palestine. Several additional figures contributed to an undercount in this census. The occupying power had still not gained full command of the country, nor was it initially acquainted with all parts of it; some sections were undoubtedly missed in the enumeration.

> Furthermore, the census was not only relatively unprecedented but was also the object of suspicion. While the Arab boycott of the census was only semi-organized many inhabitants, out of fear, were less than candid in their returns. When one examines the age–sex breakdown for the Arab population, one finds a consistent deficiency in the enumeration of males in the productive ages of life. While some may have been out of the military service, others were evidently reluctant to be enumerated for fear of conscription.

The second objection is that nowhere in his article does Gottheil refer to the census figure of 1931[68] which recorded 30,340 as being foreign-born. I assume that this figure was ignored because it did not include so-called illegal or unrecorded immigrants. In any event around 4,000 of the recorded foreign-born are non-Arabs, for example, Englishmen and Europeans. Even if we assume that all the foreign-born Arabs lived in pre-state Israel, which is a big assumption, the remaining figure of 26,000 is less than half of that reached by Gottheil.

Writing in the 1930s, Hopkins estimates the number of Arab immigrants at around 23,000, even though his period extends to 1936. Relying on official statistics, he notes that between 1922 and 1936 the number of immigrants into Palestine amounted to 260,000, of which 'it is estimated that 237,000 were Jews, 10,000 were Christians and the remaining 13,000 were Moslem and others.'[69]

It is also worth noting in this regard that the 1922 census listed 14,761 Palestinian Arabs and 6,264 Jews as residing outside the country, some of whom were on temporary business. Of the Jews, close to 20 per cent were residing in the neighbouring Arab countries, in particular Egypt.[70]

Third, a more serious shortcoming of Gottheil's methodology has to do with his use of 'political' demography. It is strange for anyone to consider internal population movement, that is, *migration*, within Palestine as being akin to *immigration*. In fact, nowhere in his article does Gottheil use the term 'migration' to refer to population movement from other parts of Palestine to pre-state Israel. Superimposing the current political boundaries of Israel on Palestine of the 1920s as a meaningful demographic category is highly questionable, for in order for one to use the term 'immigration', as Gottheil does, the experience of the Arabs who moved into Palestine between 1922 and 1931 would have to have been similar to the experience of those immigrants who moved across international boundaries or across different regions of the world, as in the European Jewish immigration into Palestine. One can hardly equate the prevalent population movement of Arabs in and out of

Palestine, to and from neighbouring Syria and Lebanon, with Zionist immigration from Europe, let alone label *internal migration* as immigration.

If Gottheil wished to say that Jewish colonies in Palestine attracted Arab workers from other parts of Palestine to work in them, as well as from neighbouring countries, then there would be no disagreement with this conclusion. In fact, the difference between the census data of 1931 concerning immigration (foreign-born Arab residents) to Palestine, and Gottheil's estimated figure, could very well be accounted for by the number of internal Arab migrants who either because of loss of land or for voluntary reasons, decided to move out of agriculture to work in Jewish centres. This shows that the economic dependency of the Arabs on the Jewish sector – a thoroughly documented phenomenon in the case of the present-day Arab sector in Israel, and shown by Gottheil[71] in another article –, is not a new feature of Arab–Jewish relations, but has its roots in early Zionist colonialization of Palestine.

Health conditions

A striking feature of Arab demography in Palestine has been the high birth rate which mainly accounts for the increase in the size of the population. As early as 1922, it was noted that the Palestinian Arabs, in particular the Muslim segment, exhibited one of the highest known birth rates in the world. It is estimated (see Table 3.2) that between 1922 and 1945 the Muslim community nearly doubled its population through natural increase, whereas the Christians increased by 72 per cent and the Jews by 28 per cent.[72]

TABLE 3.2 *Rate of natural increase per 1,000 for Arabs and Jews in Palestine (1922–45)*[73]

Year	*Muslim*	*Christians*	*Jews*
1922	24.95	19.16	16.71
1932	22.66	20.53	19.46
1942	25.31	15.66	14.13
1945	37.87	22.80	23.61

In commenting on this phenomenon, Sayigh advances a psycho-political hypothesis having to do with the Turkish occupation:[74]

> [Turkish] conscription was the form of oppression most feared and detested by the Palestinian peasants. At a time of high infant mortality, it took their young men, their most valued

> form of capital, the basis of lineage and household survival, and almost never returned them. Camp Palestinians [in Lebanon] today still recall grandfathers and great-grandfathers who died in the Turkish army. It was one of the commonest causes of orphanhood, and may be one of the reasons for still existent pressures towards early marriage, and many children.

The Arab rate of natural increase would have been greater had infant mortality been lower. Between 1927 and 1944 infant mortality among the Jews dropped by 60 per cent, reaching the figure of 63 per 1,000 in 1942–4. For the Arab communities the situation during the periods 1927–9 and 1942–4 was as follows:[75]

> The Christian infant mortality decreased by 51 per cent from 283 per 1000 to 138 per 1000; the Moslems' by 39 per cent, from 412 per 1000 to 251 per 1000. A closer look at the latter figure will reveal that during the 1942–1944 period, the Moslem child mortality rate was over 300 per 1000 in rural areas . . . [and] was under 200 per 1000 [in urban areas].

A great deal has been made of the Zionist efforts to improve the health standards of the Arab population in Palestine. In one of its conclusions, the Royal Commission looking into the causes of the 1936 disturbances noted:[76]

> Institutions founded with Jewish funds primarily to serve the [Jewish] National Home, have also served the Arab population. Hadassah [hospital], for example, treats Arab patients, notably at the tuberculosis hospital at Safad, and the Radiology Institute at Jerusalem admits Arab country folk to the clinics of its Rural Sick Benefit Fund, and does much infant welfare work for Arab mothers.

In challenging this overemphasis on Zionist health efforts in the Arab sector, Mansur quotes from a study by a Palestinian Arab physician, who noted that 'it is true that the Jews have provided extensive medical services but only an insignificant proportion thereof has affected Arabs. We do not deny the authoritative aide of some [Jewish] specialists. But is not by far the greater part of the private income of such excellent men derived from Arab patients?'[77] Mansur goes on to show that Jews benefited *more* from governmental and non-Jewish (such as missionary) hospitals than Arabs did from Jewish hospitals. In 1934, in Haifa, for example, 'the proportion of non-Jews who have been treated in Jewish dispensaries and clinics is 12 per cent while that of the Jewish treated in non-Jewish institutions is 17.3 per cent.'[78] With regard to the non-Jewish hospitals in Haifa, Mansur notes that while close to 35 per cent of all patients were Jews, Arab patients admitted to Jewish hospitals in the same city amounted to 0.7 per cent of the total patients admitted to those hospitals. The same is true with regard to Christian missionary hospitals in Jerusalem, whose Jewish intake of patients amounted to 24 per cent, while the proportion of the Arab patients admitted to Jewish hospitals in Jerusalem was 0.31 per cent.[79]

The specificity of Palestinian class relations

There is consensus among writers on pre-1948 Palestine that Arab class structure did not develop historically in the same way that European class structure evolved from feudalism. The close proximity and contact in Europe between the aristocracy and peasantry and the subsequent alliance between the aristocracy and bourgeoisie, on the one hand, and, on the other, the crystallization of an oppositionary industrial proletariat, had no parallel either in Palestinian Arab society or in the rest of the Middle East: 'And though towards the end of the 19th Century rich city merchants began to buy land for plantations, these were strictly commercial transactions, with almost no socio-political effect. Thus, unlike the ruling classes of England, Prussia, Russia, China, or Japan, the Arab ruling class had weak ties with the peasantry.'[80] More important, according to Shimoni, an interlocking or, more accurately, a unified aristocracy-bourgoisie structure, adumbrating an Arab ruling class began to take shape: 'The [Arab] ruling stratum is the same: the large landowner is a city dweller, he is also the large merchant, the banker, the lawyer and so on . . . his family controls the rest. This is unlike Europe where the opposition was between the commercial and industrial cities; agriculture versus city finance.'[81]

Although towards the latter part of the British Mandate a distinguishable stratum of Arab bourgeoisie and proletariat was beginning to emerge in the cities, its progress was checked by a more advanced and highly efficient Jewish sector which possessed the needed capital,[82] technological know-how, the protection of the Mandate authorities, and a well-organized, exclusively Jewish trade union movement, the Histadrut. 'Within fifteen years of the institution of the Mandate', Zogby remarks, 'Jewish capital had seized the initiative from this [Arab ruling] class . . . a fledgling Arab bourgeoisie could not compete with the much better financed and more modern Zionist enterprises.'[83] For this reason, it is pointed out that whereas in 1928 there were close to 2,400 Arab enterprises in Palestine, their number declined to 1,558 by 1942–3. Shimoni[84] attributes this decline to a change in the census classification system whereby small-size enterprises included in the earlier census were dropped from the 1942–3 report. Such an explanation ignores the impact of a more competitive and Zionist-financed capitalist economy upon a more traditional Arab sector. According to Smilianskaya,[85] this influence is evident in the nineteenth-century Middle East, even before the advent of Zionist colonization; European penetration in the area contributed to a decline of local industries, notably textiles. The author traces the emergence of a strata of lumpenproletariat in Syria, Lebanon and Palestine as early as the 1850s. According to this analysis, the disintegration of the feudal mode of production and the emergence of a capitalist structure began to take root during this period. It could be argued that the continued depressed levels of industrialization in the Middle East well into this century could be attributed in no small measure to foreign restructuring of the indigenous economic order through imposed European capitalism, without completely eradicating the traditional structure.

It is estimated that by the 1940s the Palestine Arab proletariat in the cities numbered between 35,000 and 37,000, of whom 6,000 worked in Arab-owned industries, 3,000 in Jewish and international concerns, 12,000 in private home services, and the rest in governmental and public works.[86] A survey conducted by the Histadrut in 1943 in Haifa showed that of 15,500 Arab workers in the city, around 5,500 were residents of Haifa, 7,000 were village commuters, and 3,000 were from outside the country.[87] The working conditions of these workers were not always ideal, to say the least. In 1935, it was estimated that in Haifa alone there were 11,000 Arab workers living in tin hovels without adequate running water or sanitation. The low wages of Arab workers could not possibly have enabled one to rent an adequate lodging facility, since it was calculated that in a place like Jaffa such rent would have amounted to two-thirds of the wages of an unskilled worker.[88]

Further evidence concerning the status of Palestine Arab villagers, is provided by Rosenfeld, who cites the work of Abramovitch and Gelphat as follows:[89]

> in 1931, 86 per cent of the Moslem Arab village population (73 per cent of the Christian Arabs) were considered to have gained their existence through agriculture. Of 122,000 earners in agriculture, 90,000 were regarded as being self-employed, 32,000 as workers. Of the latter 5,000 were shepherds, with the remainder representing agricultural servants, a worker-type between a tenant and a hired labourer, hired labourers and workers in Jewish settlements.

Rosenfeld's contrast of the occupational structure of one Arab village over two time-periods, 1920 and 1957–8, shows that whereas, in 1920, 12 per cent of the villagers were wage-earners, forty years later the proportion rose to 66 per cent. Whereas farm owners comprised 12 per cent of the villagers in 1920, in the late 1950s the percentage declined to 8 per cent. The majority of wage-earners were employed as labourers, either on farms or in cities.[90] This typifies the experience of most Israeli Arab villagers today, as will be shown in Chapter 5.

All along, the Palestinian aristocracy played a peripheral part in the social and economic development of the country. They acted mainly as a consuming stratum emulating a Western life-style. The non-productive economic role of the Palestinian ruling class was only one factor accounting for its marginal role. Throughout the four centuries of Turkish occupation, Palestine was linked economically, politically and socially to Syria and to a lesser extent to Lebanon. Damascus and Beirut assumed a more significant position in Palestinian economic life than any of Palestine's cities. When Palestinian aristocratic leadership appeared on the political scene, it came at a relatively late stage. Its fundamental aim was not to improve, but to keep undisturbed, the economic position of the peasantry, and, in contrast to the radical position adopted by the latter in its fight against Zionist settlers and British occupiers, the mode of political action of this ruling class was on the whole negotiatory and non-radical.[91]

Palestine's relatively small size and its homogeneous national composition did not prevent the presence of significant internal social cleavages. Regionalism, the clan system, village autarchy, not to mention the class structure, militated against the appearance of cross-cutting clan and group loyalties.[92] Of the various cleavages, the city–country dichotomy presented a type of social differentiation which exceeded in its overall effect any other social cleavage in creating lasting social distance between the two main sectors of Palestinian society. Sayigh remarks in her study of Palestinian refugee camps in Lebanon twenty-eight years after their dispersal from Palestine in 1948:[93]

> Yet so tenacious were the perceptions of social class differences that camp Palestinians today still use the terms *madani* and *fellah* to classify themselves and others. It is clear from the situated usage of these terms that they indicate socio-cultural differences, and not simply occupational differences.

Arguments concerning separate development

The Jewish boycott of Arab labour and Arab products (which was not always successful) gave the impression that the Jewish and Arab sectors developed separately under similar circumstances. As stated earlier, Zionist writers have used this argument to point to the non-exploitative character of Zionist colonization, and furthermore argue that the stagnation of the Arab sector is due to the internal structure of that sector. This conception of pre-1948 Palestine is not confined to Zionist writers. 'Most writers on Palestine', remarks Asad, 'have tended to represent the Mandate period in terms of the political confrontation of two national communities in which each excluded the other and maintained its own economy.'[94] Asfour, a Palestinian Arab writer, while acknowledging the so-called separate nature of the two economies, is nevertheless aware of the dependent aspect of this separateness:[95]

> With the larger inflow of capital into Palestine before the Second World War, the Arab population could have benefited indirectly to an important degree had the economy of Palestine been normally integrated. But . . . the economy in fact was split into two separate parts which intermingled only rarely and only in urban centres. Practically no Arab labourer was employed after the '20's except for seasonal work in the citrus groves in the 1930's. On the contrary, professional and trade services were largely sold by the Jews to Arabs in various towns. The Arab community on the other hand 'exported' to the Jews some agriculture products, particularly wheat, meat and vegetable oil.

Kolton, writing in 1932, grasped the essence of the relationship between the Arab and Jewish sectors:[96]

> Jewish capital which flows into the country secures the development of the country through industrialization; it fulfills the first part of the plan: it destroys in a significant way the small Arab industry, and transfers industries to new Jewish centres (soap, olive oil, textiles, etc.), without employing whatsoever, or they employ in an insignificant manner, Arab workers.

Augmenting his account of the closure of the Jewish sector to Arab workers, Kolton argues that had it not been for the internal Arab markets as well as those surrounding Arab countries, Jewish industry could not have become viable. Noting the Zionist memorandum submitted to the Simpson Committee in which it was claimed that the Jewish market is entirely dependent for its survival upon further Jewish immigration, Kolton says:[97]

> Jewish industries are built in part at the expense of Arab consumers, but they do not return to them any benefits in terms of absorbing Arab workers, and the establishment of

free markets to [absorb] the produce of the peasants. In both instances we face the problem known in the name of 'conquest of labour', the problem which lies at the heart of the relationship between Zionism and the Arabs.

Hyamson expressed this relationship in a similar way when he remarked: 'With two largely self-contained populations . . . it happened that while one mainly prospered [Jewish sector] the other largely suffered destitution.'[98] It is also clear that the nature of this asymmetrical relationship was such that the Jews were in firm control of the industrial sector. Shimoni notes in this respect that although the Arabs were attempting to break into the Jewish monopoly of the industrial sector, the imports of machinery and industrial equipment remained solely in the hands of Jews, while Arabs engaged in food imports.[99] An examination of the data in Table 3.3 confirms the uneven development of the two industrial sectors; in terms of the yield of the two sectors in Palestinian pounds, the 1942 data show that the Jewish sector's net produce approximated £P 10.5 million, while the Arab sector was £P 1.75 million.[100]

TABLE 3.3 *Share of Arab and Jewish sectors in Palestinian industry (1942)*[101]

Sectors	*Distribution of firms*	*Distribution of workers*	*Wages*	*Capital*	*Total*
	%	%	%	%	%
Jewish	55	75	83	60	79
Arab	44	17	17	10	15
Other*	1	8	—	30	6

* The remaining percentages pertain to five British firms of which three were Jewish controlled.

Although agriculture was one of the areas where the Arab economy showed signs of viability, the gap between the Jewish and the Arab sector was evident as early as 1936. According to Warriner the *per capita* income of a rural Arab (whether working in agriculture or in non-agriculture) was £7; for the Jewish worker, it was £34. In 1944, the Arab income per head of the rural population was £27, while in the Jewish sector it was £63.[102]

Overall, Kolton estimates that Jewish workers performing the same tasks as Arab workers were paid double the wages.[103] Carmi and Rosenfeld argue that in government jobs the differential in pay between Arab and Jewish workers reached 30 to 33 per cent. The rationale was that 'their standards of living are very different', or that account had to be taken of the 'peasant's cultural habits'.[104] With no strong union organization behind him, the Arab worker had no bargaining power similar to that utilized by Jewish workers in dealing with employers. In fact, with an abundance of surplus Arab labour, the employers succeeded in paying subsistence village wages to the Arab rural proletariat. It is worth quoting Carmi and Rosenfeld at some length on this, for though they see no functional connection between the developed Jewish sector and the under-developed Arab economy, they describe the situation of the Arab worker as follows:[105]

> We find, by comparing [Arab] wage statistics, that throughout the mandate period, wage rates in the new economic branches (government services, port refinery, citriculture, building, transport, etc.) approximated what was estimated to be the average yearly earning of the peasant. . . . In any branch of industry in which he worked, even the most profitable, he did not receive the labour price in that branch, that is, according to his productivity, etc., but rather he received the equivalent of the subsistence returns of a peasant. . . .
>
> During most of the mandate period, most of the potential workers remained in the villages, but they were ready to exploit any work opportunity offered at any work place, near or far. Taking into consideration that they did not compete for skilled jobs, replacement was simple, and a wide gap was maintained between the wages of skilled and unskilled workers.

However, the pace of improvement in the Arab sector was slow since capital was lacking. Warriner estimates, for example, that since an investment of £100 per working place is needed to make it economically viable and competitive, the Arab cultivator with a £7 per annum income will never be able to match Jewish settlements.[106] The extent of Jewish progress in intensive agriculture was noted by Russell who, writing in the 1940s, cited figures showing that while there was one tractor per 1,300 hectares in the whole of Palestine, the ratio in the Jewish sector was 1:120.[107] As remarked earlier, this is not to imply that Jewish agriculture was self-sufficient. It continued to rely totally on Arab grain.

Any contact that may have taken place between Arabs and Jews was in the area of citrus-growing. Smelansky[108] comments that while the Arabs taught Jewish settlers the basic skills of citrus-growing, the latter introduced the former to new methods of marketing technology. Thus, Arab citrus groves grew from 19,000 *dunums* in 1922 to 130,000 in 1945. However, Asfour notes that, overall, and except for citrus-growing, 'modern methods of the [Jewish] settlement farmer were seldom directly observed'[109] by the Arabs.

While the build-up of Jewish settlements was in progress, rural migration of Arabs to the cities was taking place. Loss of land, the inheritance system and heavy taxation had led to increasing pressure on the land. In 1930, the John Crosby Commission estimated that 44 per cent of the land was *musha'a* and 50 per cent *mafruz*; these figures had been the reverse a few years earlier, in 1923.[110] By the 1940s a Zionist report estimated that 75 per cent of the land was *mafruz*.[111] As far as rural debt was concerned,[112]

> On the basis of data collected from 26 per cent of all rural families and 12 per cent of all villages, the investigators calculated an average debt burden per family of £27, and an average yearly interest on debts of £8. The meaning of these figures can be grasped by setting them against the average yearly income of rural families, then estimated at £25–30 per annum. The total debt burden of the peasants at this time [in 1930] was calculated at £2 million.

TABLE 3.4 *Distribution of national income between Jews and Arabs by economic sectors (1936, 1944)*[113]

	1936				*1944*		
Sector	*Jews*	*Arabs*	*Other*	*Total*	*Jews*	*Arabs*	*Total*
	%	%	%	%	%	%	%
Agriculture	30.1	69.9	—	100	30.8	69.2	100
Manufact., elec.	64.4	33.5	2.1	100	88.3	11.7	100
Construction	83.2	16.8	—	100	48.2	51.8	100
Trade, transp., finance	59.2	40.8	—	100	64.2	35.8	100
Health, education	80.3	19.7	—	100	*	*	—
Government, municip.	23.3	76.7	—	100	36.0	64.0	100
Other services	—	—	—	—	77.3	22.7	100
Armed forces	—	—	—	—	53.2	46.8	100
Total	52.6	47.4	—	100	59.7	40.3	100
Population	28.1	71.9	—	100	30.4	69.6	100

* Indicates 'other services'

The pattern of national income distribution reveals two factors closely related to the picture offered above. First, as shown in Table 3.4, while Jews comprised 30 per cent of the population in 1944, they reaped close to 60 per cent of the national income. The Arabs, who were 70 per cent of the population, controlled the remaining 40 per cent of the national income. This showed no improvement over the 1936 figures.[114] Second, in contrasting the national income distribution in terms of the economic sector, we discover that while in 1936 the Arab share of manufacturing and electricity sector amounted to one-third of the income, in 1944 it declined to 12 per cent. In trade, transport, and finance, the Arab share amounted to 36 per cent, slightly less than in 1936. The Arab share of the income from the service and agricultural sectors exceeded that of the Jews. However, by any economic standards, the sign of a healthy economy is a balance in the composition of the three traditional sectors: primary, secondary and tertiary. It is clear that the Arab sectors lacked such a balance, being weakest in the important industrial sector.

The mediatory role of the British

'In order to grasp the changing organization of Arab villagers', Asad asserts, 'it is necessary to begin with a different set of concepts: the articulation of a capitalist with a non-capitalist mode of production mediated by the British colonial state.'[115] Instead of viewing the Arab sector as a dependent region characterized by immobility, a cognizance of the role of the British Mandate enables one better to understand the internal dynamics of the situation which has led to the underdevelopment of the Arab sector. Of particular importance here are the tax policies[116] of the British, which have tended to favour capital-intensive agriculture and the setting up of industrial enterprises, both of which characterized the Jewish sector more than the Arab one.

Equally relevant are the concessions made by the British to Zionist industrialists, such as the concession given to Rottenburg (a Russian Jew) in 1922 which made it possible for the Zionists to seize monopoly over the construction of the biggest electricity generating station in the country, and in turn to use this concession to give priority to equipping Jewish settlements with electricity first.[117] In the field of communications, Jewish interests managed to obtain concessions from the British for setting up a modern transportation and road system which served the Jewish settlements exclusively.[118] Mansur offers this as another example of differential treatment, condoned by the British, of the Jewish and Arab populations:[119]

> Certain roads, on the other hand, have been built on account of the [Jewish] National Home. The Jewish Agency refers to them as 'security' roads. These go from Haifa to Jaffa, from Tulkarem to Nathania, and from Affula to Nahlal in one direction and from Affula to Beisan in the other. The work on the latter was given to Jewish labourers at the cost to the treasury of £80,000, whereas an official engineer's estimate was

> £27,000 [presumably this is to meet higher wages which had to be paid to Jewish rather than Arab workers]. These roads were not built until Arab inhabitants, who might have profited from them, had been driven out of that part of the country and it had been completely Judaised.

The concept of Judaization, whereby Zionist authorities ensure the presence of Jewish majorities in certain enclaves of the country, is still an operational policy as far as the Israeli government is concerned.

A related example of how concessions gained by Jewish settlers were to the detriment of the Arab sector is the case of Tel Aviv port. At a time when the economic life of Jaffa and the living of thousands of Arab transient workers depended upon the activities of the Jaffa port, the Jewish Agency through its powerful lobby in the British Parliament and press managed to secure in 1937 a concession to build a port in Tel Aviv. Since Arab labour, under the policy of 'Jewish labour only', would not be able to secure employment in the new port, the Arab Labourers Federation protested unsuccessfully against the granting of such a concession.[120] The satellite status of Jaffa in relation to present-day Tel Aviv can be traced to the decline in importance of Jaffa in the late 1930s.

In addition to the phasing out of the Jaffa seaport, the British Mandate launched a scheme of 'town-planning' in Jaffa which resulted in the destruction of Arab homes.[121] Barbour argues further that the atrophy of Arab urban development is a function of the decline of certain vital Arab industries, such as the olive oil and soap industries in Nablus; moreover, 'Nazareth lost when the crops of the Emeq were transferred to Jewish hands.'[122]

Under the slogan of 'Jewish labour' not only did the Histadrut and other Zionist institutions manage to curtail entry of Arab workers into its organizations, but they also made sure that similar practices would be followed by Jewish contractors who carried out a disproportionate share of public and governmental contracts (see Table 3.5), at a time when the Jewish population comprised a third of the total population of Palestine.

Notorious in this regard are the activities of the major building contractor Solel Boneh, which operated with the full backing of the Jewish Agency. Solel Boneh was the target of many protests and strikes by Arab workers because of its refusal to hire other than Jewish labour. In 1937, the Union of Craftsmen and Artisans in Haifa demanded, to no avail, that Arab workers be paid identical wages to Jewish workers, that an equal number from each national group be employed in its government contracts, that Solel Boneh make public its records, and that an impartial supervisor be

TABLE 3.5 *Contracts awarded to Jews and Non-Jews (Arabs) by the government departments and four municipal corporations (1935–6)*[123]

	Non-Jews		*Jews*	
Department	*No. of contracts*	*Amount in £P*	*No. of contracts*	*Amount in £P*
Public	1,006	153,562	1,003	111,166
Palestine railways	15	42,560	8	45,500
Post and telegraph	18	4,617	13	1,170
Jaffa harbour works	4	4,026	4	13,424
Municipality				
Jerusalem	17	27,377	3	17,502
Haifa	235	12,358	300	5,015
Jaffa	14	10,867	12	14,102
Tel Aviv	—	—	127	89,220
Total	1,309	255,367	1,470	297,099

appointed to implement the terms of the contract.[124] Another confrontation between Arab workers and the Histadrut, in which violence erupted, was the 1936 strike staged by Arab workers at the Majdal Yuba quarry, which used to provide Tel Aviv with building stone. The quarry, nominally defined as state land, though in practice it had been in the possession of Palestinian Arabs, was leased to Jewish interests in the course of concessions made by the British to the Zionist settlers. In order to safeguard against the implementation of the policy of Jewish labour, the Arab unionists demanded guarantees that the transfer would not affect the 400 Arab workers in the quarry. As happened on numerous other occasions, the Arab demands were ignored and 400 Arabs were displaced by Jewish workers.[125]

There were unsuccessful attempts to organize Arab–Jewish federated trade unions. In 1926, 475 Arab workers joined the international federation of railway workers and came in contact with Jewish workers. Under the initiative of the Histadrut, the Federation of Palestine Workers was established in 1927. Its motto was that it would not engage in politics but would confine its activities to economic matters. This call to Arab workers to forget about national questions came at a time when Jewish immigration into Palestine was at the root of the economic problem faced by Arab workers. While there were internal factors associated with Arab society which made the task of unionization difficult to accomplish, an Arab–Jewish union federation, as conceived by the Zionists, was bound to fail for[126]

> the central obstacles were internal: the way the Palestine Federation of Labour was run, the composition of the workers [Jews were skilled and Arabs unskilled] and the nature of the work itself, but above all it was the purity of the majority of the [Jewish] members of the Histadrut. The slogan 100 per cent Hebrew work, not only drove Arab workers further away, but prevented the Federation from approaching many of the Arab workers who worked in Solel Boneh and in Army barracks. The approach followed by the Palestine Federation of Labour asked a forbidden request from the workers. In line with its nationalist slogans, the Histadrut asked the Arab worker to desist from nationalist activity, [to stay away] from 'politics'. Man does not survive on bread alone. The Arab worker who progressed in his social standing, was drawn by the nationalist current and became an active as well as instigating factor. He could not continue 'to stay away from politics'.

Not only did the Zionist institutions engage in discriminatory practices against Arab labour, they also ensured that the Jewish working classes were the direct beneficiaries of the disadvantaged Arabs.[127] When in 1936 the Arab workers organized a general strike, the Jewish workers acted as strike-breakers and aided the British in the construction of a barbed-wire fence along the northern and north-eastern borders of Palestine built in order to contain any possible identification with the aims of the rebellion among neighbouring Arabs in Syria, Lebanon and Jordan. Barbour summarizes the situation thus:[128]

> On the other hand, the Jewish unemployment which had resulted from the over-immigration of 1934–1937, was greatly reduced by the construction of Tel-Aviv port, by the enrolment of thousands of Jewish supernumeraries, by the demands of the military for labour and for goods by the use of Jewish workers to build the frontier fence, by the Arab transport and other strikes which led to a greatly increased demand for Jewish services, and in many other ways. It is, indeed, no exaggeration to say that only the disturbances saved the Jewish economy from a very serious crisis.

Yehuda Baur assessed in a more general way the consequences of the Arab Rebellion:[129]

> The strike led to a paradoxical development in the Jewish community. Its economic independence was strengthened. The port of Tel Aviv was built, and the expansion of the port of Haifa was speeded up. Strategic roads were built, which were very useful to the Jewish community. Jewish agriculture no

longer had to face the competition of abundant and cheap agricultural products, which the Jewish sector could not meet. The increased strength of the general strike and the revolt was in itself a severe defeat for the Arabs.

The Zionist policy of *Havlaga* (self-restraint) in 1936–9 notwithstanding, the Zionist influence became apparent in the social control agencies of the Mandate such as the police force, and in the subsequent military assistance given to the settler defence force, the *Notrim*, which in Ben-Gurion's words 'provided an excellent framework for training the Hagana'.[130] During the period of the Arab Rebellion the contribution of the Zionist settlers to the police force doubled, to be supplemented later on by close to 3,000 fully armed supernumeraries. Thus, while Palestinian Arab energies, economically and militarily, were consumed in the rebellion, the Zionists were strengthening their military and economic infrastructure ready to mount the offensive on Arab villages and cities in early 1948 – an offensive which in part contributed to the dispersion of the Palestinian Arabs.[131]

Finally, the structure of fiscal spending of the Mandatory government had a direct effect on the Arab population. As every Royal Commission set up to investigate the numerous disturbances in Palestine concluded, there seems to be a direct correlation between an influx of Jewish immigrants with no consultation of the indigenous Arabs, an economic crisis, and a violent Arab reaction. This sequence led the Mandatory government to adopt in turn more oppressive measures against the Arab population. Translated into monetary terms, this then meant a decrease in spending on social services (such as education) and a corresponding increase in budgets allotted to police and security. Since the public and social services in the

TABLE 3.6 *Relative importance of expenditure on the various government services (1933–8)*[132]

	1933–4	*1934–5*	*1935–6*	*1936–7*	*1937–8*
	%	%	%	%	%
Defence	28.4	25.3	20.0	36.6	26.1
Administerial finance	22.1	23.2	22.7	20.7	16.9
Legal services	3.7	3.1	2.4	1.9	1.8
Social services	12.0	11.9	10.2	7.8	7.4
Develop. and economic services	33.8	36.5	44.7	33.0	47.8
	100.0	100.0	100.0	100.0	100.0

Jewish sector came directly under the control of the Zionist authorities, the overall effect on the Jewish sector of changes in the Mandatory budget was not crucial. In 1933–4, the share of the social services amounted to 12 per cent; in 1937, during the height of the Arab Rebellion, the share of social services declined to 7.8 per cent and that of defence rose to 36.6 per cent (see Table 3.6). In contrast, between 1940 and 1948 the share of spending on education did not reach the 5 per cent mark.

Educational gaps

Like all other aspects of Jewish–Arab development discussed so far, it is expected that the Arab educational infrastructure will also show signs of weakness when compared to Jewish provision in this area. In 1944, of 97,400 Arab schoolchildren in the elementary stage between the ages of five to fourteen years, 32 per cent were attending school; among Jewish children it was 97 per cent. As anticipated there were differences in rates of school attendance between children coming from the cities and those living in the countryside, and between boys and girls. The figures for 1946 indicated that 85 per cent of boys and 63 per cent of girls of the elementary school age attended school. For the villages, the figures were 63 per cent and 7.5 per cent for boys and girls, respectively.[133] Not only was there this evident gap, but it was also pointed out that the level of education among the Jewish settlers was 'among the highest in the world'.[134]

TABLE 3.7 *Number of Arab pupils who applied to enter elementary schools in contrast to those who entered (1933–9)*[135]

Year	*No. of applicants*	*Secured a place*	*Per cent*
1933	14,383	8,638	60
1938	23,031	11,552	50
1939	25,488	13,222	52

Contrary to the propagated myth that the low level of education among Palestinian Arabs is due to their traditionalism and value-system (no doubt this is *partially* true, especially where the low rate of school attendance among girls is considered), the evidence presented here provides a different picture. First, as shown in Table 3.7, elementary school enrolment was dictated mostly by availability of places, a factor which the British Mandate controlled. Even at the height of the Mandate, 1945–6, only 69 per cent of Arab children who applied could secure a place.[136] This shortage is especially acute in villages, since the contribution of the Mandate government was aimed at coping with city demands. The efforts of villagers to raise their own funds to meet the educational needs of rural children were described by the John Hope Simpson report of 1930: 'The *fellah* is tremendously anxious for education for his children, and in one year alone the *fellahin* voluntarily contributed over £16,000 towards the building of schools in their villages.'[137] Between 1941 and 1945 the contribution of Arab villagers alone amounted to close to half a million pounds. Additional funds were raised by taxation imposed by local Arab bodies. These funds supplemented the decline in public services expenditure which the Mandate government had to divert from public and social services in order to cope with Arab unrest. By the late 1940s the total Arab contribution (including private education) exceeded that provided by the Mandate government.[138]

The total spending on Arab education per student is still much lower than that found in the Jewish sector. With a population of over a million, there were, in 1944–5, 71,662 Arab pupils in the public school system staffed by 1,871 teachers, housed in 478 schools, with a British government spending of £409,000. The Jewish population, numbering around half a million, had 77,968 pupils in its schools, 3,783 teachers, 573 schools, and a budget of £1,489,563, with 10 per cent of its budget contributed by the British government.[139] This contrast led Tibawi to comment that 'one-third of the population had more children at school than the other two-thirds', and 'the money spent on education of the children of one-third the population was three times the amount spent by the government on the education of the other two-thirds.'[140]

TABLE 3.8 *Development of Arab public and private schools (1925–44)*[141]

Year	*No. of schools*	*No. of pupils*
1925–6	587	38,327
1934–5	719	67,387
1937–8	779	87,498
1943–4	749	105,368

In spite of an increase in the number of Arab schools between 1925 and 1944 (see Table 3.8), the overwhelming majority of these were primary schools. By 1944, there were only 959 secondary school students, with no secondary schools in rural areas.[142] The only university in the country was the Hebrew University, which was established in 1925 to serve the Jewish community exclusively.

Conclusions

It would be erroneous to conclude, in the light of the evidence presented here, that the Arab sector of pre-1948 was dependent on Jewish colonizing efforts in its pattern of development. Palestinian peasants were not colonized by Zionist settlers in the classical sense of colonialism. The situation more resembled a dual society structure, with one part deriving benefit from the sponsoring imperial power at the expense of the other. The Arab–Jewish asymmetry which developed had no real basis in direct Zionist exploitation of the Arab sector, and it would be inaccurate to attempt an application of the classical colonialism theory to account for the eventual marginalization of the Palestinian peasantry.

How is one to account for the resulting politico-economic domination pattern in which the Palestinian Arabs occupied a subordinate place? This could be accounted for in terms of the following factors: (1) the introduction of a capitalist mode of production under foreign control in a system of peasant economy governed largely by communal ownership of the land and subsistence economy; (2) the policies of the British government (in particular its tax policies), which tended to favour an industrially oriented economy and intensive agriculture, both of which were more prevalent in the Jewish than the Arab sector; (3) the importation of capital and technology by the Zionist settlers, which made it difficult for the traditional Arab industries to survive in the face of a more advanced and efficient European-styled economy; (4) a periodic alliance between the Zionist colonists and British imperial interests in the area, on the one hand, and between the Zionists and Arab landlords, on the other, which culminated in the opposition of the aspirations of the native Palestinian population; (5) the influx of Jewish immigrants, without taking into account the economic absorptive capacity of the country, the wishes of the indigenous Palestinian Arabs and at times the policies of the British government; and (6) the presence of serious internal cleavages within the Arab sector, vertical and horizontal, based on clan–class–ethnicity, which made the task of a unified opposition to British–Zionist domination impossible.

4 The Arabs in Israeli social science writings

Various labels have been adopted to describe Israeli society: pioneering, revolutionary, egalitarian, theocratic, and colonial. Though this list is by no means exhaustive, it reflects two things: the varied nature of the labels used, and their frequent polarity.

In certain cases the labelling has been motivated by strictly partisan interests, while in others it has been sociologically based. Some writers have underscored the important changes which Israeli society has experienced over the last fifty years or so, from being 'pioneering' and 'revolutionary' during the earlier days of colonization and settlement, to becoming increasingly bureaucratized in later days and imbued with 'dynamic conservatism', to use Eisenstadt's phrase.[1] Others have argued that Israeli society is both democratic and exclusivist depending on the particular sphere of activity being discussed and the group in question. For example, when comparing the Arab minority to the Jewish majority commentators pointed out that the latter enjoys a greater degree of political, economic and social freedom, although there is a further distinction in the case of the Jews; the European Jew is more advantaged than the Oriental one.[2] It is in a similar analytical context that Tamarin,[3] Weinstock,[4] and Ghilan,[5] among others,[6] refer to an apartheid-like situation existing between Arabs and Jews in Israel.

One feature upon which Israeli sociologists agree is this: Israel is a settler society, the outcome of processes of colonization which were started by European Jewry in the latter part of the last century in a land populated predominantly by indigenous Palestinian Arabs. What is problematic, however, is the typification and interpretation of the nature and consequences of this process of colonization. On the whole, Israeli sociologists have interpreted this process as positive and benign, arguing that Zionist colonization has little in common with other processes of colonization, or more appropriately colonialism, which are discussed in the literature on the Third World and race and ethnic relations in general. We shall turn to these arguments in more detail in this and subsequent chapters. But first, let us make the following assertion: Israel is a settler society; whether or not it differs from other settler and colonial societies is an empirical and sociological question; the resolution of this question depends on the extent to which Israel shares with other settler regimes features which are sociologically characteristic of the colonial encounter between the settler and indigenous groups.

While our task in this and subsequent chapters is to examine Israeli academic, sociological, and social science writings dealing with the Arab minority, we have widened the criteria to include non-resident indigenous Arab writers as well as those who are not practising academics. This is due to the fact that there is a limited number of Arab social science academics in Israel. The writings of these authors make up the bulk of the published material on the Arabs in Israel. In terms of the general orientations of Israeli academic writers, the tendency is to project a consensual and cultural-pluralistic view of Israeli society, and the Arabs in it. The discussion will centre around the following main themes: (1) the pluralist and anticolonialist image of Israeli society, (2) the centrality of cultural and socio-psychological factors in explaining Arab behaviour, and (3) Arab writers.

The pluralist image

In terms of the models discussed in the second chapter, it is accurate to say that, on the whole, Israeli sociologists have been conscious of the plural character of their society. This recognition has to be assessed with two main qualifications, however. First, there is the premise that Zionism, as an ideology, will eventually act toward integrating Jewish settlers and immigrants into a cohesive, homogeneous society. Very few had anticipated that this process of *mizug galuyot*, or 'ingathering of exiles', would give rise to Jewish ethnic and class cleavages. Thus, it is admitted that there exists in Israel a mild form of pluralism along social and cultural, but not political or economic, lines; and that in due course this cultural pluralism will give way to lesser forms of social differentiation. More will be said about this later on.

Second, because the plural conception of Israeli society minimized economic and political differentiations, a mention of the Arabs in the context of Israeli pluralism would be accompanied by contrasting their *cultural* distinctiveness to that of the Jews; little attention was paid by Zionist writers on Palestine to the consequences of institutional separateness between Arabs and Jews which resulted in an advantaged position for the Jewish settlers relative to the indigenous Arab population; this, in turn, would help to explain, in large part, the current economic and political dependency of the Arabs in Israel.

A main theme which runs through most of the established academic research on Israeli society addresses itself to the *uniqueness* of the Jewish colonization of Palestine. In his book *Israeli Society,*[7] Eisenstadt singles out the absence of economic motives as a factor which sets Jewish colonization of Palestine apart from other forms of European colonization. 'Moreover', he says, 'the colonizing movement was not . . . primarily motivated by economic considerations but by the desire to bring about a social and national renaissance – a transformed modern society.'[8]

Writing recently, Eisenstadt isolates four 'basic contractual problems of the society', one of which addresses itself specifically to the conflict between Arabs and Jews:[9]

> First, these problems were connected with immigration and absorption; second, with the persistent problem of the development of the economy; third – with the problems of defense and establishing roots in a foreign, and even hostile, environment; and fourth with the crystallization of collective identification symbols of Israeli society which are linked to the Jewish tradition on the one hand, and the reality of the Middle East on the other.

In an attempt to resolve these persisting issues, various approaches were adopted by the Israeli élite, some of which led to increasing group solidarity and identification with the Jewish State, while others gave rise to 'cultural provincialism', 'chauvinism', and 'ideological conservatism'.[10] The crux of the problem, as seen by Eisenstadt, lies in the dominance of so-called dynamic conservatism exemplified in expanding bureaucracies whose success in coping with some of the problems they face is overshadowed by a rigid and uncompromising attitude which has typified Israel's dealings with the outside world.

Implicit in Eisenstadt's analysis is the primacy of Weber's notion of bureaucratic rationality which is alleged to be responsible for the rigid and conservative symptoms mentioned above. For Eisenstadt, Israel appears to be a case where revolutionary leaders of the pre-state period assumed the role of legitimate authorities subsequent to 1948, whereby spontaneity was replaced by routinization. In a sense, Israel's uniqueness – mentioned so often in the writings of Israeli sociologists – appears to dissolve into normality, and her problems are seen to be no different from those faced by any modern nation-state; they are in large measure the problems of bureaucracy.

While an emphasis on bureaucratic rigidity and the continuing existence of the hegemony of the East European élite – resulting in an unresponsive social system – might explain the cleavage between European and Oriental Jews, it does little to shed light on the situation of the Arabs and their built-in inequality.

Although Eisenstadt sees in Israeli society a pluralistic and heterogeneous structure (excluding the Arabs from his analysis), nevertheless it is a form of pluralism which is characterized by domination. The successive waves of Oriental Jewish immigrants who flowed into the state in the early 1950s 'mixed with the established society and the political organization as they were already established without causing significant changes; most of the immigrants were educated to accept as "given" the values of the first pioneers – the values of national brotherhood and equality'.[11]

Eisenstadt is quick to note that changes in the complexity and structure of the Jewish community in Palestine, the *Yishuv*, diluted, if it did not alter, the so-called egalitarian ideologies of the early settlers, which stressed 'non-exploitive agricultural and manual work as a major way for rejuvenating the nation'.[12]

Nevertheless, the hegemony of this East European ideology was maintained after the establishment of the state through placement of the pre-state élites in key positions in the political, economic and cultural spheres. This is the reason, according to Eisenstadt, why no effective counter-ideology succeeded in crystallizing, even though a drastic change in the demographic composition of the society was taking place.

Such continued dominance by the old élites has managed to further their grip on the definition of Israeli identity; thus analyses result which overlook the possible cleavages and even 'privatization' of some of the traditions of the other Jewish ethnic groups immigrating at later stages. In consequence, the differing interpretations of Israeli identity might eventually lead to 'socio-political cleavages', according to Eisenstadt.

As remarked earlier, nowhere in Eisenstadt's treatment of Israeli society do we find an acknowledgment of the consequences of Jewish colonization for the indigenous Palestinian Arabs; indeed, it appears from reading Eisenstadt's work that Zionist colonization has taken place largely in a social vacuum. In his lengthy discussion of the *Yishuv* in his above-mentioned book, and likewise in an earlier writing published in 1948[13] on the same topic, one finds hardly a mention of the patterns of contact between Jews and Arabs in Palestine. To the extent that he deals with the Israeli Arabs in one chapter of *Israeli Society*, the main emphasis is on cultural variations, that is, the modern Zionist settler versus the traditional Palestinian Arabs. Had he addressed himself to the phenomenon in a holistic fashion, taking into account the imperatives of Zionist colonization of Palestine, it would have been possible to explain in a more satisfactory fashion the transformation of the Palestinian Arabs in Israel from peasants to marginal proletariat, a fact of which he is aware, as the following quotation demonstrates:[14]

> One of the consequences of these changes is the development of a migrant landless peasant-proletariat consisting of those who went to the cities as part-time workers and developed trends usual in migrant labourers. Such groups tended to concentrate in areas where manpower was most needed, but while some developed into skilled workers, helped by the vocational courses of the Histradut and the government, the great majority of this floating proletariat belonged to the lower categories of unskilled workers.

Although Eisenstadt does not provide the necessary comparative evidence, he advances the contention that the Arab minority ranks lower than Oriental Jews on most indices of stratification: 'Culturally and educationally, the Arabs rank lowest by all criteria, even lagging behind the new immigrants from Asia and Africa who have the lowest educational level among the Jewish population.'[15]

A more systematic attempt to test the pluralist thesis is found in Lissak's[16] work on Israeli society, which we examine in detail below. It must be stressed, however, that this test *does not* assess the position of the Arabs in Israel. Lissak reaches the conclusion that, within the Jewish sector in Israel, pluralism is manifest along social and cultural lines, but not at the institutional level.

Mainly, institutional pluralism implies a greater degree of correspondence between, on the one hand, power distribution in society and, on the other, social class, regional and ethnic variations. It also implies a perception on the part of the citizenry that the class structure is rigid and mobility is difficult. Once the class system manifests flexibility and a degree of openness, we have, according to Lissak, social pluralism. The contrast between the two is expressed as follows:[17]

> The stratification system in a socially pluralistic society differs from that present in an institutionally pluralistic society. In the latter, the stratification structure is imposed, totalistic and its bases of evaluation are only collectivistic and ascribed; in a socially pluralistic society the system is less hierarchic, more permissive and its evaluation criteria tend to be more achieved and individualistic.

Hence, according to Lissak, a change in the institutional arrangement demands, first and foremost, a change in the political set-up.

It is possible for institutional pluralism to ensure a form of political hegemony on the central level in the face of existing pluralistic tendencies:[18]

> Different legal frameworks, marriage patterns and contradictory stratification criteria are further examples of institutional pluralism. Only on the political level, however, is the institutional pluralism limited. The ruling group, which holds the power sanctions, forces a more or less uniform political framework upon the whole population within a given territory.

'Criss-crossing allegiances' along various status dimensions such as education, income, occupation, power, and so on, are sufficient guarantees, in Lissak's view, to counter the centralization of power positions in the hands of few groups. However, comparing Israeli census data gathered from 1954 and 1965 Lissak notes differing patterns of mobility among Oriental and European Jews. The latter, together with Israeli-born Jews of Western background, dominate the professional and managerial strata of the occupational ladder, while the former are increasingly abandoning agricultural pursuits to enter production and building industries, trades, and, to a lesser extent, the service industries. Concerning inter-generational mobility the same pattern holds:[19]

> the conclusions regarding skipping and short cuts among Israeli children of Western old-timers, and, even more, amongst Western new immigrants, are extremely illustrative. Moreover, the slow mobility amongst children born in Israel to Oriental parents and amongst Oriental born is evidence of the fact that the rate of both class and inter-generational mobility in the Oriental communities is far from keeping pace with the rate of mobility amongst Israeli and Western born of the same age group.

Indeed, if anything, the children of Oriental parents experience *downward* mobility more than any other group. The gap in income distribution among the two groups has also increased between 1951 and 1964. In 1951 the monthly income of a head of an Oriental household was 88 per cent of that of Euro-American immigrants; in 1964 the ratio declined to 71 per cent. The economic gap between Oriental and European Jews persists to this day, as indicated by the continuing debate on the subject in Israel, and in our subsequent discussion of Smooha's work.[20]

Turning to mixed marriages as an index of integration, Lissak notes that from 1952 to 1962 the proportion of inter-group marriages increased from 9 to 15 per cent. However, the tendency among

Israelis of European or American origin to marry within their own group is significantly higher than that found among Israelis of Asian or African origin. Over time, the tendency of the European and American group born in Israel to marry within its own group has *increased* noticeably. Yochanan Peres' more recent findings tend to support Lissak's earlier conclusions.[21]

Using ecological dispersion as another indicator of social pluralism, Lissak finds that 'At any rate, it is clear that in the mid-sixties, the old-timers are concentrated in the older and more established cities of Israel, and also in the central areas of the country; the new cities and the new urban settlements are mainly populated by Asian-African immigrants.'[22] He goes on to quote another study which showed that established West European immigrants tended to settle in city centres, while more of the Oriental immigrants tended to gravitate to the periphery. Lissak concludes by saying that 'partial segregation is therefore an undisputable fact'.[23]

Concerning perception of, and self-placement within, the class structure, Lissak's study shows that the majority of European Jews thought of themselves as middle class, compared to 52 per cent of Israeli-born, 48 per cent of Asian immigrants, and 29 per cent of North African and other respondents.

When confronted with various images of Israeli society, low-income people held a conflict image of society, while the higher educated held an egalitarian image. This picture is complemented by another study of urban youth, ages sixteen to twenty-five, in which it is found that a 'status', in contrast to a 'class', image is more prevalent among Western than among Oriental youth.[24] Lissak notes that the former reflects a more 'dynamic' and 'complex' perception of class structure, in contrast to the rigid and simple image possessed by the latter. Lissak seems to imply that perception of social structure along class, rather than status, lines is primarily psychologically generated and denotes a low level of sophistication in the subjects. This personalistic and value-oriented perspective, essentially a structural-functional derivative, obscures the role played by objective reality, namely, as Frank Parkin[25] rightly claims, that one's perception of the class structure could actually be a reflection of the reward system and one's experience within it. Indeed, in a subsequent discussion by Lissak, Oriental youths deny the optimistic claim made by their European counterparts concerning the chances of upward mobility.[26]

Whether or not this situation in reality translates into feelings of ethnocentrism, Lissak, writing in the middle 1960s, dismisses the possibility. He notes, for example, that while the Oriental groups are in fact at the bottom of the social ladder, this does not translate itself into a hatred of the European Jews. Instead it is the Kurds and

Moroccans – both groups being Oriental Jews – who are most disliked. Overall, 'it appears that aggression and unilateral prejudices are usually directed by European-born against Asia–African born, rather than vice-versa.'[27]

Finally, Lissak tackles the extent of Oriental Jews' integration into the political structure of Israel. As a measure of 'integration', Lissak focuses on the extent to which Oriental Jews participated in the various political organizations, beginning with the *Yishuv* – the earliest organized pockets of Zionist colonization in Palestine – and continues up to the development of the present national party system in Israel. Noting the traditional 'passivity' of the Oriental Jews in participating in the affairs of the *Yishuv*, he advances the following explanation: 'This passivity, as we know, expressed in their incapacity to form effective pressure groups, while most of the social groups from the *Yishuv* period turned, with the creation of the State, into pressure groups bargaining actively in the political market.'[28]

He goes on to show that while ethnic pluralism became, with the establishment of the state, a more noticeable feature of social life in Israel, the support secured by political parties on the national level tended to be non-pluralistic. Thus, for example, the extreme right-wing Herut party, with its traditional East European leadership, tended to draw its support mostly from North African Jews.

However, because of the slowness of occupational mobility and economic progress, various forms of protest movement appeared, mostly of a localized nature. These protests were ethnically based as well as social-class-bound. The riots – by Orientals in 1958 in Haifa's Wadi Salib slum district, in 1966 in the southern port of Ashdot, and more recently in the poor districts of Jerusalem and in Tel Aviv – are indications of attempts by Oriental Jews to usurp power on the local level at least. This is manifest in the noticeable increase in the number of ethnic lists, which would signify a greater degree of political and ethnic polarization. It is in this context that the situation looks ominous for the future:[29]

> We witness here a development by which feelings of real and apparent deprivation are starting to be channelled into clearly oppositionary streams as well, besides their orientation towards organizing ethnic lists. Is it possible that in addition to the occupational and economical, we will attach a separate political label to the population of the 'second Israel'? Such a prognosis has frightening meanings for the future Israeli society, if indeed this would be the exclusive or dominant trend.

A more extensive application of the pluralist model of race relations, taking account of the Arabs, is found in Smooha's study of pluralism in Israel. An Israeli of Iraqi origin, Smooha gives greater weight in his discussion to an analysis of the Oriental–European Jewish dichotomy (something which has a direct bearing upon him), than to Arab–Jewish relations.

Smooha is certainly more critical of Israeli society and its academic sociology than either Eisenstadt or Lissak. This is true on two main levels. First, he is willing to incorporate radical perspectives into his analysis as a means of rectifying the dominant trends in Israeli sociology which he sees as being mainly ahistorical. Second, he acknowledges the coercive character of pluralism in Israel as it affects Oriental Jews and Arabs. Thus his multi-dimensional treatment of pluralism centres on legal and extra-legal differentiation, cultural diversity, socio-economic differences, power disparities and segregation.[30]

The situation of the Arabs in Israel is best described as one of 'exclusionary domination'.[31] Since the Arabs in Israel are assigned societal roles on the basis of ascriptive criteria, they constitute *vis-à-vis* the Jewish population a quasi-caste. In terms of status, power and political culture, the Arabs live in a system of '*Herrenvolk* democracy', in which democratic norms apply to the dominant but not to the subordinate group. While the Oriental Jews are in a disadvantaged position relative to the Europeans, they do not suffer from a similar ascriptive differentiation (on the basis of religion, endogamy and nationality) which applies to the Arabs in Israel. Yet the position of the Oriental Jews is better than that of the Arabs:[32]

> Membership in the Jewish quasi-caste ensures Orientals some symbolic and material gains. The status superiority of Orientals qua Jews (majority membership) over Arabs (minority members) is important. But not less important are the economic benefits. The separate facilities for Arabs or agencies for controlling them provide jobs and positions of power for Oriental Jews. Since Arabs are discriminated against in jobs for security and other reasons, Orientals have an edge in employment over Arabs.

Although Smooha sees in 'the countermeasures taken by the Israeli Government, notably military administration and expropriation of lands', a cause for Arab resentment, he resorts to the familiar themes of modernization to explain the reaction of Arabs by noting that 'the acceleration of the process of modernization and continuing rise in the standard of living infused the younger generation with frustrating nationalism.'[33]

What emerges from the above discussion is a system within Israeli society of stratification – and, by definition, of power – in which the Oriental Jew, compared to the European one, occupies a subordinate position along various dimensions of the stratification system, with the Palestinian Arabs occupying the lowest status rank.

The anti-colonialist image

An equally central theme, which is dealt with at one time or another by almost every Israeli social scientist, is whether or not Israel constitutes a colonialist society. As stated earlier, the conclusion reached, without exception, is that Israel was founded through colonization and not colonialism, and that in its present form Israel is the only true democracy in the Middle East. Any deviations from the democratic ideal are minor and, it is further claimed, will be rectified in due course.

For the purpose of illustrating the rationale behind the offered anti-colonialism image of Israel, we have focused on the writings of Tartakower,[34] Memmi,[35] Avishai,[36] and Lucas.[37] These are by no means the only sample of Zionist writings which we deal with. In the final chapter we examine the various strands of Zionist thinking as they relate to Jewish–Arab relations.

Although Memmi is neither an Israeli citizen nor associated with Israeli academia, he identified to a large extent with the State of Israel. As a Tunisian Jew, and a writer on colonialism, in this respect his views on Israel and Zionism are appropriate to examine. Avishai, a political scientist, has practised social science at one time or another in Israel; and Lucas has researched the modern history of Israel and participated in the affairs of the Histadrut and other Zionist organizations. Tartakower is one of Israel's longest-standing sociologists.

Writing in 1948, Tartakower is emphatic in rejecting the colonialist nature of the Jewish settlement in Palestine:[38]

> There have been cases of states established as a result of the occupation of the country; the occupying forces become assimilated with the local population into one nation. There also have been cases of nations deprived during a certain period of their statehood and trying to regain it; but these were nations living on their own soil and leading their own normal life. There were even cases of statehood coming into existence in consequence of colonization in an uninhabited or semi-vacant country; but then the work of colonization was done by people accustomed to hard labour, speaking the same language and protected by their former home country. Not a single one of these conditions applied to the Jewish state.

Not only does he reject the colonialist characterization of Israel, but he goes on to suggest that 'the most appropriate definition of the

Jewish state could be to call it a state by agreement.'[39] It is not clear from Tartakower's discussion when and how the agreement of the Arab population was secured in the process of reaching this consensus. Chaim Weizmann, one of Zionism's most influential ideologists, who became the first President of Israel, provides the following rationale which must have typified the attitudes of many Zionists: 'the rights which the Jewish people has been adjudged in Palestine do not depend on the consent, and cannot be subjected to the will, of the majority of its present (Arab) inhabitants.'[40] Writing a decade later, in 1960, Tartakower sees in Israel not only the fulfilment of a Messianic dream, but also a blessing to a region lacking any sort of enlightenment:[41]

> There exists, however, a second idea of a mission. . . . This is the mission to be fulfilled on behalf of civilization and progress in the Near East. In this region of over one-hundred million inhabitants, the great majority of whom starve physically and culturally and in many countries suffer exploitation by small number of owners of latifundia or rich capitalists without recourse to their own governments, the State of Israel is one of the few bright spots, probably the brightest.

Tartakower's views are shared by many liberal and conservative Western social scientists. An influential writer who echoes this view is Albert Memmi, whose book *The Colonizer and the Colonized*[42] – a study of the consequences of French colonialism in North Africa – has been praised by students of the Third World and of colonialism in general. In a lengthy interview granted to an Israeli magazine in 1972, Memmi rejected the characterization of Israel as a colonialist state, arguing that Zionism was 'from its start not only a movement of the poor strata, but also the expression of an entire oppressed people'.[43] In his reply to Maxime Rodinson,[44] a French Orientalist scholar who advanced the thesis that Israel is basically a colonialist experiment, Memmi says:[45]

> It is difficult to find in the Israel venture – unless one plays with semantics, as Rodinson did – a single indicator of the various measures depicting colonialism: no economic exploitation of child labour by a minority of settlers, no application of force to secure cheap labour, while the settlers occupy the position of managers only, no mother country [which is responsible for] either direct or indirect military rule, no suppression of the cultural rights of the indigenous population in favour of the settlers.

As far as the immediate problem facing Arabs and Jews inside Israel is concerned, Memmi calls for a fuller integration of the

Arabs into the economic life of Israel. Such integration should not be carried out at the expense of Arab cultural identification. Regarding the Palestinian question, he calls for a possible future solution through the formation in the area of a federation in which the Palestinians would have a separate state or would be incorporated into Jordan.

Bernard Avishai, at one time a lecturer in political theory at Jerusalem's Hebrew University, expounded his views on the 'myth' of Israeli colonialism in an article written for the American magazine *Dissent*. Like Memmi's remarks, Avishai's are aimed at refuting Rodinson's claims, and, at the same time, at winning over leftist dissenters who are critical of Israel.

To say as Herzl did that Palestine was 'empty' is, in Avishai's view, 'not all that far from the mark',[46] and therefore desirable environs could not be used as a proof of the colonialist intentions of Zionism. It is difficult to reconcile Avishai's claim with that of another Jewish European visitor to Palestine, Achad Ha-Am, a contemporary of Herzl and no less important a figure from the point of view of Zionism. Writing in 1891, after paying a visit to Palestine, he expressed the following concern:[47]

> Abroad, we are accustomed to believe that Israel is almost empty; nothing is grown here, and that whoever wishes to buy land could come here and buy what his heart desires. In reality, the situation is not like this. Throughout the country it is difficult to find cultivable land which is not already cultivated. . . . Abroad, we are used to believe that the Arabs are all desert people, and like a donkey they can neither see nor understand what goes on around them. This is a great error. Like any other human being, the Arab has a sharp mind and is calculating.

The fiction of the emptiness of Palestine, which later 'became an embarrassment for Herzlian Zionists',[48] is as far from being isolated in its expression as it is from being the actual truth of the time. In referring to the writings of Epstein, Smilansky, and Kalvarisky – members of the First Aliyah – Taylor notes that 'what troubled them most was the indifference and hostility of the agricultural *Yishuv* toward the indigenous population.'[49] The selective perception displayed by Herzl and others after him is a well-known phenomenon in inter-ethnic and colonial societies – a process whereby the superordinate group reduces the subordinate group to an invisible entity in order to avoid an otherwise painful reconciliation with the facts, namely, in this case, that Palestine was not desolate but, instead, inhabited by its indigenous population. In Chapter 3 we have dealt in detail with the demographic debate concerning pre-1948 Palestine and the extent of Arab and Jewish immigration into Palestine during this period.

Avishai sees a positive effect accruing to Arab peasants as a consequence of Jewish acquisition of Arab land: 'Those peasants who retained their lands quickly benefited from superior Jewish technology.'[50] Again, the substantiating evidence for this assertion is rather thin. As indicated in the previous chapter, any benefit coming to the Arab peasants was incidental and not part of a conscious attempt on the part of Jewish settlers to share their agricultural technology with the Arabs.

A more direct and contrary statement on the subject was made by the Israeli writer A. B. Yehoshua, speaking at a youth symposium held in Israel in 1973:[51]

> the beginning of the conflict was created as a result of a clash between two nationalist movements about the land not the result of intrigues by a few *Effendis* who incited the simple masses to rise against the Jews. . . . There are those who claim that it [Palestine] was desolate. To them I answer: The Negev is still empty at the present time; after twenty-five years there are only 10,000 people living in it. Is there anybody who would be prepared to give away a lump of earth from the Negev because it is desolate? The fact that we built this place and that before we came it was desolate does not impress anybody, because in the West building [a place in itself] does not entitle one to ownership. In spite of this, everyone likes to build according to his taste; let go of my freedom and I'll build the way I like in my own tempo. Even if this country was full of swamps, diseased and desolate, they [the Arabs] could say: it is fine with us this way. We like to live by ourselves.

Avishai's discussion leads him to conclude that any movement by the Israeli government toward practising colonialist policies would be the result of conditions of war and Arab extremism. Israel, in Avishai's view, mainly *reacts* and *responds* to external stimuli; and whenever she responds in a negative fashion it is because she is compelled to do so by Arab extremists:[52]

> War, not Zionism, is driving Israel step by step, expediency by expediency, to practise colonialist policies. But Jewish [rather than Zionist] colonialism is still a distant nightmare and will not materialize except as the self-fulfilled prophecy of Palestinian maximalists who still resist the very concept of Jewish national life.

Explanation of the discriminatory legal structure in Israel – as well as its one-time system of military government in the civilian

Israeli–Arab sector – on the basis of war imperatives alone is, as we will show in subsequent chapters, an impressionistic, liberal statement on the subject which typifies the attitudes of many Israeli intellectuals.

Surely S. M. Lipset, an ardent supporter of Israel, did not write the following lightly, after paying a visit to Israel:[53]

> Opinion polls taken before the Yom Kippur War indicated clearly that the majority of the Jews regarded the Arabs as an inferior people. As in other multi-ethnic societies, the long continuation within one nation, of different peoples living with sharply different levels of culture, education, and skill, produces or sustains the phenomenon described as institutionalized racism in the United States. In effect, the varying components of the social system serve to prevent the depressed group from gaining access to the good things, while they give the dominant one an ideological defense for their birth-right superiority. The Sepharadim will improve their situation, but Israel, if it ignores its Arab population and relies on a large 'external proletariat' could become a racist state.

Lipset's prognostication of the Israeli situation does not end on an optimistic note, unlike the one reached by Avishai, who says: 'Today Arabs and Jews can still be reconciled to one another in a historic Palestine precisely because the intended result of Zionist policies has been substantially achieved and class domination of one people by the other avoided.'[54]

Rather than deal in an equally passing manner with Avishai's impressionistic claims concerning the absence of Jewish class domination, we shall defer such a discussion to Chapter 5, where we examine the continuing transformation of the Arabs from peasantry to proletariat with their resulting marginalization. It is there that we will be able to substantiate that the situation is somewhat closer to the claim made by Anis Shakour, a Palestinian: 'The improvement of the economic situation [of the Arabs] has no reliable foundation and has no basis in the ownership of the means of production.'[55]

Lucas concurs with other Zionist writers in arguing against equating Zionism with colonialism. Zionism, he claims, is dissimilar from other forms of colonialism in the sense that it does not rest on the economic exploitation of indigenous Arabs. 'The most forceful expression of Zionism as implemented in Palestine was the "conquest of labour" strategy of the Histadrut. This policy secured the containment of Arab employment in the Jewish sector to a minimum. It was this which most markedly distinguished Zionism from other European settler enterprises such as those in Kenya and Rhodesia'.[56]

Jewish economic nationalism, Lucas argues, was manifest both in labour and in produce markets. To the extent that there were economic exchanges between the two sectors, it was to allow for the outlet of Arab produce in Jewish markets. Thus complete segregation and discrimination in labour relations by the Zionist institutions are cited by Lucas as necessary measures to prevent the exploitation of Arab workers.

In his discussion of the role of the Histadrut during the 1920s and 1930s Lucas shows how the Zionist socialist ideals, when they clashed with Zionist national goals, were consistently sacrificed. Arab–Jewish working-class solidarity, according to the Zionist ideologists, could not be attained on the basis of a starting point reflecting differential positions in the occupational and economic spheres. It is only when Arab workers manage to build a cohesive trade union movement and to raise their life-style and consciousness to the level of the Jewish workers that a Jewish–Arab working-class movement will materialize.

In other words, the road to Zionist socialism and non-colonial exploitation of Arab workers implied exclusionary practices on the part of the Zionists in the economic sphere, non-co-operation with the Arabs in the area of politics, and non-sharing of technological and scientific knowledge.

While the Zionist socialists such as Ben-Gurion viewed the lack of Arab unionization as a social, that is Arab, problem, the events of the thirties (when the Histadrut managed to assert its hegemony) proved that the conflict was indeed a national one and that the national socialism of the Histadrut together with Arab land expropriation crystallized Arab opposition to Zionist settlement in Palestine, which manifested itself in the Arab Revolt of 1936–9.

It must be pointed out, however, that although Lucas endorses the Zionist interpretation of the ideological motives of Jewish economic nationalism, and therefore does not incorporate either a critical or an Arab interpretation of Histadrut effects on Arab economic life, he does acknowledge the pitfalls of the Zionist doctrine:[57]

> But as socialists the Histadrut leaders preferred to look on the issue as a social rather than a national conflict. In this way they could reassure themselves that recurrent violent expressions of Arab resentment were not due to incompatibility between Zionism and Arab nationalism. Arab aspirations, they could tell themselves, were not hampered by Zionism, but by the adverse Arab political and social structure. Socialist reasoning selected the torpor of Arab society and its ruling class as the source of Arab–Jewish conflict. It was a small group of

landowners, usurers and clergy that stood in the way of the Arab masses. The moment their overlords were overthrown the Arab masses would realize that Zionism and Arab nationalism could cooperate in peace and progress. This theory was widely diffused throughout the Zionist movement but it had a special value for the labour-Zionists. By beclouding the essentially nationalist élan of their own programme their socialist reasoning enabled them to evade the logical conclusion that the Arab opposition could also be interpreted in national terms, as incipient nationalism. Incidents of cooperation with Arab peasants or workers and occasionally with intellectuals were exaggerated out of all proportion.

The Arab image: traditionalism v. modernism

In contrast to the anti-colonial and cultural-pluralist images of Israeli society which are apparent in the writings of Israeli social scientists, the thrust of most writings on the Arabs in Israel tends to rely heavily on the literature on social change, with the notions of modernity and traditionalism being considered central in such an approach.

In accounting for social change, the onus in such an approach is put on the individual actor – his psychology, culture, value-system, temperament, and so forth – and not on the social structure in which the individual is immersed.[58] To follow this reasoning to its logical conclusion, the advocate of this approach would claim that for economic, social and political developments to take place, they have to be initiated in the mental and psychic configurations of individual people. This personalistic perspective of social problems has serious repercussions, for it precludes the consideration of revolutionary institutional change as a plausible programme for development. Rather, the focus is upon pragmatic and piecemeal social engineering with a view to altering individual attitudes and behaviour, leaving the institutional framework of society almost intact.

Patai's[59] overall approach to the problems facing Israeli society, and the Middle East in general, reflects a preoccupation with cultural and psychological variables. In particular, he draws upon the literature on modernization and development as discussed both above and in an earlier chapter. He isolates familism, personal contact, aestheticism and religion as the basic components characterizing the traditional culture of the Middle East. Attachment and loyalty to an extended kinship system, reliance on interpersonal contacts, the emphasis on folk culture as part of individual aesthetic satisfaction, and adherence to religious precepts which permeate both country and city – all of these components contribute toward a traditional society which is resistant to Western-style industrialization and development. And it is the absence of such traditional cultural characteristics among Israel's European Jewry, and of modern ones among the Arabs, which ultimately leads, in Patai's view, to further conflict between Arabs and Jews.

In assessing the Oriental–European Jewish dichotomy, Patai detects, as early as the 1950s, the eventual emergence of culture-conflict between the two groups. Through the perspective of social anthropology Patai analyses the situation during the earlier days of the state's existence and isolates the roots of the conflict in terms of two opposing *Weltanschauungen*, one representing the East and the other the West – these are the factors which, in Patai's view, contributed to the Arab–Jewish discord, first in Palestine and later on in Israel.

Patai correctly anticipated the now familiar patterns of prejudice which characterize certain aspects of Oriental–European relationships. He foresaw the outcomes of the domination of Euro-culture in Israeli society. The emergence of negative stereotypes of Oriental Jews and the idealization by the latter of the symbols of the dominant European culture in Israel were some of the features which Patai saw signalling the coming of a cultural crisis in Israeli society.

Although the Oriental Jews approximated in their cultural experience the people of the Middle East, and therefore were closer in their world-view and social structure to the Arabs in Israel than to the European Jews, recent research by Israeli psychologists on the thought-patterns of Arab and Jewish children showed a process of Western acculturation taking place among Oriental Jewish children which set them apart from Israeli Arab children of rural background. Kugelmass, Lieblich and Bossik[60] compared the thought-patterns of urban Oriental children to rural Arab children and discovered an IQ lag among Arab children in all areas, ranging from performance on information, vocabulary, arithmetic to comprehension tests. Overall, Arab rural children performed poorest on abstract tests (such as arithmetic), and best on concrete tests, such as acquisition of information. However, when in a subsequent study[61] the authors matched Arab and Jewish children from a mixed city in the north of Israel, the results were quite different in that Arab children performed similarly to Jewish children; this, we might add, occurred even though the educational system is segregated. These results led the authors to stress the environmental, and not the ethnic, factors in accounting for the poorer performance of rural Arab children in the earlier study. Still, the earlier findings should be considered crucial since most Arab children in Israel reside in rural areas which have deficient educational facilities. More will be said about socialization patterns of Palestinian youth in a subsequent part of this chapter, when the contrast is made between young Palestinians living on the West Bank and those living in Israel.

What is the remedy for this situation? In the case of the Jews, Patai sees the roots of the problem in environmental factors, and not necessarily in deep psychological or cultural typifications. However, this environmental change is, in Patai's view, to be achieved along Western lines. In the case of the Oriental Jews, the reshaping process is to be conducted by the educational system, the army and the Histadrut, the Western institutions *par excellence*. While Patai advocates an East–West 'cultural synthesis', as far as the Jews are concerned the fact remains that the key institutions in Israeli society remain Western in their essence. Therefore, it is not surprising to discover that twenty years after Patai published his study on Israeli society, the institutional and cultural domination of European Jews in Israeli society has persisted and gained in strength.

When it comes to considering the situation of the Arabs, Patai, in his new book, *The Arab Mind*,[62] leans heavily on psychological-cum-cultural explanations in accounting for the stagnation and backwardness of the Arabs. According to Patai, as the title of his book clearly implies, the Arabs' problem is rooted in their mental configurations. More significant, in Patai's view, is the fact that although the Arabs are schizoid in their attitudes to the West – maintaining a love-hate relationship – they seem to be unique among all colonized or, as he prefers to call them, 'colonial' people in rejecting and even denouncing Western culture. Why is this so? It is because, according to Patai, the Arabs resent a Western culture which, not too long ago, borrowed heavily from them, eventually to surpass and subdue them. For the Arabs 'The West is a cultural upstart, and to have to learn from it is for the Arabs a position verging on dishonour.'[63]

The crux of the problem, as Patai sees it, lies in the 'modal personality' of the Arabs. This psychological view is made clear in the following lengthy quotation:[64]

> There are a number of other now familiar features in the Arab modal personality which predispose Arabs to an anti-Western stance, and which do not exist, or are present to a much smaller degree in the modal personalities of other ex-colonial nations. Among these is the proclivity to exaggeration, which not only inclines the Arabs to overemphasize and reiterate what they feel toward the West, but actually intensifies those feelings. Another is the sense of marginality which never allows an Arab to detach himself from his traditional culture and environment. . . . Closely connected with his marginality is the Arab's ambivalence toward both his own traditional culture

> and the West, which makes his hatred of the latter the stronger the more he is attracted to it. His extremely keen sense of honour is yet another factor creating in him a suspicion, of which he cannot rid himself, that by imitating the West he might be debasing himself; and since he cannot stop imitating the West, he hates it for luring him into dishonourable posture. To all this must be added the Arab's proclivity to blaming others for his own shortcomings and failure. Since the West is the most readily available scapegoat, it must take most of the blame, with that goes inevitably most of the hate.

In addressing himself more directly to Arab–Jewish contact during the pre-state period, Patai gives more credit to the Palestinian Arabs in contributing to a cultural interdependency between them and the Jews.[65] Referring to the early phases of colonization, Patai seems to reject the then popular explanation which states that in cases of culture contact, culture is usually diffused in a one-way direction from the so-called superior and technologically advanced to the 'simple and more passive' culture of the native population. If anything, he notes, it was the European Jewish settlers in the early phases of colonization who tended to assimilate – though in small numbers – to the local Arab culture. However, as the Jewish colonization of Palestine reached a more advanced stage, the economic interdependency of the two sectors increased; it is significant to note that this interdependency was asymmetrical and took place within the political, cultural and economic spheres. Thus, while the Jewish sector relied at one stage on unskilled, cheap Arab labour, and on the importation of certain agricultural produce which could not be met through the current production rates of the Jewish sector, the Arabs imported manufactured goods and had to rely more on the technological know-how of the Jewish colonizers. Here Patai notes that this asymmetrical economic relationship implied Jewish cultural penetration into the Arab sector which affected the life-style and consumption patterns of the Arab community. The upshot of all this was the underdevelopment, in the long run, of the Arab sector. The inability of the short-lived Arab co-operatives to compete against more numerous and efficient Jewish establishments, the concentration of manufacturing industries in the Jewish metropolis, the separate educational and cultural institutions – all these factors accounted for the fact that there was little diffusion of knowledge and information from the Jewish to the Arab sector. This explains in part why the Arab sector, even though it was the majority at one time, failed to develop a viable economic infrastructure and metropolitan centres. If anything, as we pointed out in the previous chapter, the once thriving handicraft and primary industries within the Arab sector had almost vanished by 1948.

The psychological reductionism which is manifest in the writings of the 'National Character' theorists – including Patai – tends to overlook, and even ignore, the historical role of colonialism in shaping the perceptions of the West by the Arabs. Instead of considering Arab attitudes as a reflection of experience with Western colonialism and imperialism, the problem is projected on to the Arab mind. Beit-Hallahmi,[66] an Israeli social-psychologist, expressed his critical attitude to this approach by referring to various writers who noted that Arab 'suspiciousness' and 'inferiority' could be due to 'arbitrary domination by local and foreign rulers over the centuries', and not to personality make-up characteristic of the Arab people in general. He went on to say with respect to the Arabs' attitudes toward Israel:[67]

> Arab suspiciousness regarding Israel can be well understood in that context: Being defeated repeatedly by a Western, technologically superior opponent, who seems to be very resourceful in finding new ways to humiliate them, and feeling victimized by stronger unknown outsiders are experiences which would contribute to clearly functional suspiciousness. In a situation when victimization and helplessness are the dominant experiences, it is better to be over-suspicious than let down one's guard. The connection between Israel and Western colonialism is not only historical and political but also psychological, since Israel brings back the same feelings of domination and helplessness.

Avineri, an Israeli political scientist, while stressing the modern–traditional confrontation between Jews and Arabs respectively, is nevertheless conscious of the role of foreign domination in inhibiting the development of Arab society, in particular in preventing the emergence of an ingredient for modernization.[68] Pursuing the same line of reasoning, Avineri claims in another essay:[69]

> Again, many unfounded claims have been made about Arab 'fantasy', 'imagination', and 'irrationality'. As such this is loose talk, and these terms do not explain much, especially if they ascribe these attributes to the 'underdeveloped' nature of Arab society. Such an identification of Westernism and rationalism is nothing more than wishful thinking. Part of the problem lies in the fact that such views imply that more Western education is a sure guarantee for 'rationality'. It is not.

It must be stated, however, that while Avineri is aware of the inhibiting role of an indirect form of colonialism, he sees in Zionism a positive catalyst in terms of furthering the process of modernization of the Middle East. A summary of Avineri's position on modernization-colonialism-Zionism and a criticism of it is dealt with in the concluding chapter.

The popularity of psychological explanations of Arab social development is apparent in many of the writings of Western social scientists on the Middle East. An extreme position in this regard is adopted by Alroy, who quotes Patai approvingly in his analysis of the Arab–Israeli conflict. Alroy traces the roots of Arab hostility to Israel back to Islam, which, in his view, is a militant, vengeful and conquering religion. He goes on to note:[70]

> To the roots of hostility toward Jewish statehood must be added the substantial emotional investment in its persistence resulting from basic personality traits peculiar to Arab peoples and from certain mechanisms associated with the prosecution of belligerency against the foe. In the opinion of foreign observers, and by their own admission, the Arabs are a fiercely vengeful people.

This one-sided explanation of Arab attitudes toward Israel, which is derived from an egocentric interpretation of Islam, and, as rightly pointed out by Said,[71] has a pseudo-Gibbonian racist ring to it, fails to account for the well-known hostility displayed throughout this century by Christian Arabs in Palestine toward Zionist colonization of the area. As noted by Ro'i and Porath,[72] two Israeli specialists in the Middle East who analysed the events in Palestine from 1908 to 1914 and from 1918 to 1929 respectively, the Christian Arab leadership waged an equally vociferous and concerted press campaign in protest against Zionist colonization of Palestine.

Alroy's thesis is more dubious when examined in the context of the contemporary ideologies of certain factions of the Palestine resistance movement, and the adoption of left-wing, secular approaches in their analysis of the Arab–Israeli conflict. If anything, as argued by Schleifer,[73] this imported secularism accounts for the social distance created between the Palestinian resistance – led by 'cultural compradors', to quote Schleifer – and the traditional Muslim masses.

Strangely enough, when Alroy is faced with evidence showing that it is not the traditional but the Western-oriented young and educated Israeli Arabs who display the greatest level of animosity to the state, he invokes psychological explanations to account for this situation too. He paraphrases approvingly an observer of the Israeli scene who, in Alroy's words, implied that 'the accelerated modernization of Arabs under the Israeli aegis is likely to produce resentment of the alien modernizer, as their exclusion from Israeli culture and identity could leave them psychologically crippled, though mentally competent.'[74]

In this respect, the concept of modernity seems to lose its theoretical viability, since it is invoked to account simultaneously for divergent and contradictory types of evidence: that is, satisfaction as well as dissatisfaction among the Arabs in Israel. Beit-Hallahmi is aware of this shortcoming. He notes that the logical outcome of Arab modernity and secularism as advanced by Israeli policymakers is that the Arabs will show a greater degree of accommodation with Israel. Yet the opposite seems to be the case:[75]

> Operationally, the prediction has been that as Arabs become more modernized, better educated, less religious, and more advanced economically, they will be more compromising *vis-à-vis* Israel. Behind it was not only a hypothesis relating Arab behaviour to various objective frustrations, but also another hypothesis relating more 'rational', compromising behaviour to modernization. Data on the effects of relative modernization on the attitude of Israeli Arabs indicate that these optimistic predictions have not been borne out by reality.

Evidence bearing on this argument will be advanced in coming chapters, when, for instance, we investigate the identity crisis of Arab youth in Israel and the emergence of protest movements among educated Arabs.

In his study of Arab political behaviour, Landau[76] makes maximum use of the culture thesis in explaining the 'problem of adaptation' and alienation of Israeli Arabs. He isolates the *hamula* (the Arab kinship system) and the traditional patronage system as the main causes of the backwardness of the Arab sector in Israel. While Landau admits that the Israeli authorities are doing little in terms of weakening the *hamula* influence, the latter, he says, will be 'weakened anyway by the very existence of a modern, dynamic state'.[77] Thus, the application of universalistic criteria such as voting and equal treatment under the law – replacing the preferential treatment based on ascribed village and kinship statuses – is bound to offset the authority patterns associated with the traditional leadership.

Following this line of reasoning, and admitting in passing that 'the adaptation and alienation of the Arabs in Israel have been conditioned in no small degree by the attitude of the Jews,'[78] Landau contends that the causes of Arab alienation are to be found mainly within the village culture and social structure. Israeli–Arab problems are the outcome of a confrontation between traditionalism and modernism, between the old and the young. Considering the problems facing the Arabs in their totality, Landau isolates the following causes: 'cultural and linguistic non-identification, consanguinity across the borders, proximity to the frontiers, the impact of the Arab–Israeli war, the influence of mass communication and the attitude of a part of the Jewish population'.[79]

In Landau's scenario, the contribution of the Israeli authorities to the problems facing the Arabs is 'attitudinal' and not a structural one rooted in the legal and institutional framework of the State of Israel. The institutionalized inequality between Arabs and Jews could be better understood as an outcome of measures adopted by the Israeli government such as the Land Appropriation Law of 1952, the Citizenship Law, the 1961 Law for the Concentration of Land, the once all-powerful Military Administration with its system of passes applied to the Arabs, and so on. To say, as Landau does, that these measures are in part the legacy of the British Mandate and in part the outcome of an unwanted necessity dictated by war circumstances does not in any way lessen their sociological importance. A clear indication of the Arab reaction to the legal, political and economic aspects of Israeli society emerges from the increase in support which the Arabs gave, and continue to give, to the New Communist List, Rakah, the only party which is not dominated by a Jewish or Zionist leadership. Protest movements which sprung up in 1961, on the eve of elections for the Fifth Knesset, such as the Movement of Intellectuals for the Defence of Democracy, the Movement of Workers and Farmers against Rising Prices and for a Rise in Salaries, the Movement of Arab Farmers against the Robbery of Land, and so on, signalled the election results for 1961, whereby Rakah increased its vote by 122 per cent compared to 1959.[80] As will be shown in Chapter 7, Rakah continued to gain in strength, particularly in national elections and in large Arab settlements.

Writing more recently on the slow process of change in the Arab villages, Bar-Gal, while admitting that 'to a certain extent there is a lack of public investment, government investment or of other sectors,' and that 'there are very few investments for productive purposes,'[81] in the Arab village, the central reason for the backwardness of Arab villages lies in the village itself, in those 'subjective' factors which typify traditional Arab attitudes: 'The important reasons which delay alteration [of Arab villages] are the subjective ones, concerning the minority population, its organizational structure, its position and attitudes. The society is founded in many cases, on the *Hamula* basis. The competition between the families is great and does not help build the village.'[82]

Applying elaborate techniques of multidimensional analysis, Jacobsen[83] reports the results of a recent study on the modernization of Arab villages in Israel. As seen by the author, the main originality of the study, in addition to the application of sophisticated analysis, is that it takes the *village* (thirty villages were sampled, chosen in a random fashion) as the basic unit of analysis, and not the individual respondent, although the survey is supplemented by 1,700 respondents chosen to represent the village residents. The methodological focus of the study is set out as follows:[84]

> Applying sociological or psychological generalizations to predict developments in large scale societies or nations, as such, is largely ineffective because the possible contingencies and intervening forces are too numerous to consider or control. Yet, these factors are also too important to ignore without drastically reducing the reliability of prediction. If, alternatively, we try to predict from the behaviour of individuals, assuming that they can be located and influenced as desired, the situation is hardly improved. For modernization to occur, the social system these individuals belong to must permit them to innovate – which, typically, is precisely what a traditional society does not do.

The analysis yielded four main dimensions associated with modernity: (1) a production dimension – having to do with the practice of agricultural technology and irrigation; (2) a social-psychological dimension – referring to attachment to village life, considering communication with and awareness of the outside world and utilization of local services; (3) an environment-orientation dimension – dealing with the degree of occupational differentiation, relationships with national organizations, and the extent to which individuals depart from the extended family pattern; and (4) a spatial dimension – having to do with the physical layout of the village in terms of zoning patterns, such as residential, farmstead and business zones.

Using these typologies, twenty of the thirty villages fell on the environment-oriented dimension, that is to say, they were villages which were capable of developing a diversified occupational structure, based on non-attachment to familial organizations. Thus, the study recommends the setting-up of 'lucrative non-agricultural employment opportunities within commuting distance from the village'.[85] Only ten villages (33 per cent) of the total number of villages sampled have the potential of developing into viable agricultural units.

The above analysis raises three questions. First, it is not clear what the attitude of the Arabs concerned would be to such a planned programme of social change. As one reviewer[86] of the complete study (incorporating ninety villages) upon which Jacobsen's article is based remarked, such an important aspect of a research having to do with directed social change was left out of the final report.

Second, to what extent is the government committed to implementing the recommendations if it continues its policy of Arab land acquisition and confiscation? Third, the study accepts as given the state of affairs in Arab villages and does not raise the fundamental questions as to why these villages have been rendered stagnant and satellite consumption units, supplying cheap unskilled labour to the Jewish metropolis. Indeed, it is inconceivable that these villages would be able to compete with the more efficient Jewish sector as long as certain aspects of the latter are heavily dependent in their economic development on exploitation of cheap Arab rural labour.

Gottheil's[87] treatment of the economic development of the Arab region in Israel points to similar results, although the theoretical framework within which he operates is not from cultural anthropology, but from developmental economics. Taking Myrdal's hypothesis of uneven economic development as a characteristic feature of developing societies, Gottheil remarks: 'A cursory reading of the Israel case suggests the applicability of the Myrdal argument.'[88] Gottheil's conclusions, showing the Arab sector to have a continuing dependent status, are based on evidence that the Arab region has been reduced to a consuming rather than producing region, and that the surplus Arab labour – which has been generated as a consequence of its displacement from agriculture and the decline in Arab agricultural holdings – has the feature of transient labour, absorbed mainly in the Jewish sector. Thus, although the Arab region has benefited from a rise in income and consumption, Gottheil remarks that unless economic development is directed to the Arab sector, the latter 'will become Israel's Appalachia'.[89]

Waschitz's writing on the Arabs in Israel, while it acknowledges the subordinate position of Arab workers as well as the Arab sector as a whole in the Israeli economy, attributes inequality to *status* and value differences, and not to basic institutional domination. Faced with evidence showing that very few of the Israeli Arabs occupy professional positions in the Israeli occupational structure, Waschitz comments:[90]

> The higher we rise in the echelons of employment, the less we find Arabs: in civil service, in the *Histadrut* administration, on university staffs. The Advisor for Arab Affairs has made a large effort to open middle and higher echelons of civil service to Arabs. But in general, the government and *Histadrut* have set the pattern for the private sector in their reluctance to accept Arabs to key positions in which Jews would be their subordinates. Openly, the reasons given are usually 'security considerations'. But the reluctance to employ white collar Arabs in general, and the fact that Arabs are employed in constructing

security installations, seem to indicate a problem of *status* not of security. [My italics]

Thus, while the lack of technological know-how in the Arab sector, and the sector's inability to compete with Jewish industry 'equipped with experience and business acumen', are acknowledged, the main impediment to Arab development lies in the 'political-national' sphere and not in the economic one. The influence of the surrounding Arab world heightens the political aspirations of the Arabs in Israel. However, in the light of 'the dual character of the Israeli polity' such aspirations become frustrated.

In the words of Waschitz, the problem of the Arabs is best understood as stemming from lack of national identification with the state. But, as he admits, even those among the Arabs who are willing to identify with the state, such as the Druze sect, do not secure the so-called 'status conferment'.[91]

> Israel is a democratic state whose basic principles guarantee equal rights and duties to all citizens, regardless of nationality. However, status and power positions are distributed according to a scale of values by which identification with a basic aim of a Jewish state (i.e., state for all Jews), and consequently, defence of this state's existence holds top priority. The psychological readiness and potential ability of various social and communal groups to play a central role in defence . . . constitute an important criterion for status conferment. Arabs as a group rank low in this sphere, even those who take part in defence functions.

In examining the socio-economic changes in the Arab sector, Rosenfeld and Flapan provide evidence which is not too dissimilar to that given by Waschitz. Of the three writers, Rosenfeld is the only practising academic, and his specialty is anthropology. However, the three are identified with the left-wing Mapam Party, which might explain their seemingly liberal approach in analysing the situation of the Arabs in Israel.

We hasten to say, however, that while the above writers document existing Jewish–Arab inequalities, their *explanations* of their phenomena do not take into account the forced displacement of Palestinian peasantry from the land, the superimposition of European and Zionist capitalist economies upon a non-capitalist Palestinian economy which resulted in a relatively underdeveloped Arab economy, and the nature of political domination exercised first by the British and then, gradually, by the Zionists.

Rosenfeld was one of the earliest Jewish writers to address himself to the transformation of the Palestinian peasantry to a rural proletariat. According to Rosenfeld, the inheritance system in the Arab sector, which has reduced the size of land holdings, and the seasonal nature of the Arab economy, explain in part the proletarianization of the Palestinian peasantry. The main causes of the class transformation are:[92]

> The influx of Jews in the 1920's (greater contact with advanced western ideas, etc., the developed importance of lime and charcoal extraction among village Arabs for, among other things, the building needs of the Jews; cheap Arab agricultural labour in Jewish settlements); the Mandatory period, especially during the World War II years (and the first, beginning of outside labour among the villagers in army camps, police work, the beginning of industry and Arab industrial workers) the State of Israel (and the tremendous growth of villagers seeking work outside their own villages; the beginning of technological changes in agriculture). The main causes for occupational change are labour market demand, and industrial and technological development, which in themselves do not stem organically from the village. The causes are connected . . . to the determining factor, that of village surplus labour.

Though Rosenfeld accepted some of these structural factors as given, he did not analyse them in any theoretical framework which would link the dependent nature of the Arab economy and its lack of viability to the colonization of the region. In concluding his essay, Rosenfeld saw a positive outcome emerging from the transformation of the Palestinian Arabs from peasantry to wage-earners (in the village studied by Rosenfeld, 12 per cent were classified as wage-earners in 1920; in 1960 the figure rose to 66 per cent): 'this has tended to draw the Arab population, and in many instances Jews and Arabs, closer together in the realization that they have common problems of wage earners.'[93] As will be shown in a later chapter, this incipient Arab–Jewish class solidarity which Rosenfeld hinted at has not materialized, and it is unlikely to do so if the current system of politico-economic domination persists.

It must be pointed out that, in certain respects, Rosenfeld departs in his analysis from other anthropological writers who analysed social change and development solely in terms of the normative aspects of Arab society, using such criteria as value-systems, kinship structure, marriage rules, and so forth. In commenting critically upon a study of Arab villages by A. Cohen,[94] a British anthropologist, Rosenfeld takes him to task for attributing the economic stagnation of the Arab sector to traditional family structure manifest in the *hamula*, the clan system prevalent in traditional Arab villages.

The persistence of the *hamula* is to be understood, according to Rosenfeld, in the context of the policies of the Israeli government which continue to enhance its life-chances:[95]

> The main difference between today's Arab population in Israel and that of the mandatory period [in Palestine] is that the Arab population was stratified during the mandate; there were urban merchants, clerks, and landowners, as well as the *fellahin* and labourers. Today these strata have been levelled; most of the first group is gone, and the population is, more or less, a single (declassed) class. The structure has become fragmented and the Arab village is not simply part of a new structure; it is a fragment of what it used to be. In terms of total population, landownership, national and religious ties, ties with urban families, or economic, social, and political structures, it is no longer the same village. Today the Arab villagers of Israel are one of the lowest strata of the lowest class. The *hamulas* remain, though in a modified form, not because class is not a fact but because changes have not been radical enough to terminate completely the traditional village social structure. The villagers did not revert to a *hamula* cleavage; they were never capable of leaving it. The fact that the Israeli government is shoring up the residual village structure is no indication of its revival.

In contrast, Flapan,[96] at one time head of the Arab Division in the Mapam Party and editor of the left-wing magazine *New Outlook*, echoed the line of his party at the time and in particular its attack on the military government, which during its eighteen years of existence – until December 1966 – compelled Arabs to obtain special passes before moving from one locality to another inside the state. Flapan called for a fuller integration of the Arabs into the economy of the state as a means of closing the gap between Arabs and Jews.

Although Flapan was aware of the impact that land dispossession was having on the social structure of Arab villages, he saw the employment of the Arab worker in the Jewish sector as the main solution to the stagnation of the Arab economy. Moreover, 'the pace of economic development and labour shortage in the Jewish sector breached the last dam between the Arab and Jewish populations.'[97] This is a curious statement, since one can hardly say, from what we know now and from what was revealed then by Rosenfeld's studies, that the occupational contrast between Arabs and Jews reflected a natural balance, since the rural Arabs continue to comprise the bulk of the lumpenproletariat of Israel. More will be said about this in later chapters.

Approaching the sociology of the Arabs in Israel through the perspective of inter-group relations and attitudinal orientations, Peres' research on the Arabs in Israel follows a familiar path charted by North American sociologists researching in the field of race and ethnic relations. Peres, a sociologist at Tel Aviv University, published individually and jointly with other colleagues – in Hebrew as well as English – a series of articles dealing with curricula in Arab schools, national-identity of Arab youth in Israel, and Arab–Jewish ethnic relations in general. Peres made extensive use in his published work of material drawn from the American-funded project on Arab education, which was launched in the mid-1960s under Eisenstadt's supervision. We shall deal in detail with Peres' work in Chapter 6, and also with that of Erik Cohen,[98] another Israeli sociologist at the Hebrew University in Jerusalem.

Although Cohen describes his methodology as anthropological, in the sense that it is based on participant observation, the research has a focus similar to that of Peres and others. Cohen's published work on the Arabs in Israel is essentially the result of an extensive case study of Acre, a mixed town in northern Israel. His research dealt with the alienation of Arab youth and the likely success of mixed marriages between Arabs and Jews; more recently he returned to Acre to study the attitudes of Arab youth toward Israel in the aftermath of the 1973 war.

In addition to the above sociologists, there is a small group of psychologists and social-psychologists working in the area of personality and prejudice, pursuing another popular perspective in the writings of North American academics in inter-ethnic relations. Tamarin,[99] Hofman,[100] and Beit-Hallahmi,[101] the latter two from Haifa University, have all addressed themselves to measuring social distance between Arabs and Jews, self-identity, ethnocentrism and so on. As pointed out earlier, Beit-Hallahmi's work is an exception to this; he attempts to incorporate wider issues in his writings criticizing the often enunciated explanations of Arab behaviour put forward by the national-character school of thought.

It is accurate to say that the general orientations, personal as well as in research terms, of the authors referred to here could be characterized as liberal. Not unlike their American counterparts, they do not hesitate to expose and even condemn prejudice and discrimination in Israeli society. However, because of lack of concern with the historical and structural features of Israeli society, as these features impinge on the Arabs in Israel, this research hardly gets at the roots of the problem. Indeed, seen in this light, the problems between Arabs and Jews appear to lie in differences in attitudes, values and understanding. The logical outcome of many of these studies, *when considered in isolation*, is that injustice appears to be rooted in the irrationality of individual men and not in the collective and institutional aspects of Israeli society which are rationally directed. We have yet to see any encompassing research on the consequences of Arab land dispossession, social mobility, inequality, delinquency, patterns of school drop-out, and the effects of political and economic domination in general.

Arab writers in Israel

It is significant to note the near-absence of Arab academics among practising social scientists in Israel. For example, in the list reproduced by Weller there is not one single Arab among the sociologists and anthropologists who teach in Israel's five universities. Since this list was compiled in the early 1970s, a total of three to four Arab social scientists have joined the staff, mainly at Haifa University. This in itself is a revealing commentary on the intellectual involvement in shaping their social life of the Arabs in Israel. This is the more important if one recognizes the fact that the majority of Arab university students enrol in departments of humanities and the social sciences. However, the fact that the greatest majority do not proceed to enter graduate programmes, together with fear (real or imaginary) of subtle reprisals if they engage in critical social science writings, might account for the lack of scholarly works by indigenous Israeli Arabs. Sabri Jiryis' critical study *The Arabs in Israel*, originally published in Hebrew in 1965 at the author's own expense, still remains in its up-dated Arabic version the only comprehensive account by an Israeli Arab of Arab social, economic, and political development in Israel.

Chomsky has remarked on Jiryis' work in an article appraising the Arab–Israeli conflict:[102]

> As for writings by Israeli Arabs or expressions of popular opinion, these too are scanty. Contrary to the claims of American Zionists, these voices have been effectively stilled. Arab intellectuals have been heavily censored, or compelled to leave the country. It is remarkable that American civil libertarians have defended these practices, or denied the facts. The most extensive discussion of the status of Arabs in Israel is in the work of Sabri Jiryis, an Israeli Arab lawyer who was confined to house arrest for over a year without charge and now lives in Beirut. . . . He gives a detailed analysis of the suppression of the civil rights of Arabs, their dispossession through expropriation in the 1950's, the blocking of efforts at independent political expression, the tight continued application of the British Mandatory laws, and so on. Jiryis

relies primarily on Israeli sources, including court records. As far as I can determine, his account is quite accurate.

Chomsky's assessment of Jiryis' work contrasts sharply with that given by Landau, who, without examining Jiryis' work in any detail, referred to it as 'political propaganda'.[103] In reviewing Jiryis' book, Ian Lustick, who researched the Arabs in Israel, differed with Jiryis on some points but overall remarked that 'In spite of such lapses the great bulk of facts reported by Jiryis are correct and well documented.'[104] We will take up Jiryis' argument in some detail in the next chapter.

The main outlet for many moderate Arab writers in Israel is the magazine *New Outlook*. Its issues contain useful information bearing on the status of the Arabs in Israel. And of course there is the large body of literature, mostly in Arabic, written by Arab poets, novelists, politicians and concerned laymen which depicts the situation of the Arabs in Israel. We shall examine some of these writings in Chapter 7.

A recent issue of *New Outlook*, which was devoted to the Arabs in Israel, included among its contributors three Israeli Arabs, one of whom, K. Nakhleh,[105] is a visiting professor at Haifa University who lives in the United States, where he received his PhD and now teaches. The other Arab contributors are non-academics.

Though not stated explicitly in the language of symbolic interactionism, Nakhleh's cultural-anthropological treatment of the emergence of a Palestinian collective identity among Israeli Arabs has a great deal in common with this tradition, in particular as articulated by Herbert Blumer. Collective identity is seen as the product of a historical process mediated through the transmission of common symbols, the sharing of values, and the crystallization of political organizations. Identifying three separate stages in Palestinian history, 1948–67, 1967–73, and post-1973, Nakhleh argues that the Palestinian collective identity came to the fore in the consciousness of Israeli Arabs as a function of historical events transpiring in the last twenty-eight years. Yet he points out that the expression of this identity is restrained by a sense of pragmatism and the recognition by the Arabs in Israel of the specific conditions under which they exist in Israel's political culture.

In another article based on field work, Nakhleh analyses in detail politics at the local level in two Arab villages in Israel. He sets out his theoretical framework thus:[106]

> My analysis is based on the sociological theoretical conflict perspective, which maintains that conflict is more applicable and has more utility (than the functional or equilibrium perspective) in the analysis of basic intergroup relationships in

> Arab villages in Israel. Palestinian Arab society has constantly been subjected to the effects of power wielded from the outside. The incompatibility in the interests of the various sectarian groups was implanted from without by the sheer creation of their groupings. Therefore, to hold that such a system behaves as a self-contained unit in generating its own mechanisms of control and harmony is inadequate.

Nakhleh provides a synthesis of the interplay between the *hamula* and the intrusion of national political parties and governmental pressure as these affect Arab villages. He notes that while the traditional social structure of the village stands in the way of village development, a crucial factor in enhancing inter-group and *hamula* conflicts is the policy of the Israeli government. It is in this context that Nakhleh remarks: 'It is therefore clear that the manipulatory tactics of national parties reinforce the tendency for faction-based conflicts in the Arab village.'[107]

The longevity of the political life of the traditional leadership, which is sustained and nourished by the regime, is apparent in the sharp contrast between the age composition of the electorate and that of the village councillors. 'Although only 9.42 per cent of those elected to Arab local councils in 1969 and 1972 were thirty years of age and under, the distribution of eligible electors for the Rameh local council in 1969 and 1973 rounds indicates that the percentage of those who were in that age category was 39.94 and 38.26, consecutively.'[108]

In a trenchant criticism of the writings of more than twenty Israeli anthropologists and sociologists who researched the Arabs in Israel, Nakhleh[109] isolates the following main themes, which are in line with our discussion so far: (1) Israeli social scientists overemphasize the ethnic-religious-sectarian aspects of the Palestinian community, for example, Christian, Muslim, and Druze; (2) they tend to explain the slow economic progress of the Arab sector by depicting Palestinian society as basically tradition-ridden, still labouring under the influence of a bygone feudalism; (3) they are reluctant to admit the sociological legitimacy of a Palestinian identity; and (4) their zealous commitment to Zionism has led most of them to present Israeli government policies as progressive.

The other two Israeli Arab contributors to the special issue of *New Outlook*, Ghanaim[110] and Bayadsi,[111] dwell on a topic of great concern to the Arab minority – the decline of village life manifested in the symptoms of social disorganization, youth delinquency and marginality in a society dominated by Zionist institutions. A perusal of the back issues of *New Outlook* reveals a frequent mention of this theme, though always couched in a tone of moderation and pragmatism, to use Nakhleh's characterization of Israeli Arabs' expression of their aspirations.

Indeed, the process of social transformation taking place in Arab villages is the topic of a PhD thesis submitted to Brandeis University by another Israeli Arab, S. Geraisy,[112] who now heads the Arab Youth Division in the Department of Social Welfare, and who not too long ago headed a committee which looked into the social problems faced by the Arab sector.

Whereas Ghanaim deals with the alienation of Arab youth villagers working in predominantly Jewish metropolises Bayadsi addresses himself to the negative differential treatment accorded to Arab villages by the Israeli government in terms of allocating funds for local authorities.

In referring to the Arab proletariat working in Jewish centres, Ghanaim has this to say:[113]

> Their working conditions are extremely hard, with no legal supervision. They work ten to twelve hours a day, six or seven days a week; most of them get their weekly or monthly wages in cash, without any pay-slip as a proof of their employment. Only a few are registered with the income tax and national insurance authorities: employers prefer to dodge taxes and to avoid assuring them social benefits. Someone injured at work, instead of receiving paid leave and compensation, is often ignored and dismissed from his job.

It is interesting to note that although Ghanaim and many Israeli Arabs like him are aware of the exploited position of Arab workers, they show a feeling of compliance to and even acceptance of the premise that the Arab should be 'realistic' and accept his place in society.[114]

> They [Arabs] build grand multinational buildings, but live in wretched hovels; this leaves a deep mark of disappointment and despondency. At first they are filled with astonishment at such a life, but when they find it is not for them, one of two things happens: either they quickly develop a sense of realism, recognizing how they can serve the purpose for which they came to town – to work, earn some money, return to build their lives in the village and, as far as possible, make use of what they saw for the benefit of the village. Or they may refuse to accept the facts and try to assimilate themselves in this [Jewish] society at all costs. In the end such a person finds himself on the outer fringe of modern society and his life will be like that of other marginal youth.

The theme of Arab political behaviour receives attention from Abu-Gosh, a political scientist who received his PhD from Princeton and is one of the few practising Arab academics in Israel. Working within the American behavioural (or, more accurately, behaviourist, as revealed in his own writing) tradition of political science, Abu-Gosh applies the familiar stimulus-organism-response trilogy, adapted from a simplified Skinnerian learning theory, to analysing the results of the 1969 elections in the Arab sector. Although Abu-Gosh manages to highlight certain peculiar features of Arab political behaviour, he is still constrained by a psychological framework inherent in all so-called American political behaviour research. For example, he describes the attitudes of Israeli Arabs to politics as follows:[115]

> Political activity has traditionally been equated with corruption and gossip, and therefore has a negative connotation. The political process which usually legitimizes authority has traditionally been associated with force. Moreover, in the traditional system the stress has been on the group rather than the individual. Certain traits in the political culture of present day Arab society can probably be traced to the traditional background. The most relevant of these to our discussion are those of being respectful or perhaps forceful, of authority, of political inefficacy and complacency.

He goes on to note that the socialization process of the Arabs in Israel has resulted in greater democratization:[116]

> However, twenty years of socialization in a modern and democratic society have had an effect on the political orientation of the younger generation in the Arab sector. They are becoming democratized and political. This is significant because the elections provide an opportunity for both the traditional and the newly acquired values to be expressed in practical ways.

This is not the place to comment on the theoretical shortcomings of political behaviour research in general. Suffice it to quote in this context a relevant remark I made on another occasion on the 'learning model' as it is understood in political socialization research:[117]

> Implied in the [stimulus-response] model is a utilitarian conception of man which in turn assumes a voluntaristic theory of action. The latter implies that people's values and behaviour are to a large extent free from coercion, and all that is needed is to seize upon available information and utilize it to maximize their gain and minimize their loss. Like the theory of free-market competition, here too the existence of monopoly over the acquisition and dissemination of information is

> overlooked. It is thus imperative to view the stimulus-response model in the context of certain constraints, the most important of which centres around the notion of manipulative socialization . . . and the relationship between the individual's experience in social structure and the range of stimuli available to him.

In contrast to the above writers, Kanaana's research on the Arabs in Israel starts from a different premise and theoretical perspective. Kanaana, an indigenous sociologist who teaches in the United States, but who has been a visiting professor at Beir-Zeit University on the West Bank, accepts as given the disadvantaged minority status of the Arabs and finds it essential to probe into their 'survival strategies'.[118]

The survival strategy adopted is a function of the social class position of the Arabs in question. In addition to urban dwellers (those living in Nazareth and mixed cities), Kanaana isolates three main classes: the landlords and rich peasants, the middle peasants, and the landless or poor peasants. Middle peasants comprise around 70 per cent of the Arabs in Israel, with the rest divided evenly among urban dwellers, landless peasants and rich peasants. The central theme which emerges from this study is that the *hamula*'s influence is not declining, but is being enhanced, and that the main cleavage in the Arab village is not between the old and the young, or even between *hamulas*; rather it is the class nature of the conflict which is pronounced, particularly the one between the middle peasantry and the declining old landlord stratum. According to Kanaana, identification with the *hamula* becomes a means by which Israeli Arabs derive psycho-social gratification. Other survival strategies adopted by the middle peasantry are reflected in the emergence of an economically independent stratum whose members are increasingly becoming wage-earners. In Kanaana's view, the group that is likely to survive least is the once rich peasants.

Though there is merit in Kanaana's thrust in attempting to depict the world-view of Israeli Arabs from the vantage point of a discriminated minority, we are still confronted by two crucial facts: (1) the survival of the *hamula* is less the result of Arab strategy than it is of conscious manipulation by the Israeli government; and (2) contrary to what Kanaana claims, one can hardly label the so-called economic independence of the middle peasantry through proletarianization and loss of land as 'survival strategy'.

In spite of the central role played by the educational system, there is little research on the nature of educational recruitment among the Arabs in Israel. Sami Mar'i, a member of the staff at Haifa University, has carried out research closing some of this gap. The latest published work has been a co-authored monograph detailing the development of Arab education in Israel since 1948. The authors note that in spite of a relative improvement in the educational standing of the Arabs in Israel, they have a long way to go before reaching the level attained in the Jewish sector. They document the high attrition rate in the Arab pre-university educational system, the high rate of failure in matriculation examinations, and the relative lack of occupational opportunities for Arab graduates of either high school or university. The post-secondary attainment of Arab youth in Israel is found to be inferior to that of the Palestinians on the West Bank and in Gaza, as well as to that in the Arab world as a whole.[119]

The impact that social change in the Arab village has had on the relationship between the educational system and the home is the topic of a 1974 paper by Mar'i. Here he acknowledges the fact that the transition from peasantry to proletariat has not been achieved through a normal process, and that the Arab proletariat has retained a 'rural mentality'. The crux of the problem, as seen by Mar'i, is the clash between a traditional Arab social structure and a modern, individualistic one which is prevalent in the Jewish sector. This has resulted in the psychological disorientation of Arab villagers and even, according to Mar'i, a loss of identity. The central problem, then, is how to develop a sense of 'individualization in Arab-rural society'. Here Mar'i falls back on the familiar theme of modernization:[120]

> The transition has been extremely difficult and drastic, accompanied by feelings of bitterness and perhaps, even by a certain sense of relative loss of identity. It took place without any appreciable self-awareness and with no concept of the reasons and logic inherent in the conditions demanding such a transition. Actually, it came about because of the demands of the new political-economic situation, in which the individual Arab in Israel found himself. It, therefore, appears that this transition caused, at least at the outset, a relative loss of evaluative behavioural orientation. The conditions, the manner and the content of the transition have apparently resulted in the fact that the sense of relative autonomy created was not real and authentic, not at all something which came about as a result of education and compelling values, but rather an illusion of autonomy coming about as a result of the rapid social-cultural changes which followed the sudden changes from an agricultural society to a society involved in an industrial economy, from internal work within the familial social-cultural context to outside work within an utterly different social-cultural

context, from an objective and subjective dependence on rigid, collective social frameworks to objective independence and personal autonomy.

The point I wish to make about this lengthy (unfinished) quotation is that it is symptomatic of a great deal of writing on the Third World which projects a view of man as pathological and psychologically inept. It is curious that Mar'i relies too heavily on the internal factors of Arab village life, invoking them as the main explanatory variables for a tension-ridden and economically backward Arab sector. Could it be that this social order surrounding the Arabs in Israel, so often viewed as voluntaristic, is in fact non-voluntaristic and shaped above all by external coercive dictates which the Arab villager has no say in, let alone being able to effect a genuine change in the political-economic environment surrounding him? Indeed, a reading of Mari's' paper shows that he is aware of the impact of the military government on the Arab sector, and the role played by the major political parties in perpetuating and manipulating traditional structures, and above all that he is aware of the dilemmas faced by Arab teachers in their role as state employees who run the risk of losing their jobs if they engage in what might be construed as 'political' activity, and the tension resulting from suspicion felt by the parents toward the teachers for being government agents. These objective factors could hardly be interpreted in terms of an Arab culture or psychology alone.

An incorporation of psychological and environmental factors in a study of achievement level of Palestinian youth is attempted in an interesting paper by Mar'i and Manna.[121] Working with eighth-graders they compared the achievement levels of two sets of Palestinian children from the same village, which was partly on the West Bank until 1967, but which was reunited after Israeli occupation. Using personality competence scales, they discovered that whereas Israeli Arab youth are more able to set goals for themselves than the Arab youth who lived in the West Bank part of the village, the latter were more prepared to invest psychological energy to attain their goals. The authors attribute the first set of differences to the higher level of modernization of Israeli Arabs, while their lower score on the latter part of the test was attributed to the Arab's minority status in Israeli society. In other words, we can say that the Israeli Arabs, realizing the limited opportunities to attain their goals that are available to them outside, opted for a 'realistically' lower level of psychological involvement. It is not so much to do with Arab culture or values *per se*. There is nothing unique about this phenomenon, for it is present among all minorities who suffer from discrimination. Black as well as poor white children in the United States, Canada, and elsewhere have been shown to exhibit similar psychological response to an environment which is not based on equality of opportunity.

Conclusions

So far, the most striking feature of Israeli sociology to emerge from this review is its bland and non-controversial character. This is true with regard to Israeli writings on the Jewish aspects of the society as well as the Arab. A thorough examination of Weller's book on Israeli sociology confirms this impression, given that the book is primarily devoted to the sociology of Jews in Israel. Radical or critical sociology, which has left its impact on recent developments in European and American sociology, does not seem to have been incorporated into the writings of Israeli sociologists. We have yet to see a C. Wright Mills or a Marcuse emerge in Israeli academia – and stay there.

While it is difficult to conclude that a picture of a monolithic sociological analysis of the Arabs in Israel emerges from the discussion presented in this chapter, the composite picture is clear enough. The central explanatory variable of Arab political, economic and social development appears to be best explained in the psycho-cultural syndrome. Little weight, if any, is accorded to objective conditions and the role of foreign domination, Zionist and otherwise, of the area.

One cannot help noting a remarkable degree of convergence between the Israeli élite's opinions concerning the Arabs in general and the images of the Arabs projected in academic research by Israeli social scientists.

Heradstreit's findings concerning the Israeli élite's perception of the Arabs are instructive in this regard. Like the majority of the social scientists whom we have been discussing in this chapter, the Israeli élite – who in the sample included academics – adhere to a traditional image of the Arabs, an image centring around 'cultural weakness', 'irrationality', and 'Arab temperament', and these are seen as the main features of Arab society:[122]

> The problem [pertaining to the Israeli–Arab conflict] was perceived by the [Israeli élite] to originate in an emotional and irrational attitude towards the relationship with Israel, resulting from what was characterized as cultural weakness. The Arab world was described as a civilization suffering from an identity crisis which bred frustration and which was in turn reflected in its great preoccupation with the State of Israel. In contrast to Israel with its high level of education and rationally

> determined acts, it was considered the Arabs allowed themselves to be guided by irrationality. . . . Those interviewed perceived a difference of mentality between Jew and Arab in relation to war and peace and considered that whereas the Jews were a pacific people, it was inherent in Arab temperament to incite conflict and war. Islam must therefore take part of the blame for this, because it preached the superiority of Moslems.

Preoccupation with the 'Arab mind' is not confined to Western Arabists or Israeli social scientists. As remarked by Edward Said,[123] *Arab* Arabists have also made use of psychological reductionism in accounting for Arab political life. Here, too, the reference point is Western cultural and political values, and the gap between Oriental and Western values is considered to reflect a state of stagnation and retardation in the development of Arab society. It must be said, however, that this trend is less prevalent among the Arab writers considered in this chapter than it is among the other Israeli social scientists.

5 The transformation of Arab class structure in Israel

In this chapter we attempt to systematize and complement existing data and findings on the Arabs in Israel. Our main purpose is to trace the changes in the social structure of the Arab community from 1948 up to the present. For this reason, we will not deal with the Palestinian Arabs in the occupied territories or elsewhere, but only those in Israel. A detailed analysis of the Mandatory period was the subject of discussion in Chapter 3. This chapter will comprise analyses of the following: (1) the demographic structure, (2) the and alienation, and (3) the proletariniazation of Israeli Arabs.

The demographic structure

One of the main problems facing any settler group, especially when this group is more urbanized and technologically advanced than the indigenous population, is how to maintain a favourable demographic balance in the total population given a traditional indigenous population with high birth rate. The difficulty of maintaining a numerically superior Jewish population was, and continues to be, the central issue facing Zionist leaders in Israel. Concentrated efforts to facilitate Jewish immigration continue to be the main mechanism by which Israel hopes to ensure the continuity of the present Jewish numerical superiority. This policy, which, until recently, was implemented successfully, did not proceed without serious problems, as the relatively small number of Jewish immigrants to Israel from England and North America shows.[1] This trickling of North American immigrants into Israel at one time prompted Ben-Gurion to attack North American Jews, who, in his view, had a duty to settle in Israel to prove their allegiance to Zionism.

In addition to the recent numerical decline in Jewish immigration (according to S. Rosen, Minister of Absorption, 32,000 immigrants came to Israel in 1974, compared to 55,000 in 1973),[2] a more alarming phenomenon as far as the Israeli government is concerned has been the increasing number of Jewish *emigrants* in recent years, or as they are labelled in Israel, *Yordim*, meaning 'those who go down'. According to Chomsky: 'Immigration has fallen sharply, by about 50% in the first half of 1975. Specifically, Russian immigration is turning elsewhere. At the same time . . . emigration is rapidly increasing, including long-term residents. Emigration in 1974 was almost triple the average of the 1967–1973 period.'[3]

Specifically, between 1968 and 1973, 7,500 Israeli Jews emigrated; nearly 12,000 emigrated in 1973, 21,000 in 1974, while 6,000 immigrated in the first five months of 1975.[4]

With around 300,000 Israeli Jews residing overseas by 1976 (defined by the Israeli Central Bureau of Statistics as those who have not returned two years after their departure), the attention of the Jewish Agency and the Israeli government turned toward inducing emigrants to return. Emigration proved to be costly in terms of the loss of high-level manpower to the Jewish State, since most of the *Yordim* are professional people of Western origin, including a sizeable number of *Sabra* (Israeli-born) emigrants. According to D. Elizur's study, for the Jewish Agency, of a sample of 500 Israeli Jews residing in France and the United States, 'the largest groups consist of persons from Europe and America (51 per cent) and those born in Israel (38 per cent). Persons from Asia and Africa make up only 7 per cent.'[5]

While *attitudinal* responses to questions dealing with emigration and intentions to return should be interpreted with great reservations (owing to the stigma attached to leaving Israel),[6] Elizur's study shows that only a minority of 22 per cent had definite plans to return; three-quarters had no such plans for the immediate future.

A study carried out in 1974[7] by the Israeli Institute of Applied Social Research on a sample of 2,000 Israeli Jews sheds further light on the reasons behind emigration: 31 per cent mentioned taxes, 28 per cent the cost of living, 22 per cent the system of government, 21 per cent the future of children, 16 per cent the military security and guerrilla activities, 18 per cent the internal gap in socio-economic conditions, 16 per cent conditions of employment, and 19 per cent military service; furthermore, there was a positive relationship between military service as a cause for emigration and the age of the respondent. A quarter of those aged between twenty and twenty-nine wanted 'very much' to remain in the country, compared to 44 per cent among the thirty- to forty-five-year-olds, and the overwhelming majority of those above fifty-five years of age.

In May 1968, the government enacted a scheme of inducements by which Jewish returnees would receive economic benefits, including travel expenses, housing, business loans, and custom-free privileges. This system, which caused a great deal of resentment among other residents who could not qualify for similar benefits, was not renewed after its official period expired in 1970. More importantly, as Nina Toren shows,[8] the system of incentives had no effect whatsoever on increasing the number of returnees. On average, she notes, the mean percentage of those returning after one year amounted to 67.6 per cent, and 87 per cent during the first two years of emigration. Of those who stayed away for more than five years, which amounts to nearly 13 per cent of the total emigrants, only 1 per cent returned. Israeli Arab emigration is more difficult to assess. Between 1949 and 1970, the official number given for declared emigrants is 5,508 (not including the substantial number of West Bank emigrants), although admittedly, like the Jews, not all Arabs declare their emigration intentions upon leaving Israel.[9] Relying on figures for Israel citizens who depart from and arrive at Israeli airports, Ian Lustick calculated that between 1948 and 1974 a total of 15,000 Israeli Arabs left the country and did not return. Averaged over the entire period, this amounts to around 5 per cent of the Arab population. However, if we consider the 1974 figure for the Arab population, it amounts to 3 per cent. While it is difficult to state categorically that these are permanent emigrants, there is no doubt that the majority continue to reside abroad. From the interviews conducted by Lustick with Israeli Arabs, it is apparent that the educated Arabs are the ones who, in the face of limited educational and occupational opportunities in Israel, decide to leave.[10]

From the point of view of the Arab population, the establishment of the state meant a drastic transformation in their relative numerical size, from a majority to a minority.

In 1914 estimates put the ratio of Arabs to Jews in Palestine in the vicinity of 13:1, with the Jewish settlers then numbering around 85,000. With the influx of Zionist settlers and organized immigration, illegal and otherwise, to Palestine, the ratio declined to 2:1 at the eve of the 1948 war.[11] Immediately after the war, and within a period of a few months in which the exodus of the majority of the Arab population was almost completed, the pattern of the population was drastically reversed, showing the Palestinians to be a minority in their own country. Thus while there were 700,000 Jews compared to 900,000 Arabs immediately before the war of 1948 (in what constitutes Israel), more than 700,000 of those Arabs became refugees.[12] From 1948, when the ratio stood at 7:1 in favour of the Jewish population, up to the present time, the percentage of Palestinian Arabs in the total population (which numbered 3,500,000 in 1974) ranged from 11 to 15 per cent. In 1974, there were 506,900 Israeli Arabs, comprising 15.1 per cent of the population. Concerning the religious composition of the Arab population, the Muslim community continues to be the majority, comprising around three-quarters of the entire Arab population in 1973, as shown in Table 5.1b.

TABLE 5.1a *Population distribution of Arabs and Jews (1948–74)*[13]

Year	*Arabs*	*Jews*	*Arabs as % of total*
1948	117,639	716,778	14.1
1960	239,169	1,911,189	11.1
1965	299,346	2,299,078	11.5
1967*	392,700*	2,383,600	14.0
1970	440,000	2,561,400	14.6
1974	506,900	2,843,100	15.1

* Approximately 69,000 Arab inhabitants of East Jerusalem are included in this figure. The figures for 1970 and 1974 likewise include East Jerusalem.

TABLE 5.1b *Religious distribution of the Arab population (1950–73)*

Year	*Muslims*	*Christians*	*Druze and others*	*Total*
	%	%	%	%
1950	69	22	9	100
1965	71	19	10	100
1967*	74	18	8	100
1973*	75	17	8	100

* Includes East Jerusalem

One of the most persistent problems facing the Zionist authorities has been how to prevent the continued existence of an all-Arab concentration in any of the six geographical districts which make up Israel. In 1948, the Northern and Southern Districts were predominantly Arab. The status of the Southern District was altered within a short period after 1948 through concentration on Jewish immigration and the building of new settlements. By 1961, the Arab population amounted to 11 per cent of the total population in the Southern District, and it declined to 9 per cent by 1971 (see Table 5.2).

The efforts of the Israeli authorities in recent years have turned to the 'Judaization of the Galilee', in pursuit of which the Jewish Agency prepared in 1973 a detailed plan for Jewish settlements in the area to be completed in the next decade or so.[14] Unlike the Southern District – where the Bedouins have been fighting a losing battle with the Zionist authorities to prevent further confiscation

TABLE 5.2a *Population distribution of Arabs and Jews by district (1948–71)*[15]

District	*1948* Jews	Arabs	Total	*1961* Jews	Arabs	Total	*1971* Jews	Arabs	Total
	%	%	%	%	%	%	%	%	%
Jerusalem	96	4	100	98	2	100	76	24	100
North	37	63	100	58	42	100	54	46	100
Haifa	84	16	100	87	13	100	84	16	100
Central	87	13	100	93	7	100	92	8	100
Tel Aviv	99	1	100	99	1	100	99	1	100
South	28	72	100	89	11	100	91	9	100

TABLE 5.2b *Distribution of Arab population by district (1948–73)*[16]

District	*1948*	*1961*	*1968*	*1973*
	%	%	%	%
Jerusalem	1.4	1.7	18.2	17.7
North	73.4	57.8	48.0	47.6
Haifa	8.4	19.4	16.3	16.4
Central	2.2	10.9	9.2	9.6
Tel Aviv	3.2	2.7	1.9	1.8
South	11.4	7.5	6.4	6.9
Total	100.0	100.0	100.0	100.0

of their land through the claims of the Israeli government that lands in the south are state lands[17] – the situation is very complex in the Galilee area. As shown in Table5.2, close to half of the Arab population lives in the northern part of the country, where most of the Arab land left is neither so-called state land nor absentee Arab property. This is not to say that expropriation and confiscation of Arab land have not taken place, as the cases of Iqrit and Kafr-Birim, two northern villages, testify.[18] Indeed, the shooting in April 1976 of Israeli Arab citizens by Israeli soldiers was in reaction to their protests over Arab land expropriation and confiscation in the Galilee. More will be said about the legal framework of the Israel model of internal colonialism in the second section of this chapter. Suffice it here to quote Chomsky on this:[19]

> To Judaise the Galilee there must be new expropriations, amounting to thousands of *dunums* of land, mainly in the area of upper Nazareth, Carmiel and Safad. The government is

considering the expropriation of 2,700 acres from privately owned land for new settlements, almost two-thirds from Arabs. Israeli Arabs naturally object, since the land expropriated will be for Jewish use, as in the past. Considerable land has already been expropriated from Arab villages in this area for Jewish settlement, for example, at the site of the all-Jewish city of Carmiel. Elsewhere, too, a village such as Um El-Fahem (in the South), which has already lost 121,000 of its 145,000 *dunums* to expropriation (leaving it with 6,000 *dunums* of arable land), is now to be deprived of another 2,000, according to the Official Gazette (*Reshumot*) of March 1975.

While such practices are not perceived as discriminatory by the Israeli government, since it claims that compensation is usually paid and, whenever possible, exchange of land is suggested, the fact remains that *such land is being taken away against the will of an indigenous national group to accommodate another settler group*; equally important is the fact that the law does not allow Arabs to engage in reciprocal practices, either through buying or, in most cases, through leasing land intended for all-Jewish settlements, as happened in the case of Upper Nazareth.[20]

TABLE 5.3 *Distribution of Arab population by area of residence (1955–73)*[21]

Year	*All-Arab villages*	*All-Arab settlements*	*Mixed settlements*	*Total*
	%	%	%	%
1955	74*	10	16	100
1961	74*	13	13	100
1971	69*	13	18	100
1973	44	31	25†	100

* Includes Bedouins, who by 1971 amounted to 10 per cent of the Arab population. A settlement has a population of 5,000 or more. Altogether there are fifteen all-Arab settlements and six mixed settlements.

† Includes East Jerusalem.

Until 1971, there had been little change in the proportion of Arabs living in mixed settlements. The 1973 (Table 5.3) figures are somewhat high owing to the inclusion in the statistics of East Jerusalem's Arab population. Still, more than three-quarters of Israel's Arabs live in segregated cities and villages. It would be misleading to interpret these figures even in the so-called mixed cities as reflecting 'integration' in any meaningful sense of the term. There is little interpersonal contact on an equal basis between Arabs and Jews in such settlements. Residential segregation, educational separateness and non-sharing in other socio-cultural and political institutions make the Israeli census label 'mixed' a misnomer. This pattern is not exclusive to the relationship between Arabs and Jews. Within the Jewish communities, V. Klaff[22] demonstrates, there exists a salient form of ethnic segregation. In towns such as Tel Aviv, Haifa and Jerusalem, the Oriental and European Jews live in separate communities.

At the centre of the demographic debate is the future development of the Arab–Jewish population structures. The demographic projections vary on this, depending on the assumptions adopted. In a recent article appraising the future demographic balance in Israel for the year 2000, in the face of various policy options emanating from the Six-Day War of 1967, Friedlander and Goldscheider[23] offer the following four possibilities: (1) If Israel were to adopt a minimalist stand in terms of its inflow of immigrants and retention of occupied territories, that is, annexing East Jerusalem and the Golan Heights only, together with a decline of Jewish immigration and fertility rate, the proportion of Jews in Israel in the year 2000 would amount to 78 per cent of the total population (the minimalist demographic assumption applied to the Arab population produces, according to the above two authors, a yearly net total in-migration of 100,000 Arabs into the occupied territories from neighbouring Arab countries and a constant high fertility rate). (2) With the same demographic minimalist position, but with maximum territories, the proportion of the Jewish population would decline to 47 per cent in a quarter of a century. (3) On the other hand, if Jewish immigration were not to be curtailed at a rate of 40,000 per year, with minimum territorial assumptions, then in the year 2000 the Jewish population will attain its maximum growth rate of 86 per cent. (4) Keeping the demographic and territorial assumptions at maximum levels, the proportion of Jewish population will amount to 66 per cent.

While the projections of Friedlander and Goldscheider estimate the total population in Israel for the year 2000 to be around seven million (using the manimalist assumption), U. Schmelz[24] gives a lower estimate. With an annual intake of 40,000 Jewish immigrants, and the usual rate of natural increase, he estimates that in 1990 the Jewish population will amount to 4,191,300, while the Arabs in Israel will reach the one million mark. Bustani's[25] estimates for 1990, based on 2.8 per cent rate of natural increase and 40,000 Jewish immigrants per year, reached the figure of 4,684,900 for the Jewish population. With a yearly rate of natural increase of 3.4 per cent among the Arab population, the latter will approximate 860,000 in the year 1990.

TABLE 5.4 *Rates of natural increase per 1,000 for Arabs and Jews (1951–73)*[26]

	Natural increase per 1,000		Live births per 1,000	
Year	Arabs	Jews	Arabs	Jews
1951	37.8	26.3	46.5	32.7
1961	42.0	16.8	49.3	22.5
1970	39.0	16.9	45.6	24.2
1973	40.7	16.8	46.6	24.2

We can see from Table 5.4 that the trend of high birth rate among the Arab population, which existed during the Mandate, continued after the establishment of Israel. In 1970 the Arab population had more than twice the rate of natural increase and almost double the rate of live births compared to the Jewish population.

TABLE 5.5 *Fertility rates per woman of child-bearing age for Arabs and Jews (1956–70)*[27]

Year	Jews	Arabs
1956	3.7	7.3
1966	3.4	8.2
1970	3.3	7.7

The high rate of fertility among Arab women (Table 5.5), together with the prevalence of large families and the decline in infant mortality, explains the preponderance of the younger age groups among the Palestinian population as shown in Table 5.6. In 1969 the average number of children in a Jewish family was 2.9, compared to 5.0 among the Arab population.[28] Likewise in 1961 around one-third of the Arab families in Israel comprised seven members or more; more than a decade later, the proportion rose to 44 per cent. The corresponding figures among the Jewish families with seven members or more were 9.8 per cent in 1961 and 7.8 per cent in 1973.

A study completed recently by Yalan[29] and colleagues, on the modernization of Arab villages in Israel, provides the attitudinal basis for the above picture. When asked to name the ideal number of children desired, 34 per cent of the sample mentioned 'as many as possible', while only 26 per cent mentioned three children or fewer, with the remaining 40 per cent opting for four, five, or more children.

It is usually remarked that it was in the area of public health that the Palestinian Arab benefited as a result of Zionist colonization.[30]

TABLE 5.6 *Family size and age distribution among Arabs and Jews in Israel (percentage)*[31]

No. of persons in family	*1973 Arabs*	*1973 Jews*	*1961 Arabs*	*1961 Jews*	*Age in years*	*1972 Arabs*	*1972 Jews*	*1960 Arabs*	*1960 Jews*
1	6.5	13.4	8.6	10.2	0–4	19.6	11.2	19.1	11.4
2	9.3	3.5	10.8	19.2	5–9	16.6	9.5	15.3	12.2
3	9.5	18.8	9.5	19.1	10–14	13.6	9.2	11.2	11.5
4	9.9	19.5	11.8	23.9	15–29	24.6	27.4	26.2	21.0
5	10.2	12.3	11.6	12.0	30–44	13.5	15.8	13.3	18.8
6	10.4	5.7	12.1	5.8	45–64	8.5	19.2	10.4	19.9
7+	44.2	7.8	35.6	9.8	65+	3.6	7.7	4.5	5.2

It must be pointed out, however, that such positive side-effects are not the outcome of total planned improvements in health standards in Palestine. The closure of the Jewish settlements to the surrounding Arab environment made it impossible for the diffusion of medical knowledge and technology to take place. The incidental and erratic patterns of improvement in the rates of infant mortality, setting the Jewish sector in a more advantageous position than the Arab sector, persist to this day.

TABLE 5.7 *Infant mortality per 1,000 live births (1955–73)*[32]

Year	*Jews*	*Arabs*
1955	32.4	62.5
1965	22.7	43.4
1972	18.8	40.2
1973	18.1	37.1

Although the trend toward reducing the infant mortality rate continued, the lag of the Arabs, compared to the Jews, persists to the present day, as shown in Table 5.7. Between 1955 and 1973 infant mortality among the Jews in Israel was almost halved, from 32.4 to 18.1 per thousand; among the Arabs the improvement was mostly noticeable between 1955 and 1965, when the infant mortality rate declined from 62.5 to 43.4 per thousand. In 1973, infant mortality among the Arabs in Israel stood at 37.1 per thousand. It must be remarked, however, that infant mortality is *higher* among Arabs in mixed cities than it is in other places.[33] Though bad nutrition is undoubtedly a main cause of the high Arab mortality rate, the data also show that while medical care is more prevalent in mixed cities than it is in all-Arab centres, it does not necessarily follow that such care is available or that it is being utilized to the same extent by Arabs as it is by Jews.

The present trend of high fertility rates among Palestinian women will undoubtedly be reduced in the future, for two main reasons. First, it is no secret that the Israeli authorities are deeply concerned about the future population balance, in the face of declining Jewish immigration and the continued high rate of Arab natural increase. A crude manifestation of this concern has been expressed by Israel Koenig, in the much talked about Koenig Report. While expulsion of the Arab population is one 'balancing' method suggested by Koenig,[34] a different and more sophisticated method is to encourage the adoption of birth control methods by Arab women, as well as encouraging the emigration of younger people.

Singerman *et al.*,[35] in writing about 'the demographic threat within', reflect the concern of many Israeli officials. They suggest that the Israeli government should adopt an 'anti-natalistic' policy to reduce the rate of Arab natural increase and prevent what they see as an eventual Arab majority in Israel within a century. By halving the current Arab and Jewish crude birth rates, these authors argue, the Jewish population will be three and a half times larger than the Arab population in a projected population size of 4.7 million by the end of this century.

A second, more indirect means of reducing the fertility rate among Arab women has to do with the induction of Palestinian women into the labour market. Since 1967, the process of female proletarianization has been on the increase, with large numbers of Palestinian women abandoning domestic work and subsistence agriculture to enter the unorganized Israeli labour force as unskilled factory and seasonal workers. Samed concludes that the Israeli government's 'encouragement of Arab female labour in social production and wage earning may be designed to lower fertility rates by raising the marriage age and reducing the time free for child care'.[36]

Although a change in the oppressive nature of traditional women's roles should in general be welcome, the end result for Palestinian women will be a system of double oppression: in addition to the male–female home hierarchy, there will be the additional burden of belonging to an exploited stratum of Arab workers in Israel.

Land alienation

In the light of the settlers' failure to acquire land through legitimate and voluntary means, it became essential, if the plans were to materialize, that new ways be devised to expand the Zionist hold on Arab land. Settlers' plans were made the more easy by the dispersion of the

Palestinian Arabs during the war of 1948.[37] Laws were immediately instituted to seize and confiscate 'absentee' Arab land and property. As we will show below, the seizure of Arab land did not affect the 'refugees' only; the Arabs who remained inside Israel were also affected by the laws, and some lost their property through a peculiar definition of 'absenteeism'. If, for example, an Arab changed his residence owing to the circumstances of the war, and yet remained inside Israel, he could still be considered an absentee.[38] Peretz, who estimates that '40 per cent of the land owned by Arab residents of Israel was confiscated by the authorities as part of the absentee property policy,'[39] comments further on this situation:[40]

> Every Arab in Palestine who had left his town or village after November 29, 1947, was liable to be classified as an absentee under the regulations. All Arabs who held property in the New City of Acre, regardless of the fact that they may never have travelled farther than the few meters to the Old City, were classified as absentees. The 30,000 Arabs who fled from one place to another within Israel, but who never left the country were also liable to have their property declared absentee. Any individual who may have gone to Beirut or Bethlehem for a one-day visit during the latter days of the (British) mandate was automatically an absentee.

Citing United Nations estimates, Peretz remarks that more than 80 per cent of Israel's total area belongs to Arab refugees. Thus 'abandoned property was one of the greatest contributions toward making Israel a viable state.'[41] It is estimated that the value, in Palestinian pounds, of movable and immovable property totals £P122,483,784.

Before we turn to the specific laws enacted for the purpose of confiscation and seizure of Arab land, let us begin with a discussion of an unanticipated feature of Zionist colonization. This concerns the failure of the Zionist authorities to attract settlers who were committed to tilling the land – land which was handed over to them for a small remuneration in the hope of 'saving' it from idleness. It became apparent in the mid-1960s that many settlers were gravitating to urban centres seeking more profitable employment. This phenomenon alarmed the Zionist leaders in Israel, especially when it became known that settlers were leasing land to Arabs. The arrangement was that Palestinian peasants would cultivate the land (which originally might have belonged to them, but was later confiscated by the authorities) in return for a payment of a portion of the crop's yield. By no means was this an easy arrangement for the Palestinian Arabs, since it involved being uprooted and in many instances involved the migration of whole families to live in shanty towns near the fields. The work pattern demanded continual work with no holiday, for pay amounting to half, or even less, of the crop's yield. The situation as a whole obliged the authorities to pass in 1967 the Agricultural Settlement Law to avert the danger of Palestinian Arab repossession of their land. In the words of the Minister of Agriculture at the time of the submission of the bill:[42]

> It is clear that in different parts of the country there are many instances of individual settlers not cultivating the land which was left in their occupancy and not themselves exploiting the quotas of water allocated to them, but transferring to others the right to cultivate and the right to exploit the water by means of leases, partnerships, or in other ways. There are many instances in which it is clear that the settler himself is engaged in work other than agriculture and obtains an income – sometimes a large income – from leasing his land and transferring his water rights obtained from the exploitation of State properties which are entrusted to him with the clear intention that he should exploit the land himself.

Although very few expressed negative reactions to this law, Uri Avenery, an independent opposition member in the Knesset, said:[43]

> There are two conflicting trends to this law; it is a Dr. Jekyll and Mr. Hyde law. To all appearances what we have is a law with an extremely positive social aim; the landlords, who, through various kinds of favouritism, have succeeded in obtaining from the Israel Land Authority State Land on cheap and easy terms, are to be compelled to return that land to the Israel Land Authority if they transfer their right to cultivate it to others. That is to say that the proposers of the law approve of the principle that the land should be in the hands of those who have friends at court or other parasites – the new class of party *Effendis*.
>
> What they really aim at are the Jewish *Effendis* and the Arab cultivators. What is meant is the land that was confiscated from the Arabs and handed over through favouritism to Jews who then leased it back to the Arabs who have thus become its cultivators.

In citing more recent evidence, Chomsky remarks:[44]

> Ten settlements were recently fined 700,000 Israeli pounds 'for illegally leasing agricultural lands to Arabs'. The Minister of Agriculture warned that 'anyone caught leasing land to Arabs will be punished' giving the estimate that 10,000 *dunums* have been leased to Arabs, 'a very serious phenomenon which must

> be fought in every way possible'. The Director of the Galilee region of the Jewish Agency announced 'that his office has sent circulars to all (Jewish) settlements in which they are warned that leasing of national lands for cultivation by Arab lessees or rental of orchards for fruit picking and marketing by Arabs is in violation of law, regulations of the settlement authorities, and the settlement movement'. The Ministry of Agriculture is reportedly undertaking an 'energetic campaign' to eliminate the 'plague' of leasing land to the Arabs.

Now it is estimated that less than 10 per cent[45] of the land in Israel is currently owned by the Arabs. The bulk of the land, including the vast area of the Negev where the Bedouins lost large tracts of land, is classified as state land. Zionist writers[46] do not hesitate to point out that the practice of designating land as state land is not a Zionist invention, but was practised by the British Mandate and the Turks before them.

It is a fact, however, that the definition of state land under the Turkish regime implied usage and transfer of the land by inheritance as long as the occupant tilled the ground. The definition of state land under Israel's rule is quite different from that of the British or the Turks and is built on exclusively national criteria. As is often pointed out, the State of Israel is not the state of its citizens, the Israelis, but the 'Sovereign State of the Jewish people'.[47]

> As the courts have repeatedly held, Israel is not the state of its citizens, in the Western sense, but rather the 'sovereign State of the Jewish people'. The legal and institutional structure of the state, as well as administrative practice, reflect this fundamental commitment to discrimination – what we would call 'racism' in discussing any other society. For the Jewish majority, Israel is indeed a democracy on the Western model, but Arabs are second-class citizens at best, in principle. Furthermore, apart from a few courageous individuals, there is little protest in Israel over the basic commitment to Jewish dominance, that is repression of the Arab minority.

In 1960, the Knesset enacted *Basic Law*: *Israel Lands*,[48] which meant that state land is defined under the principle of the Jewish National Fund, whose original constitution stipulates the inalienable right of the Jews to the land:[49]

> Two principles of Zionist colonization, both incorporated in the constitution of the Jewish Agency, are especially resented by the Arabs. These are: (i) the principle that Jewish property is inalienable; no Zionist settler may dispose of his lease to

> any one but a Jew, (ii) the principle carefully safeguarded by the powerful Jewish Federation of Labour, that only Jewish labour may be employed in Zionist colonies. The net result is that, when the Jewish National Fund makes a purchase the Arabs lose not only the land itself but also any chance of being employed on this land.

Though the principle of 'Jewish labour' continues to be operative in post-1948 Israel only on certain agricultural settlements, the 'inalienability' of Jewish property remains a cornerstone of Zionism.

A major portion of Arab land was acquired by the State of Israel through the application of a series of Laws designed to dispossess the Palestinian refugees of their property. A central law in this regard was the 1950 Absentee Property Law. According to this law, the property of the refugees was transferred to a 'custodian' who would negotiate with the government any transactions concerning the land. Later, in 1953, a Development Authority assumed 'ownership' of the property, which was gradually turned over to the state for the accommodation of Jewish immigrants.

Other laws of a similar nature which were enacted had their origins in the legal framework enforced by the British to counter the Palestinian Arab Rebellion which lasted from 1936 to 1939. The emergency regulations, passed in 1945 by the British, approved the appointment of military governors in various districts of Palestine, specifically in regions with Arab concentrations. Using the same regulations, the Israeli government through its military governors classified many regions in Palestine as 'closed' areas for security reasons. What this meant was that the land falling within these regions could not be used by the original inhabitants, and most of it was eventually confiscated, and it was later found that new Jewish settlements were set up on the same expropriated land.

The reaction of the Arabs to the Israeli land policy is expressed by Peretz in the following words:[50]

> All sections of the Israeli Arab community protested vigorously against the government's discriminatory seizure of 40 per cent of their land. Land in Military Government areas was seized by the authorities under the Defence (Emergency) Regulations of 1945 in the 'interest of public safety'. The Minister of Agriculture requisitioned land under the Emergency Regulations (Cultivation of Waste Lands) Ordinance. The Custodian of Absentee Property took control of about 300 thousand *dunums* belonging to Arab residents of Israel, as well as much of their urban property. Seizure and distribution of this land to various Jewish settlements or organizations was legalized by the Land Acquisition Law of 1953. This also, Arabs felt, was not in accord with

> the (UN) partition resolution which stated (Chap. 2, article 8) that 'No expropriation of land owned by an Arab in the Jewish State . . . shall be allowed except for public purposes. In all cases of expropriation, full co-operation as fixed by the Supreme Court shall be paid previous to dispossession'.

The intentions behind the application of these laws were clear from the outset. In 1962, Shimon Peres, the previous Prime Minister, remarked concerning the emergency laws that 'the use of Regulation 125, which served to a great extent as the basis of the Military regime (in the Arab regions) is the direct continuation of the struggle for Jewish immigration.'[51] Ben-Gurion made similar remarks in the Knesset, noting that 'the military regime exists for the defense of the right of Jewish settlement everywhere.'[52]

It is significant that although the civil rights of the Arabs in Israel were blatantly violated through a system of 'passes' enforced by the military regime, the voice of protest from the Jewish legal profession was not heard. Nowhere did we hear the echoes of protest which were voiced in 1946 by the Hebrew Lawyers' Union when it described the same measures applied by the British to Jewish settlers in the following words:[53]

> The powers given to the ruling authority in the emergency regulations deny the inhabitants of Palestine their basic human rights. These regulations undermine the foundation of law and justice, they constitute a serious danger to individual freedom and they institute a regime of arbitrariness without any judicial supervision.

One cannot, as Aharon Cohen does,[54] attribute the abolition of the military regime in 1966 to the few voices of opposition coming from a handful of concerned citizenry. Similarly, one cannot attribute it to the altruistic motives of the government. There are serious pragmatic considerations involved here. First, the concerted attack on the military government emanated from Jewish political parties. As Tamarin[55] and others note, such an attack was prompted by revelations that the military governor was engaged in vote-stacking among the Arab community, during elections, on behalf of the ruling parties. A second reason – which is argued by Dror as well as Tamarin – has to do with the increase in demand from the Jewish market for unskilled Arab labour. However, it is conceded that the relaxation of restrictions on the geographic mobility of the Arabs was done with little consideration for the eventual socio-economic integration of Arabs in the Jewish sector.

Another 1949 law, not declared invalid until 1972, enabled the Minister of Defence to declare with the approval of the Knesset's

Foreign Affairs and Security Committee that all or part of the 'protected area' – a zone stretching ten kilometres north and twenty-five kilometres south of the Thirty-first Parallel along the whole frontier – was to be a 'security zone'. In this way nearly half of the Arab Galilee area was declared a security zone.[56]

Finally, in 1949, the Minister of Agriculture was empowered by a law passed at that time to assume control of 'waste' (that is to say, uncultivated) land if he was not satisfied with the way the land was managed. A simultaneous law, the Emergency Land Regulation Law of 1949, was designed to seize Arab property located in urban centres, if, as article 2 of the law put it, 'the defense of the State, public security, the maintenance of essential supplies and essential public services, the absorption of immigrants or the rehabilitation of ex-soldiers of war invalids'[57] required the land.

Together with these two laws aiming at dispossessing the Palestinian Arabs of their property, two additional laws were enacted which aimed at defining citizenship of the state along theocratic lines. First, the Israeli Nationality Act, which was enacted in 1952, preceded by the Law of Return of 1950, meant that any Jew anywhere in the world was entitled to Israeli citizenship.[58] Palestinian Arabs, on the other hand, who had been residing in the country for generations and whose ancestors had been there for centuries, were denied this automatic right of citizenship which was granted to Jewish settlers. Another law related to the 'demographic battle', which Israel has been waging since 1948, is the 1953 National Insurance Law. On the surface, this law was intended to encourage families to have as many children as possible by awarding twenty Israeli pounds per child until the age of eighteen. When it became apparent that Arabs – who were contributing toward the scheme in taxes and insurance – were benefiting disproportionately because of the large size of their families, the law was repealed, since its latent intentions were to encourage Jewish families to have many children. In its place, the government applied the existing Discharged Soldiers Law. This meant that Jewish families alone are likely to benefit most from this family allowance since most Arabs (except for the Druze), do not serve in the armed forces. In protesting against these measures, a Jewish member of the opposition in the Knesset remarked, 'the intention (of this law) is to encourage births among one part of the population of Israel and to effect the opposite among the other part, to pay grants to the hungry children of one part of the population and withhold them from the hungry children of another part'.[59]

To assess the implications of land dispossession and the demographic structure for the Israeli Arabs, we turn in the next section to an analysis of Arab class structure and the further transformation of the Arab population from peasantry to proletariat.

Occupation and income

A central, important factor in the transformation of the class structure of the Palestinian Arabs is the emergence of a large stratum of rural proletariat, manifesting the features of migrant labourers encountered in the metropolises of colonial societies, or more recently in advanced Western industrial societies, such as Western Europe and the United States.

If we examine the 1931 British census of Palestine, we discover that close to 80 per cent of the Palestinian Arabs lived in rural areas.[60] Immediately before the end of the British Mandate in 1948, around 30 per cent (of a total of 1,300,000 Arabs) were living in cities. At the end of the Palestine war in 1948, out of approximately 170,000 Arabs who remained in Israel, 27 per cent were urban; the majority were classified rural, including a high proportion of Bedouins. The Arabs under Israeli rule constituted the remainder of close to 900,000 Palestinians who used to live in the territories held by Israel. As we noted earlier, close to 700,000 Palestinian Arabs were displaced in what used to be Palestine within current pre-1967 Israel borders.

As late as 1963, the proportion of rural Arabs in Israel amounted to 75 per cent.[61] The 1973 census shows 56 per cent of the Palestinian Arabs to be residing in urban settlements (settlements of 5,000 or more) and towns.[62] While it is true that in terms of absolute numbers the majority of the Arabs in Israel are not considered rural, it is the qualitative aspects of this shift, and the accompanying changes in social structure, which interest us in the remaining part of this section of our study.

Had this transformation reflected a *natural* shift from ruralism to urbanism, one would hardly be justified in singling it out as an important aspect of the sociological study of Palestinians. After all, many contemporary urban societies were still in the rural stage forty or fifty years ago. However, what makes the Palestinian case of special significance is the fact that this transformation took place, and continues to do so, in the context of colonization with strict patterns of domination and dependency. The urban character of the settlers, their acquisition of native land for colonization purposes, the contrasting occupational characteristics differentiating the settlers from the native population – all these factors explain the continued asymmetrical development in the social and economic spheres of the two groups, and the subsequent distortion of the original social structure of the Palestinian Arabs.

Contrary to the popular belief that what attracts the Zionist settler to Palestine is his attachment to the land and rural life, we find that as early as the 1920s the Zionists tended to cluster in urban centres. In 1931, 74 per cent lived in urban areas; in 1948 the proportion increased to 84 per cent.[63] Today the proportion of Jews living in towns and urban settlements reaches 90 per cent.[64]

Similarly, the occupational structure showed as early as 1931 a preponderance among the Zionists of individuals employed in

TABLE 5.8a *Distribution of employed Arabs and Jews by category of employment*[65]

Economic sector	*1931* Arabs	*1931* Jews
	%	%
Agriculture	57.1	18.1
Industry, crafts, construction	12.0	33.5
Transportation	6.0	6.4
Commerce	8.2	19.1
Liberal professions	2.7	11.6
Public service	3.9	2.2
Domestic service	3.2	3.5
Rent, others	6.9	5.6
	100.0	100.0

TABLE 5.8b *Distribution of employed Arabs and Jews by category of occupation*

Occupation	*1963* Arabs	*1963* Jews	*1972* Arabs	*1972* Jews
	%	%	%	%
Professional, scientific, technical	5.5	12.9	6.6	17.6
Administrative, executive, managerial, clerical	2.0	16.8	3.9	19.0
Traders, agents, salesmen	4.7	8.4	8.2	8.4
Farmers, fishermen and related work	38.0	11.8	19.9	6.9
Workers in transportation and communication	4.3	5.5	6.6	5.0
Construction, quarrymen,	—	—	26.4*	6.7
miners, craftsmen, etc.	39.3	32.1	18.4	24.0
Service, sport and recreation	6.2	12.5	10.0	12.4
	100.0	100.0	100.0	100.0

* The 1972 Israeli census separates construction workers, quarrymen and miners from craftsmen, etc. Thus among the Arabs 26.4% are in construction and mining (unskilled jobs), compared to 6.7% among the Jews.

non-agricultural pursuits (see Table 5.8). If we compare the figures of 1931 with those of 1963 and 1970, we notice that by 1963 only 38 per cent of the Arabs were employed in agriculture, and in 1973 the percentage declined to 20 per cent – that is, around one-third of the 57 per cent figure shown in 1931. The decline in the representation of this occupational group is compensated for by the significant increase in the proportion of unskilled workers, mainly those employed in construction and unskilled service industries. If we examine the 1973 figures, we discover that around a fifth of the Arabs in the Israeli labour force are employed in construction.[66] A survey of the construction industry in Haifa showed it to be comprised as follows: 36.5 per cent Israeli Jews, 42.9 per cent Israeli Arabs, and 20.5 per cent Arabs from the West Bank.[67] There has been hardly any improvement in the situation of the professional and managerial strata; if anything, Lustick's[68] comparative data show that the divergence has increased between the two groups over the last decade.

The same pattern holds if we classify the labour force in terms of *sector* of industry, rather than occupation *per se*. In 1944, 51 per cent of the Palestinian Arabs worked in the agricultural, forestry and fishery sectors. In 1955 and 1961 the percentages of Arabs in the above-mentioned sectors were 50.4 and 41.5, respectively. Among the Jewish population the corresponding percentages were 15 and 12.8. By 1973, 6.8 per cent of the Jews were employed in the agricultural sector, against 17.4 per cent of the Arabs. Here too we notice the rising proportion of Palestinian Arabs channelled into construction and unskilled jobs. Between 1950 and 1973 the proportion of Arab workers in the construction sector rose from 6 to 25.5 per cent.[69] It is important to note that while the share of Arabs in the Israeli labour force was only 9.8 per cent[70] in 1973, they provide a highly disproportionate segment of the total unskilled and semi-skilled workers in the labour force.

Though the definitions of census categories vary slightly, it is significant to note the decline in the proportion of Arabs employed in the commercial, banking and public, and personal services sectors.[71]

> In 1931 the percentage of those [Arabs] employed in those industries was 24.0 per cent of all Arab earners; in 1944 it reached 33 per cent; while in 1950 the percentage went down to 28 per cent, in 1955 to 18.9 per cent, and in 1959 to 16.7 per cent . . . rising slightly in 1968 to 17.1 per cent. There is a noticeable decline in the percentage employed in commerce and personal services and in the percentage employed in public services (from 11.0 per cent in 1944 to 8.2 per cent in 1963).

In 1973, the Arab share of the commerce and banking sector was 9.9 per cent.[72] It is this phenomenon of an unnatural class structure which prompted Waschitz to conclude that while the Jewish occupational structure in the Diaspora used to be an inverted pyramid, 'the Arab-Israeli pyramid is a truncated one.'[73]

One area where Arabs would, under normal circumstances, have been expected to make a break-through is in public service. Yet the actual picture is marked by the scarcity of Arabs in high civil service positions. Of 2,560 officials in the various ministries and agencies, only 25 were Arabs in 1972.[74] These Arabs were mostly employed either in religious courts dealing with the Arab sector, or as token members in the Arab divisions of various ministries. The pluralist character of Israel was never intended to incorporate Arab citizens into the same framework as Jews, as is evident in the dominant Zionist ideology:[75]

> Israel is both a Jewish State and a Zionist State; the character of the State having been determined by the ideological commitments that its major institutions have been designed to serve. Segmented from the Jewish community on the institutional as well as the structural level, Israeli Arabs are cut off from the main-stream of public power and purpose in Israeli society.

It is difficult to infer from the census the sociological significance of the employer/employee status of the Arabs in Israel. Waschitz remarks that 'in 1973, Arabs constituted 4.5 per cent of all self-employed in Israel.'[76] Geraisy, in his 1969 study of Um El-Fahm, an Arab settlement of around 11,000 (in 1973, its population was 14,500),[77] notes that out of 116 villagers working in Jewish metropolises, 92 per cent occupied subordinate occupational positions, and only 8 per cent were in supervisory roles, and 'for 95.8 per cent of the respondents, the supervisors were Jewish, while for 5.4 per cent they were Arabs.'[78] Nor do we know in a precise manner the extent of wage differentials between Jews and Arabs doing the same kind of work. With respect to the latter, Ben-Porath claims that it narrowed down during the mid-1960s, though differences still persist. Between 1949 and 1952, 'Arab wages were roughly 35 to 70 per cent of Jewish wages for similar work. The smallest gap is between Jewish and Arab skilled workers.'[79] It must be borne in mind that very few of the employed Arabs fall in the professional or skilled category. As indicated previously in the occupational breakdown, most of the Arab labour force is concentrated in farming and construction, occupations which rely mainly on unskilled workers. As we noted in Chapter 4, in the case of agriculture, the discrepancy in wages between Jewish and Arab agricultural workers existed as early as 1936, when a Jewish worker's income per annum amounted to five times that of an Arab.[80] A study conducted in 1960 estimated that Arabs working in agriculture earned half as much as Jews working in similar jobs.[81] It is important to note in this regard that Arab agricultural workers comprise the majority of workers in so-called 'Jewish agriculture'. According to a study for the Ministry of Agriculture, the ratio of Arab to Jewish workers in 'Jewish agriculture' is 6:10.[82]

Overall wage differentials existed as far back as the mid-1940s, when the wages of an Arab in the Arab sector amounted to half of a Jew's wage in the Jewish sector.[83] It is difficult to verify Ben-Porath's optimistic claims regarding the narrowing down of income gaps. It we compare the income distribution among the two groups, as displayed in Table 5.9,[84] we discover that between 1967 and 1973 the gap in the gross annual income of Arab and Jewish urban employees has followed an erratic pattern. In 1973, the ratio differences of Arab–Jewish income amounted to 84 per cent, in 1971 it was 66 per cent, and in 1967 the ratio difference was 74 per cent. These figures are an improvement over those given in 1963 in which, according to Zarhi and Achiezra, the average annual income of an Arab amounted to 45 per cent of that of a Jewish earner. Concerning rural employees the data is lacking. However, according to Waschitz, 'the gap would be much greater'[85] than it is among urban employees. It must be remembered, however, that because of larger families among Arabs and the smaller size of the Arab labour force to begin with, the *per capita* income of an Arab is, as we show below in Table 5.11, significantly lower than the *per capita* income of a Jewish citizen.

TABLE 5.9 *Gross annual income of Arab and Jewish urban employees in Israeli pounds*[86]

Year	*Jews*	*Arabs*	*Ratio of Arab/Jewish income* (%)
1967	9,400	7,000	74
1968	9,600	7,000	73
1969	10,500	8,400	70
1970	11,900	8,100	67
1971	12,900	8,600	66
1972	15,500	11,200	72
1973	17,600	14,900	84

Quoting from a report to the Prime Minister's office prepared in 1976 by the Arab affairs staff of the Public Council for Social Welfare, Kislev presents the following summary statistics:[87]

> The number employed in an Arab family is 60 per cent of that in the average Jewish family (taking family size into account). The low employment rate among women determines this. In contrast, among men 14 and up, 73 per cent of Arabs are employed, compared to 67 per cent of Jews. The Arabs' additional six per cent is not due to unemployment among Jews, God forbid. It stems from the addition of workers between 14 and 18 years old. Children under 14, hidden at night in the kitchens of Tel Aviv restaurants and steak houses, are not included in this statistic.

The susceptibility of the Arab worker to the whims of the Jewish market is evident from the unemployment rates displayed in Table 5.10. During economic recessions such as the ones that occurred in 1961 and again in 1967, we find that the unemployment rate among the Arabs is twice that shown to exist in the Jewish sector.

TABLE 5.10 *Unemployment rates for Arab and Jewish urban employees (1960–70)*[88]

Year	*Jews*	*Arabs*
1960	3.6	13.9
1967	9.0	19.4
1969	3.6	5.0
1970	3.4	3.2

TABLE 5.11 Per capita *income for Arabs and Jews (Israeli pounds, 1968–73)*[89]

	Population size		*Emp. labour force*		*Per capita income**		
Year	*Arab*	*Jewish*	*Arab*	*Jewish*	*Arab*	*Jewish*	*Arab/Jew*
							%
1968	406,300	2,434,800	82,800	828,100	1426	3266	43.6
1969	422,700	2,496,400	86,900	858,900	1727	3613	47.7
1971	458,500	2,636,600	94,600	902,500	1775	4415	40.2
1973	497,100	2,810,400	108,100	976,700	3240	6166	52.5

* The *per capita* income was calculated by multiplying the size of the employed labour force for each group (per year) by the average annual income given in Table 5.9, and dividing the result by the respective population size.

Now if we calculate the *per capita* income for the two groups, we discover as shown in Table 5.11 that the gap has diminished only marginally. Whereas in 1968 the *per capita* income of an Arab amounted to 43.6 per cent of that of a Jew, in 1973 it rose slightly to 52.5 per cent.

The picture which we have given above is in keeping with a comment made by a student of Israeli pluralism:[90]

> While there are no systematic studies of trends in the socio-economic gap between Arabs and Jews, there are no reasons to believe that the gap has narrowed. Since the disproportionately greater investments are made in the Jewish sector, it is possible that the gap has grown even wider over the years. For instance, in the first income survey which included Arabs (1967), Arab *per capita* income was 48 per cent of Jewish *per capita*, but four years later (1971), this per cent dropped to 41. A survey of the labour force for the period up to the mid-1960's shows that the gap in the occupational distribution of Arabs and Jews was widened.

These figures are in marked contrast to those given by Zarhi and Achiezra in their 1966 study in which they predicted that in 1973 the *per capita* income for the Arab population would amount to 70 per cent of that of the Jewish population. Of course, their projections would have been accurate (compare their predictions with the data in Table 5.9) had we not adjusted the figures, taking into account the Arab proportion of the labour force.

The role played by the Histadrut in the economic integration of Arabs is minimal. Although the Histadrut opened its doors to Arab workers in 1959, and in 1965 it allowed them to participate in the Histadrut elections, their influence within the organization's decision-making apparatus is negligible:[91]

> Yet one should not infer from such activities that the Histadrut has made an important contribution toward the integration of Arabs and Jews in Israel. Rather its overall pattern of operation, activities and decision-making still reflects its character as an organic part of the Zionist movement and its primary commitment to the development of a strong Jewish working class and a strong Jewish economy. . . . Most importantly, of the thousands of Histadrut owned firms and factories, not one is located in an Arab village. After sixteen years of full membership there are now only five Arabs on the 168 members Histadrut Executive, and no Arab members of the 18-man Central Committee of the Histadrut. Nor are there any Arabs among the over 600 managers and directors-general of Hevrat

> Ovdim industries. Actually the Histadrut *per se* does not involve itself with the Arab population . . . rather there exists a special Histadrut 'Arab Department' that has responsibility for the Arab sector.

This is not to imply that the Histadrut is not visible in the Arab sector; far from it. It acts as one of the many Zionist social-control institutions operating in the Arab sector. It aims through its cultural, educational and labour councils to pacify Arab activists and neutralize the influence of Rakah. In 1969 the Histadrut could list among its various activities in the Arab sector 40 sports organizations, 100 trained Arab youth leaders, more than 6,000 Arab youth in its scout organizations, 17 Arab secretaries affiliated with its labour councils, and 200 scholarships granted to Arab high school and university students, not to mention the activities of its Arabic publishing houses.[92]

Standards of living

One indicator of the economic well-being of a population is its spending and consumption patterns. Up-to-date figures distinguishing between the Arab and the Jewish population concerning spending patterns are not available to this author. However, the results of a 1956/7 survey on family expenditures reveal that the 'average monthly expenditure per individual member in an Arab family was about half the expenditure in a Jewish family, being £39 Israeli and £76 Israeli respectively.'[93] If we examine the types of expenditure, we discover that 60 per cent of Arab spending is devoted to food and shelter (50per cent to food alone), whereas among the Jewish population spending on food and shelter amounts to 49 per cent of the total monthly spending.

Living conditions, measured in terms of number of persons per room, reveal the lop-sided nature of the contrast between the Arab and Jewish populations. In 1973[94] while 25 per cent of the Arab population lived four or more persons in one room, the corresponding figure for the Jewish population was 1.5 per cent. Similarly, while close to 50 per cent of the Jewish population were distributed, on the average, at one person or less per room, among the Arab population it was 15.4 per cent. If we compare these figures with those of 1968, we notice that while there has been a marked improvement in the situation of the Jewish population there has been hardly any such improvement in the situation of the Arabs. In 1968, 75 per cent of the Arab population lived two persons or more per room, compared to 71 per cent in 1973. The respective figures for the Jewish population are 29 per cent for 1968 and 21 per cent for 1973.[95]

Even if we compare the most recent figures with those of 1961, we notice that as far as the Arabs are concerned the picture did not change that much. In 1961, 30 per cent of urban Arabs lived, on the average, at fewer than two persons per room, while the corresponding proportion among urban Jews reached 62 per cent. Among rural Jews and Arabs the respective figures were 51 and 13 per cent.[96] In terms of population density in towns, Kislev provides the following picture:[97]

> In Arab Nazareth live about 40,000 people, and the built-up area is 71,24 *dunums*. Upper Nazareth [a Jewish town] has about 16,500 residents or 9,000 *dunums per capita*: 178 square meters in Nazareth and 548 in Upper Nazareth. The situation is no better in the Arab villages of the area: 149 square meters *per capita* in Kfar Kana, 156 in Ein Mahil, 165 in Mashad and 160 in Tur'an. Only in Kfar Rina is the built-up area per inhabitant a little higher: 250 square meters, still less than half that of Upper Nazareth.

Although the government-commissioned report from which Kislev quotes recommended the abandonment of further expropriation of Arab land, the Rabin government at the time did precisely the opposite.

Another accepted comparative indicator of the standard of living is the ownership of durable goods among various sub-groups of the population. Except for ownership of radios, which extends to around 80 per cent of the Arab and 90 per cent of the Jewish population, the comparison across the remaining consumer items shows a striking lag in the living standards of the Arab population. Table 5.12 shows that the proportion of Jews to Arabs in terms of ownership of various commodities varied from 10:1 in the case of telephones, to 4:1 in the case of electric refrigerators, and to 5:1 in the case of private cars and so on.

TABLE 5.12 *Ownership of durable goods by Jews and Arabs (1970)*[98]

	Jews	*Arabs*
	%	%
Telephones	38.1	3.4
Private cars	16.7	3.1
Television	53.4	14.3
Electric refrigerators	95.5	26.8
Washing machines	46.1	11.8
Gas ranges	88.5	60.7

Proletarianization

The transformation of the Palestinian peasantry into a stratum of marginal proletariat has had two serious implications as far as the indigenous Arab population are concerned. First, they were uprooted from traditional village life. As early as 1961, around 50 per cent of Arab workers were geographically mobile and worked in areas outside their residences. For 1970, the figure for migratory male Arab workers was around 59 per cent, with the overwhelming majority coming from rural regions.[99] In 1961, for example, 21.5 per cent of commuting workers in the Arab labour force came from urban centres, compared to 78.5 per cent who came from rural areas.[100] Of those employed in the construction industry, close to 77 per cent worked away from home in 1961.[101] According to a governmental survey conducted in 1965, those who were considered to be transient workers amounted to '27,000, that is, one-half of the Arab workers, which proportion included 23,500 males; 69 per cent of these mobile workers came from rural areas, 13 per cent from Nazareth and Shfa'amer, 10 per cent were Bedouins and the remaining 8 per cent lived in cities.'[102] At the initiative of the government, plans were drafted in 1963 to organize residential living for those village proletariat who worked in the cities. However, a referendum[103] carried out among 116 Arab village workers in 1964 showed that very few workers were prepared to make the move away from the village, and as a consequence a parliamentary committee looking into the matter of Arab workers' residences concluded in 1968 that the initial idea of a government subsidy to build such residences was not a viable one. Instead, the government promised to look into securing cheaper transportation rates from and to the villages. It is estimated that now around 90 per cent of Arab village workers commute each day from their villages to Jewish towns and cities in order to work.[104] Geraisy[105] gives a somewhat lower estimate. His survey of Arab villages gives an overall figure of 70 per cent, although among the age group fifteen to twenty-five the percentage of those working outside their villages reaches 90 per cent. According to Waschitz, 'such a situation makes Arabs vulnerable to any contraction of employment; the "non-local" Arab villager will be the first to be fired (for example, in the Haifa port, this year).'[106] These findings bring into question a recent statement by Toledano, the Prime Minister's Adviser on Arab Affairs, who cited official census figures showing that close to 50,000 Arab workers (that is, half of the officially registered Arab labour force) are engaged in Jewish enterprises located in the Jewish sector.[107]

Two main causes lie behind the dislocation of Arab workers: economic stagnation of the Arab sector and continuing expropriation of Arab land. An example of how expropriation of Arab land affected the occupational structure of one Arab community, which is not atypical, is the case of Taibeh, an Arab village in the Triangle:[108]

> In 1949 the village had 4,900 residents, and 33,000 *dunums* of land. Today, over 15,000 residents and 19,000 *dunums*. Thus the change in occupational structure. Until 1949, over half of the village lived off agricultural work. Today – only 10 per cent. But this 'employment revolution' did not occur so much naturally as it was the result of land strangulation. Most of the 90 per cent who do not work in [Arab] agriculture are not even employed in the village itself. They work in construction, [Jewish] agriculture, restaurants – in cities, in Jewish moshavim and Kibbutzim, like other Israeli Arabs.

Kislev argues that most of this land expropriation was carried out through the application of the 1950 Absentee Property Law, according to which 'absentee' residents are either those who may have continued to live in Israel (between 1948 and 1950), but in a different location from the one they originally inhabited; those who left for a neighbouring Arab country but eventually returned; or those who, because of boundary adjustments (such as that which took place between Israel and Jordan after the 1948 war), were outside the borders when the state was declared but were eventually 'united with their land'. Taibeh is an example of the latter case, the differenc, being that the Arab inhabitants were not 'united with their land' and continued to be counted as absentee, or 'present-absent', because technically they were outside the state-declared boundaries of 1948. Overall, Kislev estimates that there are between 1,200 and 1,300 land registration suits pending between the Israeli Arab population and the Israel Land Authority.

Further evidence bearing upon the process of Arab proletarianization is provided by two separate studies conducted in the early 1970s, one at the Hebrew University and the other at the Technion; both came up with results similar to those discovered almost a decade ago by Rosenfeld. It is possible to summarize the findings of these latter studies as follows:[109] (*a*) the Arab village is losing its traditional character very quickly; (*b*) toward the end of the British Mandate, the Arab village was more developed than it is today; (*c*) the Arab agricultural workers suffer from the lack of having a permanent place of work; (*d*) as to work relations between Arabs and Jews in cities, the Arab attaches importance to them while, in most cases, the Jew does not; (*e*) by the age of forty to forty-five, the Arab villager who works in construction or in the different service industries is found to be an 'old man', having spent twenty-five years working; (*f*) out of ninety-four villages sampled in the Technion study, only twenty villages had an acceptable level of modernization.

The second feature of the distortion of social structure among the native Palestinian Arabs is in the transformation of the Arab village into an economically stagnant unit. Writing more than a decade ago, Ben-Porath commented: 'The present structure of the Arab sector is such that it generates only limited demand for educated manpower and the potential source of demand is the Government and the Jewish sector.'[110]

All the evidence shows that Ben-Porath's observation still holds now. In commenting on the underdevelopment of the Arab region and the deterioration of its economic position relative to pre-1948, Gottheil comments:[111]

> Although it is clear that Arab incomes and consumption have increased considerably since the formation of the State, it is also clear that the Arab region, as a producing region, has declined relative to the rest of the economy. Arabs are increasingly leaving their villages for employment opportunities in the Jewish sector, and although their consumption of houses, automobiles, refrigerators, televisions, food and clothes has increased, construction of factories, expansion of agricultural acreage and the development of local services in the Arab region have not. This circumstance, incidentally, contrasts with the experience of the Mandate Period. While the Jewish economy during 1922–1931 was expanding rapidly . . . , the development of the Arab economy in Palestine was also substantial. The extent of Arab participation in the industrialization process is reflected in the growth, from 1918 to 1929, of 1,373 new Arab-owned enterprises. Although clearly of smaller scale than the Jewish enterprise, they nonetheless represented over 70 per cent of the total Arab enterprises. But since 1948 disparity between the Jewish and Arab regions in Israel has increased rather than diminished.

An additional factor which would account for the economic lag of the Arab village is discussed by Lustick. He focuses on the tremendous gap in the inflow of capital in the form of government subsidies to Arab villages as an important factor in slowing down, or even preventing, the industrialization of many Arab villages. Out of 105 Arab villages, only 43 are supplied with electricity, while 20 other villages are still at the planning stage, thus slightly less than half of the Arab villages have no immediate or future plans to acquire electricity. While Jewish villages and settlements have access to funds from the government as well as the Jewish Agency, Arab villages, if they embark on programmes of improving social services, have to borrow money in loans repaid in full with added interest to meet the costs of these programmes. For example, since the total budget for an Arab village council amounts to slightly more than half a million Israeli pounds, it becomes next to impossible to try and install an electricity network in the village when the connection to the nearest grid could cost anywhere from I£0.5 million to I£3 million. It is estimated that since 1948, more than $1,200,000,000 were granted by the Jewish Agency alone towards the development of Jewish settlements.[112] It is unlikely that such an inflow of capital will ever be channelled into Arab villages. Overall, within the last fifteen years, out of the government's budget totalling billions of Israeli pounds, a meagre sum of I£15 million Israeli pounds has been spent in improving Arab villages.[113] Bayadsi, an Israeli Arab, confirms the above picture:[114]

> A Ministry of Interior report on Municipalities in Israel during 1971/1972 reveals that the total grants allocated by the Ministry to local authorities amounted to I£158,580,000, of which the Arab sector received a total of I£1,785,000 or 1.1 per cent of the total, while the population included within the Arab local authorities is as much as 11 per cent of the entire population governed by local authorities in Israel. In the matter of loans, the Arab minority's share is minute. Again, the Interior Ministry's report for 1971/1972 shows that the Ministry made loans to cover deficits in local authorities' budgets to an amount of I£50,185,500. The Arab villages had no share at all of these loans. The Ministry of the Interior also granted loans for the repayment of indebtedness to an amount of I£60,897,000 to Jewish local authorities, while Arab local authorities received nothing for this purpose.

Supporters of the Israeli government's policy toward the Arab sector remark that Arab villages are underdeveloped because of the unwillingness of Arab local councils to levy taxes on their residents. Table 5.13 does not support this claim entirely. While the *per capita* property tax levied on Jewish towns is higher than that collected from Arab towns (a fact which shows that Jewish centres are richer than their Arab counterparts), the main contrast is in terms of grants *per capita* where the Arab share is minuscule compared to grants given to Jewish localities. If we consider two comparable towns, Yavneh, a Jewish town of 10,100 inhabitants, and Taibeh, an Arab town of 11,700, with *equivalent* property tax, the *per capita* grant given to the Jewish town exceeds that given to the Arab one in the ratio of 122:7.

The economic well-being of the Jewish and Arab sectors is a function of the extent to which each sector is politically organized,

TABLE 5.13 *Share of selected Jewish and Arab towns, in terms of* per capita *grant and property tax (Israeli pounds)*[115]

Towns	*Population in thousands*	*Grant per capita*	*Property tax per capita*
Jewish			
Or-Jehuda	12.3	123	23
Bet-Shean	11.3	194	10
Bet-Shemesh	10.1	174	11
Hod-Hasharon	13.5	94	50
Tirat-Hacarmel	14.6	129	25
Yavneh	10.1	122	17
Nes Tziona	11.7	85	34
Upper Nazareth	14.8	105	30
Afula	17.4	119	35
Pardes Hana	13.6	133	29
Kiryat Gat	19.2	178	21
Kiryat Tivon	9.8	55	48
Arab			
Um El-Fahm	13.3	7	11
Taibeh	11.7	7	17
Baqa	7.6	7	23
Daliat Al-Carmel	6.2	10	12
Tira	8.3	7	25
Tanra	8.6	8	18
Majar	6.4	18	15
Sahknin	8.4	5	8
Arabe	6.0	2	8

TABLE 5.14 *Arab and Jewish localities* with no local councils (1953–71)*[116]

Year	*Number of cities, villages and settlements*		*Cities, villages and settlements with no local councils*	
	Jewish	*Arab*	*Jewish*	*Arab*
			%	%
1953	742	112	12.5	79.5
1957	802	111	5.0	73.0
1960	780	112	2.9	59.8
1966	774	103	1.7	44.7
1971	781	104	1.1	28.8

* Excluding Arabs in East Jerusalem

in particular on the local level. Here too we note that the Arab and Jewish villages have developed in separate directions. As late as 1963, around seventy Arab villages, that is, more than half of the entire number of Arab villages, had no local councils. As shown in Table 5.14, around 29 per cent of the Arab localities in 1971 had no local councils. In contrasting the two sectors, it must be borne in mind that the patterns of development are not a new phenomenon. They existed prior to 1948 where the Jewish sector had already included the development of local councils in pockets of Zionist settlements. After all, the idea of local councils is a Western concept of political and social participation, which was imported into the region on a large scale by the Zionist settlers. Within the Arab sector, there were two localities that had municipal councils as early as 1948: Nazareth and Shfa'amer.

The most drastic change has occurred in the magnitude of decline in the number of Arab villages and settlements in the area now constituting Israel. In 1945, there were 863 villages; as shown in Table 5.14 there are now close to 104 villages and settlements. The Zionist takeover and destruction of Arab villages has been greatly facilitated by the mass exodus of the Palestinians. Peretz points out that 'of the 370 new Jewish settlements established between 1948 and the beginning of 1953, 350 were on absentee property.'[117]

In contrast to the Jewish villages, it is claimed, Arab villages were run according to clan and family units, or the *hamulas*, and had in them many of the traditional structures which prevented industrialization and the development of mass-based participation in local affairs. Family feuds and traditional value-systems are usually cited by the Israeli authorities and social scientists alike as the main reasons for the economic backwardness of the Arab sector. It is not our purpose in this study to investigate the sociological bases of the *hamula* and its place in Arab village life. Asad's, Rosenfeld's, and Nakhleh's works, which were discussed in this study, make it clear that if an adequate explanation concerning the social structures of Arab villages is sought, one has to turn to studying the role of political economy, and move away from current approaches fashionable in socio-anthropological writings which emphasize the centrality of values and kinship systems.

It is in this context that we find it difficult to ignore the role of the Israeli government, including the dominant political parties, who have capitalized on, and even perpetuated, the presence of the *hamula* phenomenon to the detriment of the economic development of Arab villages. Contrary to Cohen's[118] conclusions regarding *hamula* revival under Israeli rule, it is plausible to argue that the *hamula* phenomenon existed all along, side by side with social class cleavages, and that its continued existence is due to governmental policies as indicated by the following comment made by Lustick:[119]

> Perhaps the single most important factor explaining the political longevity of the traditional *hamula* framework is the support that *hamula* leaders have received from the government, specifically from the military government, the office of the advisor to the Prime Minister on Arab Affairs, and politicos in the Mapai-Labour Party and in the Histadrut's Arab Department.

Sabri Jiryis[120] demonstrates in detail the extent of manipulation of local leaders in Arab villages by the ruling parties. The introduction of 'whole scale democracy' in Arab villages has had debilitating effects on the efficiency levels of the various councils. For example, in 1965 and 1969 a total of 252 and 195 voting lists were included in local elections, respectively. In 1965, 154 lists won, and in 1969, 151. In other words, the average number of lists for each village totalled five, which made it impossible to conduct the affairs of the councils with any efficiency. Instead of (and perhaps in addition to) family feuds, the Israelis have managed to introduce political party feuds; in both cases, the results are similar in their overall effect. In some instances the Communist parties have formed coalitions with Arab nationalist elements in order to confront Zionist-based political parties. In such cases, the Ministry of the Interior would interfere and upset the political balance by reclassifying the status of the village so as to justify the election of additional members, thus annulling the existing balance. In one such case, cited by Jiryis, the local council of Kufer Yassif village, which was led by an Arab nationalist-Communist coalition, appealed to the Israeli Supreme Court against government interference in the political affairs of the village (by deposing the elected mayor), and won its case.

In Jiryis'[121] view another reason for the government's reluctance to take definite steps in increasing the scope and number of local councils in the Arab sector is the fact that the setting up of local councils implies recognition of the existence and legitimacy of that particular village. This has implications concerning the size of the land holdings by the village inhabitants and the extent of the local councils' jurisdiction. Such final steps might impede future designs of the government to confiscate Arab land and relocate Arab villagers, as has been done in more than one case, for the sake of settling incoming Jewish immigrants. Bayadsi's comments are relevant here:[122]

> In spite of the Planning and Construction Act in 1965, and its practical implementation as of 1966, local town-planning committees have yet to be established in a number of Arab

villages. Most Arab villages have no approved zoning plan and no status has been accorded to any local zoning committee in any Arab local council, in spite of the fact that in most large local councils in the Jewish sector the authority has also been designated as a local zoning committee.

While the authoritarian structure of the *hamula* makes it amenable as a tool for co-option of Arab élites, the central factor in such a process remains the dependent economic relationship which all Arabs have with Zionist institutions. Bearing in mind that the state is the main employer, followed by the Histadrut through its affiliated industries, and that both of these institutions are Jewish-cotrnolled, the Arabs have little chance of securing employment in an economically stagnant, non-Jewish labour market. To a very large extent, the co-option of Arabs is carried out in a highly symbolic and personalized manner which does not require a commitment on the part of the Arabs to participate in political norms. A clear indication of this phenomenon is the absence of permanent Zionist affiliated parties in the Arab sector. These lists are usually organized under high-sounding labels on the eve of the elections, depending on the immediate issues in the Arab sector, and the particular relationship which Zionist parties (in particular the Labour Party) happen to have with the *hamulas*.

In addition to co-option as a method of control, the Israeli government resorts to a 'divide and rule' policy. This policy is clearly reflected in the preferential treatment accorded to the Muslim Druze sect on the assumption that they are not Arabs. For example, although the Druze comprise around 10 per cent of the Muslim population, they receive disproportionate help in terms of government subsidies and local development programmes and in the handling of their religious affairs. Concerning the latter, the Druze, who number around 33,000, have six religious judges, whereas the 300,000 other Muslims have five similar judges to handle their religious affairs. The *per capita* government grant to Druze villages in 1973–4 amounted to I£30, whereas for 'co-operative' Christian and Muslim villages it was I£10. And 'of the five Arab villages in 1974 in which sizeable light industries were located, three of the villages were Druze.'[123]

In return for these side-payments, the co-opted élites render useful services. In addition to delivering Arab votes to Zionist parties, as Lustick notes, Arabs act as informers on other Arabs who are politically active and oppose the Zionist regime. Arab Members of Knesset are asked to deliver to the Arab community ritualistic speeches of praise on behalf of the state on public occasions. After the Land Day strikes in 1976, an Arab Member of Knesset affiliated with the Labour Party condemned the strike, while another Druze member asked that the Community Party, Rakah, be declared illegal in view of its involvement in the organization of the strike. These are only examples of the latest political behaviour of co-opted Arab élites, for the Knesset records contain many previous examples of Arab members siding with Zionist parties against the interests of the Arab population.[124]

Up to 1971, only 3 Arab villages, out of a total of 104, have been land-surveyed, 49 other villages are still in the planning stages, while the rest have not even been considered. In those villages which have not been land-surveyed and incorporated into the municipal or local council government structure, the day-to-day disadvantages for the inhabitants are obvious. It is difficult in the absence of clear-cut zoning and ordinance laws to secure licences to build and develop village land. In those instances when the villagers 'violated' non-existent zoning regulations they discovered, to their sorrow, that their houses could be – and were in fact – demolished. Toledano, the Prime Minister's Adviser on Arab Affairs, confirmed the execution of these measures. In a recent interview, he admitted that not too long ago eighteen houses were demolished in one Arab village due to the violation of zoning laws.[125]

TABLE 5.15 *Jewish and Arab cultivated land and value of agricultural output (1950–71)*[126]

Year	*Cultivated land* Jewish	Arab	*Value of agric. output* Jewish	Arab	*Value per* dunum Jewish	Arab	*percent diff.* Jewish/Arab
1950–1	2,705*	645*	65,172†	5,798*	24.09‡	8.99‡	186
1954–5	2,965	625	353,237	24,168	119.13	38.67	208
1958–9	3,350	755	671,245	41,767	200.36	55.32	262
1962–3	3,185	820	1,102,997	58,330	346.31	71.13	387
1966–7	3,273	865	1,516,272	98,563	464.27	113.95	307
1970–1	3,387	774	2,393,200	116,700	706.58	150.97	368

* Thousands of *dunums*
† Thousands of Israeli pounds
‡ Israeli pounds

The economic lag of the Arab sector is not confined to income differentials or to a distorted occupational structure, as we have seen above, but also to a highly marginalized agricultural sector, which has been traditionally the back bone of the Palestinian Arab economy. Although a far larger proportion of Arabs live in rural areas, compared to Jews, neither the size of land owned nor the productivity of cultivated land shows the same pattern. Table 5.15 shows clearly the infinitesimal size of Arab cultivated land, when compared to Jewish land. Between 1950 and 1971 the average cultivated land in the Jewish sector exceeded that found in the Arab agricultural sector by more than 400 per cent. Similarly, the agricultural yield in the Jewish sector exceeds that found in the Arab sector, on average, by 289 per cent for a two-decade period, 1951–71. In 1971 it reached as high as 368 per cent.

Even in such areas as tobacco growing, one of the most successful traditional agricultural pursuits among the Palestinian Arabs, we discover that although in terms of tonnage the Arabs produce more than the Jews, in terms of price per ton the situation of the Arabs deteriorated during the last two decades. Whereas in 1961 the difference in the price of a ton of tobacco was I£685 in favour of the Jewish farmer, in 1971 the difference amounts to I£1,444.[127]

It is to be expected, in the light of the previous discussion, that the actual consumption of water for irrigation purposes will differ drastically in the two sectors. Table 5.16 demonstrates that between 1962 and 1970 the Arab proportion of the consumption of water for agricultural purposes remained around 1 per cent of the total water consumption in Israel.

TABLE 5.16 *Millions of cubic metres of water consumption in Jewish and Arab agricultural sectors (1962–70)*[128]

	1962	*1964–5*	*1966–7*	*1967–8*	*1968–9*	*1969–70*
	%	%	%	%	%	%
Jewish	99.1	99	98.9	98.7	98.7	98.6
Arab	0.9	1	1.1	1.3	1.3	1.4
	100.0	100.0	100.0	100.0	100.0	100.0
Cubic metres (in millions)	1,144	1,075	1,203	1,133	1,236	1,248

Conclusions

Basically, we have tried to show in this chapter that the sociological characteristics of the Arab minority in Israel define it as an internal colony. This, we might add, is irrespective of whether or not the Zionist colonization of Palestine aimed in its original plans to reduce the indigenous Arabs to the status of a colonized minority.

Weinstock,[129] for example, refers to Israel as a 'deviant' form of Western colonialism, arguing that, considering the writings of earlier

Zionist leaders, the aims of the original settlers were not to exploit and subjugate the native Palestinian Arabs, but to replace them with a Jewish population. Although we concur with Weinstock that this does not make it a lesser form of domination, it is important for the development of theory of settler societies that we shift the emphasis from considering interpretations of the pronouncements of Zionist leaders as the guiding principle of how the Zionist colonization of Palestine actually proceeded, to assessing important unanticipated consequences of this process. Even if one appreciates the socialist context of the call for 'Jewish labour', 'Jewish economy', and 'Jewish agriculture' as necessary mechanisms for the eventual creation of a natural Jewish occupational pyramid, devoid of the exploitation of Arab labour (a claim that Borochovists and Gordon's followers advance),[130] one cannot but echo Warriner's[131] remarks made during the 1940s that it is a strange form of socialism built on sectarianism and Jewish exclusivity.

It would be too fatalistic to accept the claim, as the Israeli historian J. Talmon[132] does, that because other states in recent history were founded by the sword through annexation, military conquest and border modifications, the case of Israel must be accepted as another instance of this normal state of affairs. Talmon seems to be conscious of one side of the eventualities of history, and he seems to be willing to grant history a licence of immorality and *fait accompli*. However, to accept the normality of a Northern Ireland, a Rhodesia, a South Africa, and so forth, is to show an unlimited capacity to generalize from the sins of history and colonialism in the name of the nation-state.

Although it is true that the present distortion of the Arab class structure in Israel is the outcome of a longer historical process of colonization whose roots could be located in the past century, the fact remains that the post-1948 period has managed to transform Palestinian Arab peasantry into a lumpenproletariat with a 'declassed' status while at the same time diminishing the likely emergence of a viable bourgeoisie.

The upshot of all this is that while Israel *claims* to have solved the perennial problem of creating a natural occupational structure among its Jews, it has done so at the expense of creating an unnatural Palestinian Arab class structure.

6 Prejudice, education and social disorganization

The bases for prejudice can be social as well as legal. In the latter sense, prejudice is discerned from the legal practices of a society. In Israel's case Tamarin refers to three areas in which legal codes condone discriminatory practices: (1) 'denial of some basic human rights by segregatory and other laws, (2) violation of the freedom of conscience by religious coercion and (3) discriminatory regulations concerning the Arab minority'.[1]

These forms of discrimination could be found in various religious laws affecting Arabs and Jews, such as those prohibiting mixed marriages between Jews and non-Jews which, according to Tamarin, create a 'situation of apartheid'. Furthermore, the presence of religious courts which are empowered to handle exclusively matters pertaining to marriage, divorce and inheritance, enhances the close connection between the state and religion, thus giving rise to theocracy whereby an individual's behaviour is regulated by ascriptive rather than universalistic criteria.[2]

With regard to legal discrimination against the Arab minority, Tamarin refers to various kinds of legislation, some forms of which were discussed in the previous chapter, whereby the Arabs in Israel are treated differentially in matters concerning land and property ownership, rights of movement, and so on.

Prejudice which is social rather than legal in its essence is our main concern in this chapter. Its sanctions emanate from the private and public behaviour of members of one group toward another. Although such behaviour does not find support in explicitly formulated rules and regulations, it nevertheless exists in the form of tradition. Segregation in housing and residential living, discrimination in education and occupational opportunity, the creation of negative stereotypes – all these are forms of prejudice which are to be found in the cultural and value matrix of a society. It is the latent (in contrast to the manifest) form of such prejudice which makes its study more problematic.

Specifically, in our argument we will deal with three areas: (1) images of the Arabs in Israel and inter-ethnic relations, (2) the structure of Arab educational opportunities, and (3) Arab social disorganization.

Images and inter-ethnic contact

A cursory examination of findings concerning the way Israeli Jews and Arabs perceive each other, and themselves, reveals patterns which are not too dissimilar from those found in other plural societies where cleavages along ethnic, racial, national, and economic lines predominate. This is especially so in cases where the plural order of a society has been buttressed by an institutional separation, and where this separation has been accompanied by the subordination of one or more groups in society by a dominant group.

The main consequence of such an institutional set-up is the emergence of a coercive social structure in which the dominant group asserts its position through a hegemonic value-system which permeates central socialization agencies; the schools, the media, the polity and economy. The upshot of this is the development of a dependent relationship in which the life-style of the subordinate group is shaped by the needs and aspirations of those in positions of dominance. This is particularly true in instances where the level of technology and know-how of the dominant group surpasses that of the subordinate group.

According to the scheme outlined in Chapter 2, a main feature of a settler regime is that it creates in the public eye a mythology which dehumanizes the culture and way of life of the native people. Thus, the native is masked by a negative stereotypical image that is utilized to justify his exploitation. Needless to say, this negative image, producing an inferior perception of the self, is often internalized by the native people. The 'mark of oppression', a concept prevalent in endless empirical research on black children in the United States, best exemplifies the psychological outcomes of an oppressive social structure. Black children are known to internalize – as early as the age of three or four – a negative image of themselves by ego-idealizing white children sharing their surroundings.[3] An entire folklore emerges to reinforce the negative stereotyping of members of the subordinate group. In describing the situation of the Arabs in Algeria under the colonial regime of the French settlers, J. Cohen says:[4]

> In North Africa, colonialism has created a stereotype to which the name 'Arab' has been given. What is an Arab? The

> descendants of the famous conquerors of the Middle Ages? Not at all; he is merely the strange creature clad in tattered *djellabah* and filthy head cloth. His wife is swathed in a white robe and his children go barefoot. There is no mistaking him. Everything about him, both physical and moral, testifies to his essentially 'Arab' qualities. . . . Not only is he dirty, but he is also a liar, thief, lazy and aggressive. . . . Don't entrust him with any difficult task, since he has neither the inclination nor the ability to carry it out; he would only make 'an Arab's job of it' . . . an expression which has passed into current usage.

Indeed this expression did, for it has become an accepted part of the folklore in Israel; the Hebrew saying *avoda araviet* is almost a literal translation of 'an Arab's job', and it is used among Israeli Jews as a derogatory statement describing extreme incompetence and lack of skill in the performance of tasks.

Herbert Blumer distinguishes four types of feeling associated with prejudice among the dominant group: superiority, alien-ness, claim to privilege, and suspicion. These entail the following:[5]

> The feeling of superiority places the subordinate group below, the feeling of alienation places them beyond, the feeling of proprietary claim excludes them from the prerogative of position; and the fear of encroachment is an emotional recoil from the endangering of group position.

There is no implication that at the root of all the attitudes of the dominant group there are scientific theories to back up their position or to explain the rather low level of accomplishment of the subordinate group. In any case, whether or not there are correlations between the 'tested' attitudes and the genetic make-up of individuals is irrelevant to our argument; apart from the fact that the correlations appear insignificant, it is the case that such as do exist, indicate variations in form and style of thought rather than in absolute content and magnitude of ability. What matters in a society, however, is what people *believe* to be true.

The evidence concerning the stigmatization of specific ethnic groups in settler societies is abundant in the literature. Content analysis of children's textbooks in North America[6] testifies to the negative depiction of blacks, Indians, Arabs and other minority groups. In the Israeli case similarly extensive research is lacking, although the limited amount of literature available points to a similar situation. In commenting on the values transmitted in storybooks for Jewish children in Israel, Maroz remarks that the racist content of such popular books is not all that different from that once revealed in school textbooks used by Arab refugee children in pre-1967 Gaza:[7]

> One of the most shocking phenomena in the area of children's literature in this country is the books published every now and then, and which are eagerly snatched by children, whose topic is always how the mighty child or children defeat the funny and thick-headed Arabs who seek to kill us for their personal pleasure.

A review of attitudes toward the Arabs in Israeli children's books, referred to by Segal,[8] revealed a similar negative stereotyping of Arabs. Segal's own discussion of the image of Arabs in Israeli fiction leads her to a similar conclusion, namely that the Jewish attitude is characterized by an 'almost neurotic suspicion of Arabs'.[9]

In her treatment of the Arabs in modern Hebrew literature, Yona Bachur notes that while Zionist writers of the 1920s – Moshe Smilansky, for example – depicted the Arab way of life and, in certain cases, focused upon confrontation between Jews and Arabs, 'not a single writer in this period (including Israel's Nobel Laureate, S. Y. Agnon, who totally ignored the Arab question) treated the theme from the standpoint of coexistence between the two national groups who found themselves sharing the same homeland.'[10]

As Yudkin[11] and others[12] have noted, a turning point in Israeli fiction became evident in the literary output of post-1967. Of significance is the work of A. B. Yehoshua, in particular his story *Facing the Forests*, in which he depicts sympathetically the status of dispossessed Palestinian Arab villagers; *My Michael* is another 1968 novel written by a younger Sabra, Amos Oz, in which the Arab–Jewish theme is central.

Turning to survey data, a recent attitudinal study[13] of ethnic relations in Israel demonstrates the rather high level of hostility exhibited by the Jewish population toward the Arabs. More than 80 per cent of those sampled by Yochanan Peres agreed to the proposition 'Arabs will not reach the level of progress of Jews,' and 90 per cent preferred to see fewer Arabs remain in Israel. A similar negative attitudinal pattern holds true with respect to mixed marriages, friendship and integrated residential living. It must be stressed that with respect to the last three areas, Oriental Jews expressed a greater social distance from Arabs than European Jews.

According to the same survey, close to 90 per cent of the sample endorsed the proposition 'Arabs understand only force.'[14] This observation is significant since it reflects a perception of the Arab as being irrational, unbending, and only amenable to physical rather than intellectual means of discourse. These aggregate data are highlighted by an additional piece of evidence based on an incident which took place in Acre, one of the mixed towns in the north of Israel, and a place that has been heralded as successful in terms of maintaining ethnic integration. During the height of guerrilla activities in Israel between 1969–1970, a confrontation between Jewish and Arab youth took place in Acre which culminated in a mob attack by the former on the latter. When questioned by a journalist, a member of the Jewish gang talked about the Arab youth in this fashion:[15]

> You have to beat them in order to teach them where they belong, so that they know their place. If we continue to be lenient toward them, we will wake up one day to discover that the city has been taken over by al-Fateh. . . . We have reached the conclusion that it is impossible to continue to tolerate the situation. They have to fear us, otherwise out [from the country] they will go.

In reviewing Israeli public opinion data over a five-year period, 1967–72, Jacob's[16] findings shed additional light on inter-ethnic feeling. He notes that whereas approximately half of the Jewish sample were willing to befriend Arabs, close to three-quarters indicated that they had never been visited by Arabs, and slightly more than half said that they had never been in an Arab home.

It is difficult to offer a precise interpretation of these results, since probing questions were not used in the survey to find out if the patterns of visiting were voluntary or dictated by necessity. However, when examining the impact of *contact* on inter-ethnic feeling, Jacob notes that the overall effect on the Jewish sample was to increase the social distance.[17]

The results of a national survey conducted in 1971 on 1,177 Jewish adults lend support to this picture by showing a similar attitudinal pattern.[18] Here we note that antipathy toward Arabs is a function of the situation – the more intimate the hypothesized contact, the greater the ethnocentric feeling. It is shown that 84 per cent of those sampled would be bothered if a friend or relative married an Arab; 74 per cent if their children befriended Arabs; 54 per cent if Jewish children were taught by Arab teachers; 49 per cent if Arabs moved next door. Finally, about a quarter of those sampled expressed unease at having to work with Arabs or sit next to them on the bus.

It is typical of most public-opinion data in Israel that they do not include Arab respondents in their universe of sampling. This is true of the data analysed by Jacob. Therefore it is difficult for us to compare Arab and Jewish responses on similar items. However, a study by Yalan[19] and colleagues, of rural Arabs in Israel, shows more than 90 per cent of the sampled Arabs to be willing to befriend Jews; when it comes to appraising the Jewish attitudes to Arabs as perceived by Arabs themselves, the picture which emerges is quite realistic when contrasted with Jacob's data. Forty-two per cent of the Arabs think that either all or some of the Jews in Israel will be prepared to befriend Arabs.

This asymmetrical positive predisposition of the Arabs toward Jews is highlighted by the following quotation from Hofman's study of Arab and Jewish youth in the north of Israel:[20]

> Arabs, more often than Jews, claim to be fostering relations with their opposites, to do nothing to avoid them, and even to find the outlook of life in Israel unsatisfactory without them. Asymmetry also finds expression in the way intentions are perceived. Jews seem to be underestimating Arab intentions; Arabs seem to be quite accurate in their attributions to Jews. Again asymmetry characterized mutual evaluations. The Israeli Jew is judged positive by both Arabs and Jews; the Israeli Arab is a positive concept to Arabs, but a neutral and undifferentiated one to Jews.

If mixed marriages are to be any indication of a future trend which will ultimately improve Arab–Jewish relations in Israel, Erik Cohen's[21] study of thirteen mixed marriages in one bi-national community provides disappointing conclusions. He shows how most of the couples whom he studied – and the findings are significantly more decisive among Jewish women in his sample, who comprised all the female partners in these mixed marriages – were marginal people in society as well as in their own communities, and this further gave rise to hostile attitudes and rejection of one partner by the other. In most cases, Cohen points out, the marriages broke down.

It is interesting to note – as an Israeli Arab activist working for Jewish–Arab understanding, Fouzi El-Asmar, remarks, basing the comment on his personal experience – that even contact among Arab and Jewish intellectuals is bound to produce little tangible result in terms of changing the solitude of the two groups, unless such contact is anchored in specific political action: 'the problem of the bad relationship between Jews and Arabs could not be understood or removed by means of a friendly talk between Jews and Arabs who meet once a week for a cup of tea together.'[22]

A study by Peres and Levy[23] sheds further light on Arab–Jewish relations. The results of the study were based on a simulated situation in which Arab and Jewish university students participated and were asked to give their reaction to what it is like to be an Arab or a Jew in Israel. The following observations emerged: (1) Both Jews and Arabs agreed on the Arab minority's inferior image; both intellectually and culturally the Jews emphasized their superiority; the ethnocentricity of the Jews 'expresses itself in the positive affinity of the majority member to his group, its heritage and symbols, together with a feeling of superiority and prejudice towards outsiders, especially Arabs.'[24] (2) Concerning political values, the Arabs voiced criticism which aimed 'at the very foundations of the

State.' It is this critical attitude which bewildered the Jewish youth, and was considered by them to be further proof of the disloyalty of the Arab minority.

There is no doubt, according to Peres and Levy, that the bases of the above stereotyped images are to be located in the differential power position of each of the two groups in the social structure: 'Our findings in general would seem to support the view that the content of the stereotype cannot be understood solely on the basis of the unconscious needs of its creator, that is derived to a considerable extent from the role each performs in relation to the other within the social and political context.'[25]

Working on the same topic, Tamarin[26] reaches an identical conclusion concerning the stereotype image of the Arabs in Israel. Of the various groups in Tamarin's sample, the religious high school students exhibited the highest level of xenophobia; the least xenophobic were the pre-1948 immigrants with a high level of education. In comparing the attitude of Oriental children born in Israel with that of their elders born in the Arab countries, the former appear to be more hostile to Arabs. This finding supports Tamarin's contention that the educational system and the general religious climate in Israel do not foster tolerance. Indeed, in discussing his teacher sample, he had this to say concerning the teacher's image of Arabs: 'The alienness of the [Arab] is seen in a more apartheid manner [compared to the 'Goy'], as a primitive, poor, exotically interesting and hostile figure but lacking the vividness and affective tone of immediate experience.'[27]

What are the consequences of this for the Arab population? Let us begin by presenting evidence of a qualitative nature which was gathered by Erik Cohen[28] in his study of the Arab youth in the city where the above-mentioned confrontation took place. Cohen documented vividly through his in-depth interview method the extent of the identity crisis which the Arab youth are undergoing. He comes to the conclusion that their predicament is attributable to objective structural factors producing, for instance, future occupational uncertainty, lack of educational preparedness because of a deficient, separate and segregated educational system, and failure to compete successfully with Jewish counterparts in the job market and in entry to higher educational institutions. Thus, Arab youth 'feel that they are excluded from society-wide participation, discriminated against by the institutions and even if they tried hard they would not be given a fair chance.'[29]

Cohen sees preoccupation with sexual matters among the Arab youth as a reaction to inability to cope with an uncertain future, and at the same time a reaction to a traditional familial moral order. Attempts to gain sexual gratification are pursued through establishing contacts with Jewish girls, which contacts in most cases are short-lived and also arouse the anger of Jewish boys, thus complicating an already tense Arab–Jewish relationship. Some of the youth resolve this dilemma by establishing contacts with tourist girls who frequently visit the historic city of Acre. The main purpose behind such relationships is to get the tourist girls to act as sponsors for facilitating the emigration of these youth to Europe and North America. Thus, for a minority, personal problems, and problems of the future, are resolved by moving to a new environment thought to be less hostile and more open to the fulfilment of their needs.

For other researchers, such as Peres,[30] the situation leads to an identification by Israeli Arabs with 'extreme nationalistic ideology'. The casual relationship could very well be seen in a different way: it is precisely because of the suppression of cultural and nationalistic sentiment that the Arab youth in Israel, and in particular its educated segment, feels atomized and alienated.

Educational opportunities

A great deal has been made of the relatively high level of educational achievement of the Arabs in Israel, compared to the Arabs in neighbouring states. The implications of this achievement are questionable on two fronts: first, the educational comparison should be made between Arabs and Jews inside Israel, for it is the latter who, in terms of occupational and educational attainment, are considered to be a reference point for the former. And, if Israel is a truly egalitarian society, the same measure when applied to judge *all* its citizens should not reveal stark ethnically systematic differences. Second, even if we carry out the comparison cross-nationally, it should be between Palestinians inside Israel and those Palestinians outside it.

Let us deal with the second point first. Recent statistics on higher education in Israel put the proportion of Arab university students (totalling 990) at 2 per cent of an estimated total of 44,326 university students attending the four major universities in Israel in 1972–3.[31] This is a rather low proportion, to say the least, when one realizes that the Arab population in Israel comprises around 15 per cent of the total population. A comparison between the Palestinians inside Israel and those outside it shows, according to a recent survey,[32] that there are approximately 50,000 Palestinians attending institutions of higher education in the Arab countries and in other parts of the world.

The claim that the Palestinians in Israel enjoy better educational opportunities does not seem to hold, even in the eyes of the Palestinians living in Israel. In an attitudinal study,[33] a sample of Arabs living in Israel were asked to assess their 'progress in the educational and family spheres' over the last two decades, compared to that of Palestinians living on the West Bank. Sixty per cent of the sample rated the conditions of the Palestinians outside Israel as superior.

The state of Arab education in Israel is best highlighted, as we said, through comparison with that in the Jewish sector. A group of researchers at the Hebrew University reached the following conclusions:[34]

> In spite of the impressive increase in the [absolute] number of Arab students, it is worth noting that the magnitude of those not attending [primary] schools, specially among girls, is extremely high when compared to the corresponding Jewish population. Also, the level of education in the two sectors is not on a par. In addition to the fact that fewer Arab students reach the high school level, fewer of these pass the matriculation examinations. In 1965, 70 per cent of the Arab students failed their matriculations. Such a percentage provides an improvement relative to previous years; in 1962, for example, 90 per cent of the Arab students failed.

Detailed statistical studies concerning patterns of educational recruitment in the Arab sector are not available. A general inspection of the level of education among the two groups shows a striking gap. As Table 6.1 shows, around one-third of the Arab population have no schooling, compared to a minority of 8 per cent among the Jews. Those with post-secondary education comprise 4 per cent of the Arab population, compared to 15 per cent among the Jewish. However, in some underdeveloped Arab villages the illiteracy rate could be as high as 70 per cent among adults twenty years of age and above.[35] Overall, the average level of educational attainment of the Arabs in 1971 was 55 per cent of that of the Jews.[36]

A comparison between Arab and Jewish youth falling within the compulsory education age (five to fourteen years) provides us with the following picture, as shown in Table 6.2. While the situation of the Arabs in Israel in this context is better than that of the Arab world in general (62.1 per cent of those of school age in school in the Arab world in 1967, compared to 83.5 per cent for the Arabs in Israel), it is almost identical to the figures given for the Palestinians on the West Bank and in Gaza.[37] Of those aged fourteen to seventeen in post-primary schools, the rates for the Arabs in 1969–70 were 192.1 per 1,000; for Jews, the rates were 588.4 per 1,000.[38]

To appreciate the magnitude of school drop-out, failure, and repetition of classes in the Arab sector, one needs detailed statistical data by age-cohort over the years to construct proper flow diagrams describing the educational progress from grade one until the end of

TABLE 6.1 *Population aged 14 and over by years of schooling*[39]

	Jews		*Arabs*	
Years of schooling	*1961*	*1973*	*1961*	*1973*
	%	%	%	%
0	12.6	8.3	49.5	32.4
1–4	7.5	5.5	13.9	12.8
5–8	35.4	27.6	27.5	32.2
9–12	34.6	43.4	7.6	17.4
13–15		9.3		3.3
	9.9		1.5	
16+		5.9		0.9
	100.0	100.0	100.0	100.0

TABLE 6.2 *Jewish and Arab youth of compulsory education age attending school (5–15 years of age)*[40]

Years	*Jews*	*Arabs*
	%	%
1954–5	91.4	63.0*
1960–1	94.3	75.3
1966–7	97.8	78.3
1970–1	95.0	75.6

* These figures refer to state-run schools as well as privately operated schools. On the whole, around one-fifth of Arab pupils (including those in East Jerusalem) within the above age range attend private schools.

high school. Such detailed breakdown, taking into account repetition and failure rates, is not available to the author. However, it is possible to give a general example showing the remarkable rate of Arab attrition after completing primary schooling where compulsory education ceases to be in effect.

Of 47,802 Jewish students who started grade one in 1961–2, 43,926, that is, 92 per cent, entered grade nine, with 26,308 completing grade twelve, that is, 60 per cent. Among 6,993 Arab pupils starting grade one in 1961–2, a cumulative of 2,671 students, that is, 38.2 per cent, dropped out before entering grade nine (see Table 6.3). Of the latter, 1,925 completed grade twelve, that is, 27 per cent of the initial group. It is interesting to note that once Arab pupils start their secondary education, their attrition rate in proportional terms is almost identical to that for the Jewish group.[41]

The Arab–Jewish contrast of high school enrolment is far from representing the natural balance of both age groups in the population

TABLE 6.3 *Rate of attrition among Arab students, grades 1–8 (1952–69)*[42]

	(1952–9)			*(1962–9)*	
Year	*Per cent yearly attrition*	*Cumulative attrition*	*Year*	*Per cent yearly attrition*	*Cumulative attrition*
	%	%		%	%
1952	—	—	1962	—	—
1953	7.9	7.9	1963	0.5	0.5
1954	13.1	20.0	1964	4.7	5.2
1955	13.1	30.4	1965	3.2	8.2
1956	7.7	35.8	1966	4.9	12.7
1957	13.4	44.4	1967	8.1	19.7
1958	18.7	54.7	1968	9.2	27.1
1959	29.0	67.8	1969	15.2	38.2
Average yearly attrition = 9.7 per cent			Average yearly attrition = 5.5 per cent		

as a whole. This is in spite of the fact that there has been an improvement from 1952. As Table 6.4 shows, Arab high school students comprised 0.7 per cent of the high school population in Israel in 1952, and 9.7 per cent in 1974. This slight improvement shown in the statistics reflects in part a change in the census classification, and not any substantial remedying of the Arab public high school system. As of 1970, private secondary schools were included in the statistics, and as of 1969 the data covered East Jerusalem schools as well.

TABLE 6.4 *Composition of high school population by ethnicity (1952–74)*[43]

Year	*Jews*	*Arabs*	*Total*
	%	%	%
1952	99.3	0.7	100.0
1961	97.8	2.2	100.0
1965	98.0	2.0	100.0
1969	96.8	3.2	100.0
1974	90.3	9.7	100.0

These discrepancies are not confined to primary and secondary education, but are also apparent in a glaring fashion in comparing the success rates of Arab and Jewish university-destined students, as revealed in Table 6.5.

TABLE 6.5 *Holders of matriculation certificates (1954–73)*[44]

	Absolute		*Per 10,000 population*	
Year	*Arabs*	*Jews*	*Arabs*	*Jews*
1954–5	38	2,520	1.9	15.8
1957–8	60	2,698	2.7	14.9
1960–1	94	3,464	3.8	17.9
1966–7	144	10,588	4.4	44.4
1970–1	250	10,693	5.5	40.6
1972–3	600	12,000	12.5	43.6

The figures in Table 6.5 concerning the proportion of successful high school graduates are self-explanatory and they provide further evidence of a backward educational system in the Arab sector. As late as 1971, the Jewish pass rate in the government-supervised matriculation examinations exceeded that of the Arab youth by about 8 times; in 1973 it declined to 3.5 times that of the Arab youth. It must be stated, however, that in certain individual cases when the high school facilities and staffing are adequate, the Israeli Arab success rate in matriculation examinations could be quite high.

For example, in 1971 in the village of Rameh, fifty high school students passed their examinations out of a total of fifty-seven who originally sat for the tests. Still, recent figures show the success rate of Palestinian students on the West Bank to be 80 per cent, while that of the Israeli Arabs was around 20 per cent.[45]

Arab university graduates in Israel comprise 0.1 per cent of the entire minority population, whereas Jewish university graduates comprise 1.32 per cent of the Jewish population.[46] The total number of Arab university graduates in Israel amounted to 600 by the end of 1971.[47] Of the 990 Arab university students in 1972–3, close to 90 per cent are BA students, with 11 per cent working toward an MA, 1 per cent toward a diploma, and 4 out of 990 working toward a PhD.[48] The contrast with Jewish university students is shown in Table 6.6.

It is interesting to compare these results with those obtained from Palestinians in the Diaspora. Of a sample of 9,715 respondents

TABLE 6.6 *Arab and Jewish students in academic institutions by level of study (1972–3)*[49]

	Total	*BA*	*MA*	*PhD*	*Diploma*
Arab	990	867 (88%)	108 (11%)	4 (0.004%)	11 (1%)
Jewish	43,372	31,675 (73%)	8,258 (19%)	2,474 (5.7%)	976 (2.3%)

participating in the survey conducted by the Palestine Liberation Organization Research Centre, 82 per cent were BA students, 6.9 per cent MA, 9.6 per cent PhD, and 1.5 per cent post-doctorate.[50]

The study completed two years ago for the office of the Prime Minister's Adviser on Arab Affairs estimates that with an average yearly increase in university enrolment among Arab students of 15–25 per cent, by the end of the 1970s there will be close to 2,000 Arab university graduates.[51] These projections are slightly inflated, for, as shown in Table 6.7, the yearly increase in enrolment declined to 11 per cent between 1972–3 and 1973–4.

TABLE 6.7 *Absolute number of Arab students in Israeli universities and corresponding percentage increases (1968–74)*[52]

	1968–9	*1969–70*	*1970–1*	*1971–2*	*1972–3*	*1973–4*
No. of students	440	608	735	807	990	1099
Percentage increase		38%	21%	9.7%	23%	11%

The gradual increase in the absolute number of Arab university students notwithstanding, the discrepancy between Arab and Jews is striking (see Table 6.8). Here the comparison with other Arab countries is instructive. In Jordan, where the majority of the population is Palestinian, the rate in 1971 reached 1,210 university students per 100,000. As early as 1966, Syria and Egypt surpassed the rates of the Arabs in Israel, reaching 600 per 100,000. Among Palestinian villages that were split in 1948 and again united under Israeli control in 1967, it was found that on the Israeli side the rate was 472 per 100,000, while in those parts which were on the West Bank side the rate reached 3,000 per 100,000 – exceeding by far that given for the Jewish population in Israel.[53]

TABLE 6.8 *Arab and Jewish university students per 100,000 population (1971–3)*[54]

Year	*Jews*	*Arabs*
1971	1520	132
1972	1655	150
1973	1741	200

Many factors contribute to the low level of educational attainment among the Arab population in Israel. Though conventional writings on the subject tend to single out Arab traditionalism, in particular the pressure on Arab women to withdraw early from school, there are equally important reasons having to do with structural factors such as poverty and the need to send children to work at an early age, the inadequate training of Arab teachers, and the lack of proper educational facilities owing to the Israeli government's unwillingness to provide the sums of money required to increase and improve educational facilities in the Arab sector.

Regarding teacher qualifications, Harari notes that there are twice as many unqualified Arabs as there are Jewish teachers, 50.7 % to 26.8 % in 1969–70.[55] In terms of numbers of pupils per class, Table 6.9 shows that compared to Jewish schools, Arab classes are significantly more crowded, in particular at the primary level.

TABLE 6.9 *Number of pupils per class at the primary and secondary levels (1972–3)*[56]

No. of pupils per class	*Jewish* Primary	Secondary	*Arab* Primary	Secondary
	%	%	%	%
Up to 20	27.6	27.2	6.7	12.3
20–39	68.7	66.9	80.6	73.7
40+	3.7	5.9	12.7	14.0
	100.0	100.0	100.0	100.0
Total no. of classes	15,278	5,200	3,305	1,166

Even those Arab students who eventually enter universities – the institutions of universalistic criteria *par excellence* – continue to face discrimination. For 'security' reasons, Arab students are barred from enrolling in certain science faculties, such as electronics, aeronautics, and related disciplines. This factor, together with employment problems, forces Arab students to turn in increasing numbers to the arts and humanities. The Shiloah study, referred to above and carried out for the Prime Minister's office, shows that of all Arab university graduates, 70 per cent specialized in humanities and social sciences, a proportion greater than that found in the general Israeli student population.[57] In contrast to this, the Palestine Liberation Organization study shows that among BA students, 58 per cent are in the humanities and social sciences; 43 per cent of those who are MA students are in the social sciences; and the 14 per cent who are doctoral and post-doctoral students specialize mainly in medical sciences.[58]

The crisis of mismatched educational training and occupational placement is another feature of the profile of Arab university graduates in Israel. While this problem is also present in the Jewish sector, it is accentuated among Arab graduates, where high school teaching seems to be the main employment outlet. Eighty-four per cent of Arab graduates in the humanities and social sciences are employed as teachers. Of the natural science graduates, only one-third are working directly in their profession; among graduates of engineering it is 64 per cent.[59]

Here again, a comparison between Palestinians inside Israel and those outside it on the West Bank is instructive. Mar'i and Dhahir discovered that the average earning potential of an Arab university graduate is only 9 per cent higher than that of an Israeli Arab with no university education. On the West Bank, the earnings of a university graduate are 300 per cent higher than those of a non-university graduate. No doubt the wide gap in the earnings of Palestinians on the West Bank is partly accounted for by an inegalitarian and polarized class structure. But the data also show that the Palestinian university graduate has a better chance of upward mobility and of employment (usually attained by working in the Arab world) in line with his university education.[60]

The socio-political predicament facing Arab university graduates is reflected in the following conclusion reached by the author of the Shiloah study:[61]

> The resulting picture is indeed chilling. Some of them [Arab students] asserted that as professional men, their political activities were subject to restrictions and pressures, the freedom of expression which they enjoyed was limited, and political considerations dictated the future of any minorities graduate in Israel. One should remember that these serious accusations have been made in the past, especially among the Arabs of Israel who sought to attack the government for its policy towards the Arab and Druze minority.

The report goes on to say on the same page:

> Moreover, since the Six-Day War, the active part played by the intelligentsia against the State has been felt. It is possible that the events of October 1973 will leave an impression on Israeli Arabs in general, and on the academics in particular. It is possible that in the future, one expression of the changes

occurring will be an increase in the pro-Palestinian position among the intelligentsia and academic circles.

Together with this structural differentiation there is a parallel manipulation of cultural and national symbols characterizing Arabs and Arab history. A candid opinion depicting the state of cultural deprivation experienced by young Arabs in Israel is conveyed in an interview with an Arab teacher. Among the points he raised were the following: First, Arab schools are compelled to teach the history of Zionism as depicted in the Jewish experience and the early plans to set up a Jewish homeland. Second, when Arab children come in contact with their own history, they learn about it through a negative perspective. Here the stress is placed on the violent aspects of Arab behaviour. Third, Arab children are made to ignore their own cultural and literary achievements by having to devote a great deal of time to memorizing poems which deal exclusively with Jewish history. Finally, in the words of the Arab teacher, 'in all the books used in Arab schools, the emphasis is put on the historical rights of the Jews to Eretz-Israel. . . . The Arab child is not taught that he too has the right to this land, a land his ancestors have cultivated for decades.'[62]

The extent of cultural control experienced by Arab youth in Israel is documented in a convincing fashion in the patterns of curricula in Arab and Jewish schools. Tables 6.10 and 6.11 show the powerful role schools play in fostering an image of the subordinate nature of the Arab pupil's cultural background. What is striking about these findings is their confirmation of the Arab pupil's total submergence in the Jewish culture at the expense of learning about his own traditions. This is accomplished through a complete obliviousness in Jewish schools to Arab history and culture. A meagre 2 per cent of the total number of hours in Jewish schools are devoted to Arab history, compared to 20 per cent in Arab schools. By the same token, the total number of hours spent on teaching Hebrew literature in Arab schools is almost equal to that spent in Jewish schools. The total number of hours devoted to studying Arab literature and language in Jewish schools is so insignificant as not to merit mention by the authors of this study.

The Arab minority's reaction to this cultural and economic domination manifests itself in various expected ways. One extensive research study[63] demonstrates the presence of a level of hostility toward the state among Israel's Arab youth which is high compared to that felt by their parents. This comes out in parent–child contrast on questions such as 'Does Israel have the right to exist?' where more than half of the parents gave an unequivocal 'yes', compared to only a quarter of the youth in the sample. Among the educated

TABLE 6.10 *Hours devoted to study of Jewish, Arab and world history in Jewish and Arab schools, according to faculties*[64]

Topic taught	Faculty of Humanities		Faculty of Sciences	
	Jewish schools	Arab schools	Jewish schools	Arab schools
	%	%	%	%
Jewish history	38.8	20.2	40.9	20.6
Arab history	1.4	19.1	2.1	19.5
World history	59.8	60.7	57.0	59.9
Total	100.0	100.0	100.0	100.0
No. of hours	416	416	384	384

TABLE 6.11 *Hours spent on literature and languages in Jewish and Arab schools in Israel, according to faculties*[65]

Topic taught	Faculty of Humanities			Faculty of Sciences		
	Hebrew in Jewish schools	Hebrew in Arab schools	Arabic in Arab schools	Hebrew in Jewish schools	Hebrew in Arab schools	Arabic in Arab schools
	%	%	%	%	%	%
Literature	60.6	66.4	51.0	58.0	66.4	51.0
Language	39.4	33.6	49.0	42.0	33.6	49.0
Total	100.0	100.0	100.0	100.0	100.0	100.0
No. of hours	768	512	824	608	512	824

youth, the level of animosity toward the state is higher than that found among the working youth. Sampling the same subjects before and after the 1967 war showed that the level of national consciousness was apparently raised among the Israeli Arabs. Whereas in 1966 the majority chose the category 'Israeli' to describe themselves, in 1967 this category receded to the last position on the list, with 'Arab' coming first. The proportion of those Arabs who 'felt at home inside Israel' dropped from 62 to 31 per cent after the 1967 war. Finally, a sizeable minority of about one-fifth of the Israeli Arab youth thought of themselves as 'Palestinians'. No doubt if identical studies were to be made after the 1973 war, the results would show an even stronger sense of Palestinianism among Israeli Arabs.[66] In a subsequent paper by Peres based on the same survey of high school students, he notes that after the 1967 war, 36 per cent of those sampled opted for a separate state of their own in the territory of Palestine.[67]

If we regard these findings in the light of other research on the political awareness of minority groups in general,[68] we notice a striking similarity. Current research on the political orientations of black children in the United States produced results indicative of alienation, disaffection, and lack of identification with basic American political symbols. These were salient features of the attitudes of the economically deprived white American child.

A different picture is given to us in a pilot study concerning the self-identity of the Arabs in Israel. John Hofman[69] says that the Arab youth have a positive perception of themselves which is ultimately translated into 'a good relationship towards Israeli citizenship'. In spite of the competent 'self' which young Arabs in Israel seem to have, Hofman finds a significant social distance between Arabs and Jews. When asked to choose the 'most sympathetic' group from a list of nationalities, the Arabs placed the Jews at the farthest end of the list. It is difficult to reconcile the positive attitude postulated above with additional findings in Hofman's study in which the Arab youth attributed a superior status to the Israeli Jews, who were rated as the most knowledgeable, most advanced, most strong, most beautiful and most stubborn. This is all the more significant when we take cognizance of the findings of another group of researchers which portray the perception of Arabs by young Jews thus: 'It appears that Arabs were rated lower on nearly all traits, significantly so on courage, good looks, intelligence, good-naturedness, pleasantness, manners, truthfulness, successfulness, self-confidence, permissiveness, reliability, leadership, cheerfulness, and capacity for hard work.'[70]

The attitudes of these youth truly reveal the social climate in the country, if the following responses – derived from the Jewish adult sample referred to earlier – are any indication: 53 per cent said that Arabs are lazier than Israelis; 74 per cent that Arabs are less intelligent; 68 per cent that Arabs feel blind hatred toward the Jews; 75 per cent that Arabs are crueller; 88 per cent that Arabs are not as brave; 66 per cent that Arabs are more dishonest than Israelis; and 67 per cent believed that Arabs are inferior to Israelis.[71]

As mentioned earlier, these findings are not all that different from those made in studies of black and white children in the United States. What is most significant in the Israeli case is the emergence of a similar, though less extreme, pattern within the *Jewish* population. In a society where Oriental Jews comprise around half of the Jewish population, it is striking to see how the main cultural institutions reinforce, in what is essentially a Middle Eastern society, an idealized image of the European Jew. When asked to identify a typical Israeli, more than half of the Oriental children in a recent study chose the European child, and there was a sharp increase in such a preference as a function of age.[72]

The 'Sabra superman' image, to quote Tamarin, appears also in a comparison between the stereotype image of the Israeli-born Jew and that of the Jew in the Diaspora:[73]

> A comparison of the two stereotypes which we have come to know here will bring to light almost item by item, a complete contrast between the two figures; on the one hand [in the case of the Sabra] we have strength, joy of life, a feeling of complete security, sociability; and on the other [in the case of the Diaspora Jew] – weakness, fear, sadness, insecurity, humiliation and seclusion. The one figure possesses superior traits and the other inferior ones, not even arousing sympathy in its suffering.

Social disorganization

Criminal behaviour provides one of the best indicators of the mental and socio-psychological well-being of a community. Sociologists have noted that social disorganization in the form of norm-breaking, juvenile delinquency and crime are likely to be correlated with a social group of disadvantaged status, be it educational, economic or even cultural disadvantage of that group *vis-à-vis* the rest of society. From the discussion so far, it should be evident that the Arab population in Israel provides us with an excellent test case.

It can be seen from Table 6.12 that in recent years the rate of conviction of main offenders amongs the Arab population was more than double the rate among the Jewish population. This is true for both adults and juveniles. As early as 1961, the rates for juvenile and adult offenders among the Arab population were 14 per 1,000 and

28.6 per 1,000, respectively; for the Jewish population in the same year the figures were 8 per 1,000 for juveniles and 10 per 1,000 for adults.[74]

TABLE 6.12 *Convictions for main offenders per 1,000 population, ages 9 and above (1951–69)*[75]

	Arabs		*Jews*	
Year	*Absolute offenders*	*Rate per 1,000*	*Absolute offenders*	*Rate per 1,000*
1951	2,312	15.2	7,080	8.3
1960	6,249	27.4	11,841	9.9
1969	5,555	19.0	14,791	7.2

In noting the disproportionately higher number of Arab juvenile offenders, compared to their Jewish counterparts, Reifen[76] attributes the differential rates to two different systems of police processing procedures. Among Jewish offenders, close to half of the cases are dropped before trial, whereas among the Arabs, only one-fifth of juvenile offenders' cases are dropped. Jewish probation officers, according to Reifen, are more likely to request out-of-court administration arrangements; Arab probation officers are faced with different circumstances:[77]

> Now if the [Arab] probation officer pursued the same policy in relation to asking for cases to be dropped before trial as does his Jewish colleague, i.e., applying the same sort of yardstick in the merit of each case, he would soon find himself the centre of a controversy which would imperil his function. Keeping in mind the clan system of Arab society and the constant quarrels between clans, any action in favour of not having a case brought before the court could be suspected of being the result of intervention by a rival clan.

While Reifen acknowledges that Arab juvenile delinquent behaviour is related primarily 'to the social and political situation rather than to personal problems'[78] the central contributing factor is village culture and its increasing clash with urban and modern Jewish cultures. The objective socio-economic conditions of the Arabs reflected in their marginal status in the power structure of Israeli society is not given its due credit in accounting for Arab patterns of social disorganization. The village and *hamula* seem to be at the centre of Arab deviant behaviour. Writing more recently, Palgi and Fuchs summarize Reifen's study by remarking that border escape to neighbouring Arab states is due to '(1) maladjustment at home and a desire to take revenge on one's parents; (2) failure at school; and (3) adolescent tensions'.[79]

The 'culture conflict' thesis has been applied to Oriental Jews[80] as well as to Israeli Arabs, both of whom come from traditional Middle Eastern cultures which are at odds with the dominant Euro-culture of Israeli society. Thus, Shoham, Segal and Rahav conclude that delinquent behaviour among Israeli Arab villagers is a function in descending order of the following factors: modernization–traditionalism, religiosity, attitudes toward women and contact with women, and attitudes concerning the education of women. The more 'secular' and less educated the Arab villager is, the more likely it is that he will manifest deviant behaviour: 'On the other hand, low education and lower-status occupation would make the village workers more susceptible to culture conflict because they do not have the solid normative foundations of the high-status occupation and higher education of the population.'[81]

The point we are making here, and which we have been making all along, is not that cultural factors are irrelevant in explaining deviant behaviour – indeed, cultural variables have a place in regulating Arab deviant behaviour – but that the relevance of these factors is not that which is argued by most Israeli social scientists and policy-makers. The Israeli legal system, while built in large part on inherited British law, nevertheless perpetuated existing Arab customary law. Disputes involving Arab villagers are usually settled within two competing frameworks – the Israeli one and traditional Arab law – thus subjecting the offender in many cases to a double jeopardy. Although the Arab traditional legal system has proven to be efficient in resolving intra-*hamula* disputes, it has contributed to severe indebtedness. In one of the murder cases analysed by Nakhleh, the settlement of the case according to Arab law involved a payment of I£13,000 to the injured party. While such a penalty is borne collectively by the *hamula*, there is no doubt that the economic burden it produces will be felt by the entire community for a long time. Surely the eradication of such a system through the application of a universal secular law is preferable. The Israeli government seems to be countenancing traditional Arab law without completely accepting its legality or attempting to abolish it. For example, in the murder case referred to above, government officials as well as representatives of the police were present at the *Sulha*, the traditional ceremony of settlement, in which money was paid to the injured party. In another *Sulha*, the chief of police presided and acted as a guarantor to the agreement.[82]

Moreover, it is in the context of indigenous Arab social class transformation, and the Arabs' marginalized status as a colonized minority, that so-called culture conflict must be understood. Considering the culture thesis in isolation is bound to lead to prescribing a false solution, as is well known to students of plural societies and colonial regimes. Remedying deviant and delinquent behaviour places the onus upon the colonized minorities, whose value-systems and social structure have to adapt through various agencies of social control, in order to eradicate their traditional structure which, according to this thesis, is at the root of their social problems. Fanon's[83] well-known discussion of deviant behaviour in colonial situations comes close to describing the experience of the rural proletariat among Israel's Arabs.

Returning to the theme of crime differentials, a detailed examination by Drapkin and Landau[84] of drug offenders in Israel up to 1964 shows that while the Israeli Arab cases comprised only 80 out of a total of 318 cases, the proportion of Arabs among offenders (Jews and Arabs) *born in Israel* reaches the 75 per cent mark.

Focussing on homicide offenders and victims, three Israeli criminologists[85] found that among the 279 cases they examined between 1950 and 1964, the proportion of Arab offenders (in terms of the size of the Arab population) exceeded that of Jewish offenders, taking the figures respectively, by more than six times. It is significant to note that offences committed by Arabs are directed mainly against other Arabs. According to Adam, violence directed against other members of the in-group is due to repressed aggression among the colonized; the following words in his discussion of South Africa are relevant to the Arabs in Israel:[86]

> The necessity for migratory workers to live alone and leave their families behind in the reserves has had more severe consequences for the rural families than for the urban dweller who soon finds substitutes. One effect of such repressions is that the crime rate in the urban locations has risen drastically to a level that is probably the highest in the world. The frustration generated by this imposed coercion is increasingly released through aggression against the in-group members, since they are the most vulnerable persons.

However, if one examines the nature of the offences, the Israeli Prison Service publication for 1972 shows (Table 6.13) that close to half of the adult Arab offenders commit offences which could be considered political in nature, involving, among other things, violation of emergency laws, trespassing, infringement of government military regulations, possession of weapons and explosives, sabotage activities, and so on. Therefore, one is justified in saying that the 'deviant' behaviour of the Arabs is in large measure a direct response to the oppressive political atmosphere surrounding them, and not a direct outcome of an inadequate value-system or their deficient personality make-up.

TABLE 6.13 *Distribution of offenders (imprisoned and detained) according to type of offence (1972)*[87]

Offence	Adults		Juveniles	
	Jews	Arabs	Jews	Arabs
	%	%	%	%
Against public order	7	50	10	29
Against the person	19	22	9	11
Against morality	9	5	7	5
Against property	53	20	65	44
Forgery and embezzlement	7	2	1	—
Other	5	1	8	11
	100	100	100	100
Number of cases	1,441	631	737	235

Conclusions

We have tried to show, in spite of a rather limited amount of data, that the plural character of Israeli society has consequences which are very familiar to the student of ethnic, racial and national conflicts. A social order which is established on claims of privilege by a dominant group and which suppresses the legitimate claims of the indigenous population is bound to espouse an ideology of superiority which is further used to perpetuate an oppressive socio-political system.

It would be a mistake to conjure up an image of a passive subordinate group in such a social order. History and contemporary events in the Middle East and elsewhere tell us otherwise. Oppressed people manage eventually to rise and regain their sense of competence and mastery over their destiny. But, to be complete, such a process requires the alteration of objective social conditions which in turn would transform people's consciousness. In looking at social structure correlates of personal identity and sense of competence, M. Brewster Smith asserts that a sense of competence will come about only as the result of three ingredients being present: power, respect and opportunity: 'Opportunity corresponds to hope and provides its warrant. Respect by others . . . more important in this regard than love or approval . . . provides the social ground for respect of self. And power is the kingpin of the system. Power receives respect and guarantees access to opportunity'.[88]

On the face of it, this sounds like a utopian vision of a liberal social scientist. It is a fact, however, that a real transformation of the image of an oppressed group can take place, as Judith Porter[89] discovered in a recent study of black children in the United States. The effects of exposure to Black Power ideology have been felt among black children of proletarian background, and Porter finds in the phrase 'Black is beautiful' wider applications than a mere learning of an empty slogan. As a result of the Black Power movement some black children have managed in growing up to develop an image of themselves as competent. And it is no accident that North American Indians are adopting 'Red Power' as their motto.

Whether or not the Arabs in Israel manage to build a power base to alter the oppressive social order inhibiting them is yet to be seen. One thing is clear: the task facing Palestinians is a formidable one; but if any change is to come about it has to emanate from within the oppressed group. Paternalistic solutions do not reflect the aspirations of groups discriminated against and disadvantaged.

7 The politicization of Israeli Arabs

Of the many problems faced by the Arabs in Israel, none is more serious or more specific to their situation than the lack of viable political organizations with which to articulate their aspirations on an equal footing with Jewish citizens of the state.

In seeking an explanation for the absence of an effective independent Arab political movement, the following factors stand out as important: (1) While contemporary Zionist political parties existed prior to 1948, there were no corresponding party developments among the Palestinian Arabs, although nascent political bodies existed during the British Mandate. (2) The familial, rather than mass-based, support of Arab political organizations hindered the articulation of national goals which would transcend familial and sectional rivalries. (3) The pre-1948 Palestinian Arab leadership all but left during the 1948 exodus. The only remaining Arab leaders were Communists, although they too were not well known to the Arabs of Palestine.[1] Together with anti-Zionist Jewish Communists they formed, immediately after the war of 1948, the Israel Communist Party (Maqi). (4) Although the traditionalism of the Arab sector is responsible in part for the failure to organize non-sectarian political parties, devoid of familial and religious cleavages, as of 1948 the conscious policies of the Israeli government have effectively neutralized the various attempts made by Israeli Arabs to organize independent Arab opposition parties.

Except for the New Communist List, Rakah, which split from Maqi in 1965,[2] the rest of the political parties in Israel are Zionist in essence. Of the many Zionist parties only Mapam has since 1952 accepted Arabs as equal members. However, the impact of Arab members in the policy-making body of the party is negligible. Since joining the ruling labour coalition in 1968, Mapam has been increasingly identified in the eyes of Israeli Arabs with the government.

hence the decline in Arab support for it. The bulk of the Zionist parties have adopted the method of creating separate Arab lists organized under the tutelage of the main Jewish parties. These Arab lists operate under a peculiar system of party patronage. Such political machines are run by Jewish party bosses, and Arab candidates, usually heads of *hamulas*, deliver Arab votes in return for favours to themselves and their followers.

The Arab response to the dominant Zionist political culture was threefold. First, it led to an increase in the strength of Rakah among the Arabs; second, it gave rise to an unsuccessful attempt to launch an independent Arab movement; third, it led to the steady development of a politicized intelligentsia.

Identification with the Communist Party

TABLE 7.1 *Arab Communist vote for Maqi and Rakah*[3]

Year	*Maqi*	*Year*	*Rakah*
1949	22.2%	1965	23.6%
1955	15.6	1969	29.6
1961	22.0	1973	37.0

In spite of the dominance of the Zionist parties in terms of numbers, organization, and availability of resources, Arab support of the Communist Party increased, particularly after the 1965 split when Israeli Arab Communists played a major part in the leadership of the newly formed pro-Moscow party, Rakah. Thus, while the proportion of Jewish votes cast in favour of the Communist Party was around 2 per cent throughout the period 1948–73, more than one-third of the Arab vote went to the Arab-Jewish Communist Party in 1973. This led to the election of four Knesset members in 1973, two Arabs and two Jews. The all-Jewish Communist Party, Maqi, secured one seat in 1973.[4]

It is significant to note that while the Arab vote has been moving increasingly in the direction of the extreme left, the political complexion of Israel as a whole has reflected an increase in the strength of the right-wing elements of the political spectrum (see Table 7.2).

Still, the fact remains that the majority of the Arab votes are channelled in the direction of Zionist parties, in particular the Alignment bloc and their affiliated Arab lists. In 1965 these parties (including Mapam, which was not in the Alignment at the time) secured close to two-thirds of the Arab votes, whereas in 1973 support declined to less than half.[5]

TABLE 7.2 *Distribution of votes and Knesset seats (1949–69, 1973)*[6]

Bloc	Votes 1949–69 (average)	Votes 1973	Seats 1949–69 (average)	Seats 1973
	%	%		
Alignment*	49.7	39.6	61.2	51
Likud†	25.2	36.1	31.2	46
Religious‡	14.1	12.1	17.0	15
Communist	3.7	4.8	4.4	5
Other	7.3	7.4	6.2	3
	100.0	100.0	120	120

* The Alignment is a coalition of labour Zionist political parties. It includes Mapai (the main Labour political party in this group), Mapam, Ahdut ha-Avoda and Rafi. The latter, an offshoot of Mapai, was formed in 1965 by David Ben-Gurion.

† Refers to the right-wing coalition led by Herut. Other parties in the coalition are the General Zionists, the Independent Liberal Party and the Progressive Party.

‡ This is an amalgamation of religious parties dominated by the National Religious Party; this coalition also includes Agudat Israel and Poali Agudat Israel, the latter being an extreme religious party with socialist tendencies.

TABLE 7.3 *Distribution of Arab vote by size of community (1965–73)*[7]

Vote	Cities 1965	Cities 1969	Cities 1973	Urban settlements 1965	Urban settlements 1969	Urban settlements 1973	Large villages 1965	Large villages 1969	Large villages 1973
	%	%	%	%	%	%	%	%	%
Alignment	48.3	44.5	33.7	49.2	38.5	39.6	63.7	50.0	40.4
Rakah	42	45.9	55.1	41.3	50.5	41.9	23.1	31.7	40.9
Other	9.7	9.6	11.2	9.5	11.0	18.5	13.2	18.3	18.7
	100.0	100.0	100.0	100.0	100.0	100.0	100.0	100.0	100.0

Vote	Small villages 1965	Small villages 1969	Small villages 1973	Bedouins 1965	Bedouins 1969	Bedouins 1973
	%	%	%	%	%	%
Alignment	75.2	69.5	63.0	83.0	75.7	78.8
Rakah	13.1	13.1	18.7	4.5	5.1	6.5
Other	11.7	17.4	18.3	12.5	19.2	14.7
	100.0	100.0	100.0	100.0	100.0	100.0

More than one commentator has observed that Arab support for the Communist Party and the decline of Arab support for the Alignment is correlated with the level of urbanization in the Arab sector.[8] This observation is borne out in the data presented in

Table 7.3. In large villages, for example, Communist Party support rose from 23 per cent in 1965 to 41 per cent in 1973, equalling the combined vote obtained from the Arabs in the Alignment parties. It is among voters in small villages and Bedouin tribes that the Zionist parties obtain the largest portion of Arab votes. It thus becomes incumbent upon the Zionist parties, out of self-interest, to enhance the traditional character of the Arab sector. For it is the loyalty of chiefs of tribes and heads of *hamulas* that is essential if the Arab vote is to be sectionalized and directed away from supporting oppositionary parties of a non-Zionist nature.

If we compare the Arab with the Jewish vote in terms of regional distribution, we discover an inverse pattern. In contrast to the Arab sector, Jewish voters in rural areas support mainly left-wing parties (not necessarily Communist, rather Mapam and Ahdut ha-Avoda), while Jewish urban dwellers tend to favour right-of-centre political parties.[9] This is particularly true in poor urban areas. For example, in 1973 the Labour Alignment lost 9 per cent of votes gained in 1969 in poor areas and large cities, whereas its support among the well-to-do in cities remained the same. The right-wing Likud coalition increased its vote among poor Jewish urban voters. In Jerusalem, for example, it doubled its vote in 1973, from 22 to 43 per cent, in Tel Aviv's poor districts it rose from 32 to 41 per cent, and in Haifa's from 29 to 37 per cent.[10]

The pervading influence of the Zionist parties is more apparent on the local and trade union (Histadrut) levels than it is on the national electoral level, as is revealed in Tables 7.4 and 7.5. For local councils, the number of lists went up from 160 in 1969 to 211 in 1973. The average number of lists per village increased from 4.8 in 1969 to 5.7 in 1973. *Hamula*-headed lists affiliated with the ruling Zionist coalitions received 73 per cent of the Arab vote for local councils in 1969, and 77 per cent in 1973. In contrast, and with the exception of Nazareth, the overall Arab Communist vote on the local level dropped from 8.2 per cent in 1969 to 7.1 per cent in 1973.[11]

As shown in Table 7.5 an examination of the Arab trade union voting pattern reveals a similar correlation between size of locality and strength of Rakah – the larger the community, the larger the Communist vote. This is also true in regions with high Arab concentrations. In areas such as Galilee, Nazareth and the Triangle, between 37 and 39 per cent of the Histadrut Arab vote was cast in favour of the Communist Party. Among Bedouins and in so-called mixed cities and in other isolated localities, support for Alignment parties in the Histadrut ranged from 70 to 90 per cent. Overall, in 1969, 31 per cent of the Histadrut Arab votes were Communist, compared to 27 per cent in 1973. Of the total 76,843 Arabs eligible for voting in 1973, 76 per cent participated.[12]

TABLE 7.4 *Comparison between Arab Communist vote for Knesset and local councils for selected localities (1973)*[13]

Locality	*Knesset*	*Local*	*Locality*	*Knesset*	*Local*
	%	%		%	%
Nazareth	58	67.3*	Yirka†	19	5.8
Um El-Fahm	53	15	Al-Buqaya	45	12.7
Baqa al-Gharbiyya	47	7.2	Qalansawa	68	6.5
Daliyat al-Karmil†	9	—	Kafr Yasif	62	21.1
Taiyyba	52	10.4	Rame	44	20.9
Tira	47	7.9	Yafi	62	25.9

* The results refer to the election held in 1975, in which the National Democratic Front composed of Rakah and other nationalist elements scored a victory under the leadership of the new mayor, Tawfik Zayyad, who is also Rakah Knesset member.

† These are Druze villages in which the Israeli government has had some success in dissociating from the rest of the Arab element as shown in the low Communist vote. Yet, as Landau notes, Communist votes among the Druze have been on the increase.[14]

TABLE 7.5 *Distribution of Arab votes for twelfth Histadrut election by size of community (1973)*[15]

Size of community	*Alignment*	*Communist*	*Other*
	%	%	%
Cities	62.4	27.3	10.3
500+	57.8	31.7	10.5
300–499	57.1	24.5	18.4
200–299	75.3	12.8	11.9
37–200	82.5	6.3	11.2

TABLE 7.6 *Eligible Histadrut Arab members (1960–73)*[16]

Year	*Arab members*	*Arab members and dependants as % of Arab population*
1960	21,246	20.5
1965	39,564	31.3
1973	76,843	35.3*

* The figure for 1973 was reached by extrapolation. Assuming a family dependency ratio of 2.3 for each Histadrut member for 1960 and 1965, we get 176,738 Arab members and families affiliated with Histadrut-sponsored organizations, that is to say, around one-third of the total Arab population in Israel. Among the Jewish population, the Histadrut covers 90 per cent of the eligible labour force, and includes around two-thirds of the Jewish population.[17]

TABLE 7.7 *Age distribution of candidates and elected members for local councils (1973)*[18]

Age	*Candidates*	*Elected*
	%	%
Below 30	22.5	9.3
30–40	40.0	33.2
40–50	27.6	37.1
50–60	6.9	15.4
60+	3.0	5.0
	100.0	100.0

The traditional character of Arab politics on the village level is also apparent in the age distribution of elected local council members as shown in Table 7.7. In 1969, 8.3 per cent of those elected were under thirty. In 1973, there was an increase in one percentage point in the representation of this group. It is worth noting that in 1969 as well as in 1973, a quarter of the candidates were of this age group, corresponding closely to the fact that 25 per cent of the Arab population as a whole was aged between fifteen and twenty-nine.[19] While there has been a slight shift in the age composition of the elected membership on the local level, the hegemony of established family members is as powerful as ever. Harari argues that incorporation of faithful younger people has been carried out without disturbing the dominance of the traditional Arab leadership in village politics.[20]

In concluding this section, it should be remarked that while Rakah has espoused Palestinian nationalism and anti-Zionist doctrines, and at times pan-Arab socialist principles, it would be a mistake to call it a revolutionary party. It operates within the constitutional framework of the state, and in 1969 it supported a government bill in which campaign expenditures were financed by public funds. As Jiryis notes, Rakah did not hesitate to dissociate itself from, and even expel, Arab party members who engaged in violent protest activities and were accused by the authorities of endangering state security.[21] Its literary organs refused on more than one occasion to publish articles, written by Israeli Arabs, which the Communist Party perceived to be extremely nationalistic.[22]

While the strength of Rakah from the point of view of the Arabs is that it is the only oppositionary, non-Zionist party which articulates their grievances, in a different way this is also its inherent weakness in a regime dominated by Zionist ideology. Members of Rakah, a pro-Soviet party, are labelled by the public, the press and government officials as traitors. Shmuel Toledano, the Prime Minister's Adviser on Arab Affairs, referred to Rakah supporters in 1974 as 'enemies of the State'.[23] The inefficacy of Rakah, what one Israeli writer termed 'the opposite of a pressure group',[24] is expressed by Lustick thus:[25]

> Indeed the separation of Rakah from the rest of the society is so complete and its illegitimacy so widely accepted that its existence serves basically to reinforce the institutional isolation of Arabs from the Jewish sector. . . . This means that Jewish groups that publicly solicit Arab political support risk losing Jewish votes as a result. After the Yom Kippur War several socio-political protest movements developed in Israel calling for thoroughgoing reforms and a fundamental re-examination of Government policy in all sectors of society. However, these groups were uniformly silent on the internal 'Arab problem', and attempts by non-Communist Arabs to join these organizations were rebuffed out of fear by their organizers that they would thereby lose legitimacy and support in the Jewish sector.

The al-Ard movement

Palestinian nationalist feelings among the Arabs in Israel have found outlets in modes of expression other than through the Communist Party proper. The first to be noted is the al-Ard ('the land') movement, an all-Arab organization whose purpose was to articulate the grievances of the Arabs in Israel along national lines. Its genesis goes back to 1958, when an Arab public committee was set up to protest against the imprisonment of Israeli Arabs in the aftermath of bloody clashes with the police during May Day demonstrations which were held in Nazareth. An alliance between Arab Communists and nationalists was forged in a new organization called the Popular Front. When attempts were made officially to register the organization, the quest was denied by the authorities. Landau describes the reaction of the authorities to the Front thus:[26]

> The Israeli authorities, for their part, took steps to discourage the political activity of the Front, which they regarded as potentially subversive. The military administration refused to grant some Front activists travel permits, which resulted in their being unable to attend meetings or lectures far from their regular residence; a few were even detained for investigation.

It is important to stress the background which gave rise to overt political action on the part of Israeli Arabs at this juncture. First, there was the large-scale confiscation of Arab land which took place during the first decade of the state's existence.[27] Second, the educational and occupational opportunities were quite limited at the time, which drove some Arab youth to attempt escapes across the border. In more than one case, these attempts led to the killing of Arab youths by Israeli border guards.[28] Third, the strict application of the military rule, which led to restrictions of Arab movement, justified selective banishment and even detention of Israeli Arab citizens and aroused a great deal of Arab resentment. This policy was responsible in part for the tragic shooting in 1956 of fifty-one Arab civilians, including women and children, in the village of Kafr Qasim. Israeli Arab villagers returning to their homes from the fields, and unaware of sudden curfew restrictions, were systematically shot by border police.[29] Fourth, the general level of politicization in the region, ushered in by Nasser's ascent to power in Egypt in 1952, affected the Arabs in Israel as well. Fifth, Israel's collusion with France and Britain in the Sinai invasion and the government's support of French policies during the Algerian war of liberation put Israel, in the eyes of its Arab citizens, in the enemy camp.

Hostile government and press reactions, as well as an internal ideological split (between the Communists and nationalists), resulted in the disintegration of the Front and the attempt to create a new organization, al-Ard, which would be more nationalistically oriented. The response of the authorities was evident from the declarations made in early 1960 by Shmuel Divon, the Prime Minister's Adviser on Arab Affairs at the time. At a press conference in Tel Aviv he described al-Ard as 'a Nasserite group whose purpose is to provoke the Arabs of Israel'.[30] Soon thereafter, the authorities confiscated the movement's publications and brought to trial and convicted six of their editorial members.

The al-Ard group appealed against the government's refusal to grant it a legal permit to register. The case was heard by the Supreme Court, and the ruling was in favour of al-Ard. An unsuccessful attempt to reverse the Supreme Court's ruling was made by the government in 1962.

When a subsequent request was made by al-Ard to secure a permit to publish a newspaper it was denied by the government. This time the government invoked the 1945 Emergency Regulations to refuse al-Ard permission to register as an association and to put out publications. In 1964 the Supreme Court refused to hear the case, arguing that the issue did not lie within its jurisdiction. Having no legal recourse open to them under the 1945 Emergency Regulations, the al-Ard group publicized its case internationally by circulating a petition to foreign embassies in Israel and to the United Nations. Ultimately the organization was banned in the same year. Late in 1964 the Supreme Court delivered its decision against al-Ard. Three of its leaders were subsequently arrested after the capture of infiltrators from across the border who, according to the Israeli government, had orders to contact the organizers of al-Ard.[31] However, no formal accusation was made and the arrested leaders were subsequently released to be put under house detention.[32]

A year later, in 1965, the al-Ard group presented a parliamentary slate of candidates to participate in the elections for the Sixth Knesset under the name the 'Arab Socialist List'. Here too the government reacted swiftly by getting the military governor to banish four al-Ard candidates for 'provocative activities against the State'.[33] The finale of an attempt to set up an independent Arab movement in Israel came when three members of al-Ard were convicted in December 1967 for giving shelter to Palestinian guerrillas. The outcome of all this was that the leadership became atomized and at least four of al-Ard's key members left Israel in the early 1970s, three of them affiliating themselves with the Palestine Liberation Organization in one way or another.

The main source of hostility toward the al-Ard movement, as reflected in the Israeli press, the courts and public opinion, is that 'the essential aim of al-Ard is to struggle for Palestinian Arab nationalism, ignoring the will of the Jewish majority in Israel as well as the State's authorities.'[34] More specifically in the eyes of the Supreme Court, the movement represented an 'illegal association denying the very existence of the State of Israel'.[35]

Apparently, the item in the constitution of al-Ard which led to the above interpretation has to do with the way al-Ard spelled out the Palestinian issue:[36]

> An equitable solution to the Palestinian problem has to be found by considering the problem as an indivisible part which has to be solved in line with the wishes of the Palestinian people, to respond to its aspirations and interests, to restore to it its autonomy, to guarantee its complete and legitimate rights for being the main factor responsible for deciding its destiny in line with the high ideals of the Arab nation.

But the programme of al-Ard also stipulated, 'recognition of the United Nations decision of 29 November 1947, which would provide a solution which would maintain the rights of both Israeli-Jewish and Palestinian-Arab people and would strengthen the stability and peace of the area.'[37]

These and other statements made by leaders of al-Ard are advanced by Israeli Arab activists to counter the criticism levelled against them by the authorities and the Jewish public that they do not recognize Israel's right to exist. Basically, the al-Ard group perceived the action of the Israeli government as discriminatory and designed to stifle Arab political opposition which calls for the right of the Palestinians to an independent state, similar to that guaranteed to the Jews by the United Nations. It is worth noting that a decade later, in 1975, a previous, prominent member of al-Ard, Sabri Jiryis, who left Israel and became an official in the Palestine Liberation Organization, went on to advocate the same idea for an independent Palestinian State alongside Israel, this time from Beirut, Lebanon.[38] The idea had a mixed reception among the Palestinians; it was totally rejected by militant Palestinians. Among certain segments of the left and liberals in Israel, as well as outside it, the belated reaction was positive this time.[39]

Students

When in 1971 Arab university students and graduates launched the Arab Academic Union in Israel, Michael Assaf, an old-time functionary of the Labour Party and a frequent writer on Arab affairs, remarked that those who had prompted the setting up of the Union were 'the orphans' of the al-Ard movement.[40] While his intention was to deride Arab intellectuals, there is a core of truth in this, for the *ideas* espoused (and not necessarily the personnel involved, except for one prominent member) by the student organizations are essentially the same as those advocated by al-Ard. Basically, they call for an end to confiscation of Arab land, improvement in the situation of the Arab minority, and recognition that the Arabs in Israel are part of the Palestinian people and the Arab nation.[41] In essence, these objectives are identical to those articulated in 1958 by the first Arab Student Committee set up at the Hebrew University.

The initial reactions to the idea of a national union of Arab university students and graduates – by the press and the Prime Minister's Adviser on Arab Affairs at the time – were negative. The founding meeting attracted 80 out of 1,000 to 1,500 invited participants. While the authorities considered this low turnout to be an indication of Arab indifference to the idea, the organizers attributed low attendance to the hostile press campaign and fear by the Arabs of government reprisals. It was assumed that those who attended the founding meeting of an organization that had been associated in the public mind with the banned al-Ard risked harassment by the government and eventual denial of job opportunities, particularly since most Arab university graduates go on to become state-employed teachers.[42]

Nevertheless, Arab student organizations do exist on the six Israeli university campuses, although they are not all recognized as legitimate organizations by university administrations. The position taken by university administrations is that there is one union, the

Israeli Union of Students, which speaks in the name of all students. However, Arab students retort that such unions are dominated by the majority Jewish students who do not cater to the specific needs of Arab students so that separatism between Arabs and Jews is equally visible in the University. Ideological rifts split the Arab from the Jewish students and as a result the Arab–Israeli conflict is transferred in microcosm to the campuses.

The extent of antagonism between Arab and Jewish university students was revealed, as it has been many times, in early 1975 at the Bar-Ilan campus in Tel Aviv and at the Technion in Haifa. In the latter case, clashes occurred between the two groups when Jewish students forced the cancellation of an Arab student meeting to protest against the arrest of an Arab fellow student.[43] At Bar-Ilan, tension erupted in the wake of a demonstration by Arab students. In commenting on the clashes, the Dean at Bar-Ilan University noted that 'tension arose between Arab and Jewish students and administration when they (Arab students) distributed leaflets in the aftermath of the (guerrilla) attack on the Savoy Hotel.'[44] The Arab students' view was that the pamphlets were directed against administrative detention and house arrests imposed upon Arab citizens. In commenting on these clashes, an Arab student leader had this to say at the national meeting of Arab students held at Nazareth and attended by 500 people:[45]

> We consider ourselves an indivisible part of the Palestinian people. As long as they [the Israeli government] don't recognize our right to support our brethren in refugee camps – there will be no calm on campuses. If the Jewish university students have the right to demonstrate in support of [Jewish] settlements [in the occupied territories] it is our right to demonstrate against them.

In the same year a meeting was held in Tel Aviv in solidarity with Arab university students, which was also attended by sympathetic Jewish personalities. As described by one newspaper, this was a 'protest meeting for equality between Arab and Jewish university students regarding admission criteria, student housing, availability of suitable work for Arab students, and the right to organize on the campus'.[46]

A second factor which contributes to the lack of rapport between Arab and Jewish students has to do with the rather conservative nature of Jewish students. According to Amnon Rubinstein, the Dean of the Law School at Tel Aviv University, Jewish university graduates[47]

> are not interested in seeing social and political change take place. Likewise they do not even take a stand on controversial

> matters, and quite often they consider their professors left wing, simply because they refuse to align themselves in the direction of the conservative right. Students abroad have worked to change fundamental structures which govern the relationship between men; they have supported the rights of minorities and the persecuted, and as a result the treatment of minorities has undergone change. They revolted against the symbols of domination not only in the university but in other places. In contrast, the Israeli student did not even express an opinion on matters of this sort.

The above remarks are in agreement with the results of recent research on the socio-political orientations of the Israeli student. In the study based on a sample of students from Rubinstein's own university, we discover, for example, that there is little identification of the Israeli student with the student left movement in general. The philosophy of the Israeli student is typified by instrumentalism and individualism.[48]

It is accurate to say that while the Arab Israeli student suffers from socio-psychological tensions which are experienced by the rest of the Arab minority in Israel, his sense of relative deprivation is unique to his student position; his frame of reference is the Jewish Israeli student. Whether it is university lodgings, employment opportunities, treatment by the university administration, or attitudes of Jewish classmates,[49] the Arab university student compares his position with that of other students around him who are of a similar social status. According to the Shiloah study:[50]

> The feeling of discrimination is strengthened when the Arab graduates compare their own position and degree of absorption with the position of their Jewish counterparts and fellow-students. The findings confirm the assumption that the younger generation of Israeli Arabs measure their own position by comparison with Jewish society and not with that of their parents' generation.

An overriding concern of Arab university students is the identity problem – Who am I? This problem is expressed by an Arab student at Haifa University:[51]

> An Arab in Iraq, Egypt or Syria doesn't have any problem in defining his nationality. In Arabic, nationality has two meanings: *Wataniya*, meaning the link to one's homeland – for a Syrian, being Syria: and *Qa'umiya*, meaning overall Arab nationality, or pan-Arabism. If an Israeli Arab wishes to be *Watani*, he has to oppose the existence of the State of Israel. His *Watan* is Palestine and the people of Palestine are a part

> of the Arab people. For a thinking Israeli Arab, there is no self-determination. He is in a place that was called Palestine 23 years ago, and called Israel now. I was born in this country, but I feel like a stranger in my homeland. The Israeli Jew believes that he was born in his homeland, and I believe I was born in mine. Why shouldn't this be a homeland for both of us? Both of us have the same right to exist.

This national identity conflict is also experienced by Arab schoolteachers, who comprise the largest stratum of white-collar, and by definition middle-class, employees of the state. As Mar'i notes, two opposing forces operate on Arab teachers in the Zionist State: one dictating that as an intelligentsia they have a duty to instil in the young a sense of Palestinian national pride, but another dictating that as employees and citizens of the state they have to ensure loyalty to the state through their actions by inculcating in the young norms which are directed toward identifying with the state. A teacher quoted by Mar'i remarked: 'When I educate my pupils toward loyalty to the State I am considered a traitor . . . and when I emphasize the national character of my pupils and try to nurture in them a sense of national pride, I am told I am a traitor.'[52] The latter type of accusation is levelled by state authorities, and the former by the parents and average villagers, both of whom tend to perceive Arab teachers as government agents who live off the Israeli regime.

The image of the teacher as a government agent is enhanced by the fact that, as Mar'i explains, schoolteachers find it necessary to associate themselves with party politics, particularly the politics of the Alignment parties. A teaching job in the Arab sector is contingent in large measure upon giving support to Zionist parties. Here lies the crux of party patronage as an effective method of control in the Arab sector. Through controlling teachers' appointments (contracts are given on a yearly basis) the ruling Zionist parties ensure that radical, independent, or nationalist Arab teachers are kept out of the teaching profession.

The identity issue is going to be more acute in the future. Whatever evidence there is points to the re-emergence of Palestinian identity among the Arabs in Israel. Some Israeli Jews, though a small but significant minority, are willing to acknowledge this fact. A. B. Yehoshua, Dean of Students at Haifa University, brings the Palestinianism of the Arabs in Israel to the forefront and calls for its recognition, although he does not offer any institutional delineation for it: 'The concept of an "Israeli Arab" is a fictitious one – there should be no such concept. There are only Palestinian Arabs. We must restore to the Arab in Israel his true identity, instead of robbing him of it.'[53]

It is interesting to note that Arab students see the Oriental Jews from the Arab countries as possible allies, simply because of their cultural background and economic position in society. The Arab Students' Committee at Tel Aviv University published an editorial in their newspaper in June 1976, along these lines. The background to the editorial was the Land Day demonstrations held on 30 March 1976 to protest against government land confiscation, in which six Israeli Arabs were shot to death by the police, while others were injured. In part, the editorial in the student newspaper read:[54]

> Do our brothers, the Oriental Jews, and all other working class Jewish masses in the country, know that the criminal hand which kills the Palestinian Arabs in the occupied territories and in the Green Line [pre-1967 Israel] is the very hand which fired at the Jewish workers who were on strike in Ashkelon last year? That it is the very hand which maintains the social, political and ethnic groups between Sefaradim and Ashkenazim? That it is the very workers and the Jewish masses in the poor neighbourhoods where they struggle for bread and milk and for social, political and economic equality?

After attacking the Law of Return and discrimination against Arab students, the editorial went on to say:

> mutual recognition of the human and national rights of both peoples is the right way to end the existing conflict, which will be attained only by uniting the masses of both people in a common struggle – against Zionism, against Arab bourgeoisie and against imperialism – for the establishment of a socialist society for both peoples in the country where both live.

Needless to say, such rhetoric fell on deaf ears. The Oriental Jewish community is the main supporter of Menachem Begin's Herut, the extreme right-wing party. It will be some time before such an alliance crystallizes, if it ever does. The Israeli 'Black Panthers', a left-wing radical movement composed of Oriental Jews, at one time began to show some signs of politicization (not necessarily identification with the Israeli Arabs) until its leaders were eventually co-opted by the authorities. Writing in the publication of Matzpen (another left-wing movement, dominated by Western European Jews) in 1973, a leader of the 'Black Panthers' echoed sentiments not too dissimilar from those expressed by Arab students.[55] One analyst, in commenting on the 'Black Panther' phenomenon in Israel, remarked, rather optimistically, about Oriental radicalism: 'Well, social revolution, voting for Rakah, and cooperation with the Arabs against the establishment. . . . Indeed, a new image of the "Black Panthers" movement.'[56]

Overall, the direct impact of Arab students within the Arab community, in terms of political action, is minimal. However, there is a great deal of identification on the ideational level between the students and the needs of the Arab community. But only a small minority of Arab university students from Haifa University who were studied by Nakhleh carried through their expressed sense of responsibility toward the Arab community.[57] The reasons for this could be varied, ranging from lack of a coherent programme to reluctance to incur the wrath of their parents as well as the authorities for diverting their educational energies into what many people would construe as political acts.

Still, some change was effected through student action. For example, while adopting non-political criteria (such as basing membership on residence and the fact that members had to be university graduates), the Nazareth League of University Graduates was crucial in 1975 in forging a coalition with the Communists and other elements which rid the city of an Alignment-sponsored city administration known for its inefficiency and corruption.

Writers

A group which complements and even overlaps with university students, in terms of their politicizing role, is Arab writers in Israel, notably poets. E. A. Simon refers to the Arab intelligentsia in Israel as the 'intellectual proletariat'.[58] There is a basis for this classification, since most Arab writers in Israel tend to be villagers who were in their formative years when Israel came into being, and who had neither university titles nor aristocratic background. In a sense their status in the Arab community is achieved rather than ascribed. They earned status by defending the Arab minority's cause through their writings, usually at a high personal price.

Writers such as Rashid Husain, Samih Qasim, Mahmud Darwish and Tawfiq Zayyad fall in this category. What unites these writers is the politicized nature of their writings and the fact that they have resorted mainly to poetry as a medium for expressing their criticisms of the Israeli government's policy toward the Arabs in Israel. Not all commentators share the Arab intellectuals' view of their situation in Israel. Landau says:[59]

> Although Arab intellectuals may be slow to admit it, they have themselves, in a great measure, to blame for their comparative isolation. In the village, for instance, the local leaders are not the sole cause of their lack of influence. Arab intellectuals contribute but little to integration in the Arab village, whose backwardness they openly despise.

There are Arab writers in Israel, albeit a small minority, who support the state and condone the policies of the Israeli government through their writings.[60] Their status and influence within the Arab community is less noticeable and they (like other Arab politicians who affiliate themselves with Zionist parties) are usually labelled by the Arabs as collaborators. Some of those writers who started on the path of conciliation – and many did in the state's first decade – ended up as critics of the government and champions of the Arab minority's cause. As mentioned above, almost without exception, radical Israeli Arab writers served time in Israeli gaols, had their movements restricted, lost their jobs, and in some cases underwent either house detention or so-called administrative arrest.

Relying on Fanon's theory of a colonized culture, Cooley identifies three stages in the development of Palestinian literature. First to be identified is the state of 'unqualified assimilation' whereby the colonized writer attempts to emulate the dominant culture of the colonizer, and in some cases perceives himself to be a part of it. Second, the writer goes through a phase in which he 'decides to remember what he is'. This stage is characterized by questioning the borrowed world-view which the writer applies to interpret his experience. Finally, the 'fighting stage' reflects the writer's revolutionary role in which he provides his colonized people with a new interpretation of reality, one that is revolutionary in essence and at variance with the incorporated value-system.[61]

Roughly, one could say that the first two stages characterized most Arab writings in Israel during the first decade of Israel's existence. During this period, literary output was apolitical and in some respect apologist. The third stage is what typifies current Palestinian writings inside Israel as well as outside it:[62]

> In the early years of the State, most of the Arab literature was non-political. In so far as an attitude towards the Jews was expressed, it was in a view of friendship and with a declared wish for mutual good-will and close co-operation; this was addressed to Arabs and Jews alike. More recently, especially in the 1960's, Arab literature is increasingly concerned (avowed by or indirectly) with the confrontation between Jews and Arabs, Zionism and Arab nationalism.

Poetry, rather than the novel, has been the most prevalent mode of critical literary expression among the Arabs in Israel. The reasons are structural and historical. In the former case, the absence of a viable Arab novel in Israel is due not only 'to the fact that poetry as an art vehicle is more effective and suitable for diffusion, but because [of] the publishing conditions surrounding Arab writers in the occupied land',[63] as the late Kanafani, a well-known Palestinian writer, has remarked. Thus, there are no independent Arab publishing houses in Israel, similar to those which exist in the Jewish sector. Almost all political parties, from Communists to Zionists, operate their corresponding Arab publishing houses. Moreover, some of the Arab religious organizations participate in Arabic publishing. Rakah, and to a lesser extent Mapam, have provided an outlet for radical Arab literature. However, in all cases the party line prevailed in terms of what was allowed to be published. In the case of Mapam, its Arabic publishing efforts at one time included pirating books published in the Arab world. In this way, Israeli Arab readers had a limited access to non-political writings emanating from the neighbouring countries, in particular from Egypt.

The slow development of the Arab novel has also to do with the historical experience of the Arabs in Israel as a colonized minority. As Fanon argues, poetry is the first to emerge as a mode of protest, to be followed by short stories and then the novel. Poetic expression, according to Fanon, is best suited for tragic and lamentary portrayal of the colonized's experience; hence it is the first to appear in the sequence of literary articulation.[64]

Still, this does not fully account for the Palestinian novel's failure to develop. Another reason which could be advanced in this regard is not unique to the Palestinian experience, and underscores the situation in other Arab countries as well, where the novel is slow to develop: of all the Arab countries, Egypt is the only centre which has managed to produce a significant stratum of literati whose influence extended beyond Egypt and whose mark was made on Arab society as early as the 1920s. The rise of the novel in Egypt is associated with the relative stability of Egypt, the duration of its institutions, inefficient though they may be, and, most important, the existence of literary traditions which developed in the context of an urban culture characteristic of big cities. While all of these factors did not crystallize in Palestine, it is the absence of the latter which contributed most to the stagnation of Palestinian literature. Flourishing Arab cities of an urban-industrial character and with institutions for higher learning did not develop in either pre- or post-1948 Palestine.

The truncated nature of the current Palestinian class structure and its distorted form of urbanization are not likely to give rise to a viable Palestinian literary movement in Israel in the near future.

Finally, one should perhaps state that in order for literature in general to flourish, and the novel in particular, a climate favourable for the free expression and exchange of ideas should prevail. In this respect the Arabs in Israel share the predicament of their Arab brethren in the rest of the Arab world. While in the latter case the crudest forms of thought-control are exercised, in the former it is the sophisticated form of Israeli censorship in the name of state security which is operative.

The limitations on Arab writings in Israel notwithstanding, Israeli Arab poetry stands out as the most powerful testimony of Arab aspirations. In Cooley's words, these 'captive' examples of literature 'helped begin a literary revolution in the Arab world almost by themselves. Palestinian intellectuals and Arab critics generally consider the "captive" poetry, written under Israeli occupation, as best representing their spirit and aim.'[65]

Through the use of symbolism and allegory Arab writers have skilfully managed to write protest poetry and to communicate with the readership under the watchful eyes of the Israeli censor. The symbolism was diverse in its origin and tended to incorporate Muslim and Christian symbols as well as Greek legends and mythology. Moreover, a substantial part of its symbolism has been borrowed from Third World experience.

It is significant that Arab literature in Israel developed in complete isolation from its Jewish counterpart. The institutional means available to the Jewish writer, in the form of government grants given to the Hebrew Writers' Union, are not put at the disposal of Arab writers in Israel. In fact they are denied membership of the Hebrew Writers' Union under the pretext that the Union is only for writers in the Hebrew language. This is in spite of the fact that some Arab writers did write in Hebrew – including one of the most militant writers, the late Rashid Husain[66] – and the fact that some of the Jewish members of the Hebrew Writers' Union do not publish in Hebrew but in Yiddish and other European languages.[67]

Three central themes appear in Israeli Arab poetry: criticism of traditional Arab leadership, in particular the role played by those who collaborate with the Israeli authorities and who are portrayed as standing in the way of Israeli Arab progress; exposition of the Israeli government's treatment of the Arab population; and an identification with revolutionary movements in the Third World. At one stage Arab literature concerned itself also with Arab–Jewish co-operation toward solving the Middle East impasse.[68]

A more extensive treatment of Arab poetry in Israel as a form of protest literature has been carried out by other writers. Suffice it here to offer samples from such works which have already appeared in English. Samih Qasim – a Druze poet whose poetry included scathing attacks on those members of his sect who collaborated with the Israeli government and agreed to accept the label of non-Arab for themselves – in an analysis of his experience in Israeli gaols and the periods of job discrimination he had to undergo for his political activity, made his point in the form of a dialogue between a Jew and a Palestinian Arab. In the same poem he rejects the assumption that the Arabs have to pay the price for Western persecution of Jews; he condemns land confiscation and negative stereotyping of Arabs, yet he shows readiness on the part of Arabs to forgive the Jews for mistreating them:[69]

My grandparents were burnt in
  Auschwitz
My heart is with them, but remove
  the chains from my body
What's in your hand?
A handful of seeds,
Anger colours your face
That's the colour of the earth
Mold your sword into a ploughshare
You have left no land
You are a criminal!
I killed not, I murdered not, I
  oppressed not!
You are an Arab, you are a dog!
May God save you – try the taste of
  love and make way for the sun!

Rashid Husain, who advocated a bi-nationalist state and called more than once upon 'Jewish compatriots' to join in opposing 'those who colonized both our people and humbled them together',[70] earned a world-wide reputation as a writer and a critic of the Israeli government's attitude toward the Arabs. His efforts to bridge the gap between Arabs and Jews were reflected in his literary abilities as well as in his close personal associations with liberal Israeli Jews.[71] He translated Hebrew literature into Arabic and even attempted writing poetry in Hebrew. Yet his disillusionment with the prospects for harmonious Jewish–Arab relations inside Israel as well as outside it typified his ultimate attitudes until his death in New York in early 1977, while working as an official for the Palestine Liberation Organization. His poem 'Flowers from Hell', published in the late 1950s, depicts in tragic terms the bitter experience of the Palestinian refugees:[72]

In dark tents, in chains, in the
  shadow of hell
They have imprisoned my people
  and ordered them to silence.
They threatened my people with
  soldiers' whips, with sure death,
And with hunger, if they complained.

They have gone away, but they told
my people: 'Live happily in Hell.'
These orphan children, do you see
them?
They and misery have been
companions for years.
They have tired of praying and no
one hearing,
'Who are you, little children? Who
has tormented you so?'
'We are budding flowers from
hell,' they said.
Among these tents the sun will
forge an eternal path,
For the millions whom they
considered not human beings.
The sun will march down in a
caravan of golden life,
And with the dew of love,
we shall quench the fires of hell.

To those Arabs who collaborate with the Israeli government, he has this to say in 'The Executioner':[73]

Give me a rope, a hammer,
a steel bar,
For I shall build gallows,
Among my people a group still
lingers
That feeds on shame and walks
with downcast heads.
Let's stretch their necks!
How can we keep in our midst
One who licks every palm
he meets?

Mahmud Darwish is the youngest of the three poets whom we are considering here. Like Husain, he too has left Israel, and he is currently working at the Palestine Liberation Organization Research Centre in Lebanon. Of the various protest poems he has written, none is as well known and powerful in its impact as 'Investigation', written in 1964. The poem consists of a monologue depicting the experience of an Israeli Arab at the hands of an Israeli police interrogator:[74]

Write, down,
I am an Arab

My card number is 50,000
I have eight children,
The next will come next summer,
Are you angry?

Write down,
I am an Arab
I cut stone with comrade labourers,
I squeeze the rock
To get a loaf
To get a loaf,
To get a book,
For my eight children.
But I do not plead charity
And I do not cringe
Under your sway.
Are you angry?

Write down,
I am an Arab,
I am a name without a title,
Steadfast in a frenzied world.

My roots sink deep
Beyond the ages,
Beyond time.

. . .

And please write down
On top of all,
I hate nobody,
I rob nobody,
But when I starve
I eat the flesh of my marauders
Beware,
Beware my hunger,
Beware my wrath.

The forceful character of Israeli Arab literature has been recognized by many, including Israeli writers. But it was Cooley who noted that it compared 'with literature of the so-called inner "emigration" of anti-Fascist European authors in Europe of the 1930s'.[75]

Conclusions

Basically, three types of politicization were discussed in this chapter: identification with the Communist Party, an attempt to establish a nationalist movement, and an increase in the Arab intelligentsia's involvement in the political affairs of the Arab community. Within a hegemonic Zionist political culture, where deviation from a Zionist definition of political precepts is neither encouraged nor tolerated, it would be unrealistic to expect Arab efforts in this direction to be a complete success. However, neither could they be considered a total failure. While the extent of Arab politicization has not solved the predicaments facing Arabs in Israel as a subordinate group, they have at least managed to keep alive a sense of Palestinian identity and attachment to the homeland, things which have been difficult to sustain in the absence of an experienced Israeli Arab leadership, and an open political culture.

It would be presumptuous to attribute whatever Arab politicization there is solely to the intellectual élites among the Arabs in Israel. As a matter of fact one of the weaknesses of this élite was, and continues to be, its inability to establish an effective grass-roots political movement which would encompass the majority rural-proletariat of the Arab masses. Only then would Arab solidarity take on a dimension which would be difficult for the Israeli authorities to contend with. The Land Day protests and the general strike which took place in April 1976 may have been championed by Arab élites, but their success is due primarily to the united front exhibited by the peasantry. Forced alienation from the land may yet prove to be the crucial catalyst in any future Arab uprisings in Israel.

8 Toward a sociology of the Palestinians

No other social movement in this century has affected Arab–Jewish relations as has Zionism. Yet, significantly, the question of Jewish–Arab relations has assumed a minor role in the writings of key Zionist ideologists,[1] even when one takes into account the interest shown by a limited group of Jewish activists including the philosopher Martin Buber, Judah Magnes, the first President of the Hebrew University and, to some extent, Arthur Ruppin, in the idea of bi-nationalism.[2]

Like any other doctrine, Zionism is difficult to place within one simple ideological construct. As far as the Zionist attitude toward the Arabs is concerned, existing writings suggest four possible meanings and interpretations.

First, there are those writers who see Zionism as embracing two oppositionary trends, a conservative and a liberal one, or a 'fundamentalist' and a 'universalist', to quote Shanin.[3] It is claimed by such writers that in pre-1948 Palestine, universalism dominated Zionist thinking:[4]

> The Zionist socialists and liberals declared their commitment to live together with the Arabs, the actual programmes varying from a Jewish state treating an Arab minority as equals, usually with a Palestinian state at its side, to a Jewish–Arab state of two nations in the whole of Palestine in the Brit Shalom and Hashomer Hatzair view. This approach has found its fullest political expression in the official policies of Havlaga (self-restraint in Hebrew) in accordance with which during 1936/1938 Arab military struggle, the Haganah Jewish armed units were ordered not to retaliate over and above self-defence for 'we shall have to live together in the future'. (This was only partially observed but was significant all the same). . . .

But, as the events unfolded in Palestine, the universalists of so-called labour Zionism, particularly in post-1948 Palestine, moved gradually to adopting and implementing fundamentalist principles. Thus, while publicly espousing liberal and secular values calling for accommodation with the Arabs, the policies adopted in Israel toward the Arab minority were on the whole inegalitarian. Shanin goes on to argue that this sliding back to fundamentalist principles is the result of unfulfilled 'suspension' of liberal ideologies by labour Zionists for pragmatic reasons, with internal division within the Zionist movement, and the onslaught of the persecution of European Jewry.

A second group of writers[5] argues that Zionism is essentially an offshoot of Western colonialism and nineteenth-century imperialism, which was bound to produce the existing chauvinistic and exclusivist structures in Israeli society. The only viable solution to the Palestinian–Israeli conflict is either the establishment of a bi-national secular state in all of Palestine, or at least the setting up of an independent Palestinian state in post-1967 occupied Palestine.

Between the above-mentioned groups of writers, it is possible to isolate a third group[6] who typify the bulk of Western and so-called 'liberal' social scientists. The view adhered to by this group is basically shared by Shanin, at least regarding pre-1948 Palestine. The assumption is that the Zionist venture in Palestine would have benefited Arabs and Jews alike had it not been for the intransigence of the Palestinian Arabs and later of neighbouring Arab states. The flaw, according to this popular interpretation, does not lie in the original premises and tenets of Zionism, which were basically egalitarian, but in the Arab reaction to it.

The disadvantaged status of the Arab minority in Israel is due, in the eyes of this group, to the state of war existing between Israel and its neighbours. The Arab–Jewish problem is basically a problem of prejudice which will be solved with proper education. More important, it is further claimed that the Arab–Jewish problem is essentially a problem between states, with the Palestinian factor incorporated as a minor component.

Among the more articulate spokesmen of this group there is at least a willingness to acknowledge a discrepancy between what should have taken place in Palestine and what actually transpired. In the dialogue with his two Egyptian interlocutors, who are called by the pseudonym Mahmoud Hussain, the Israeli historian Saul Friedlander had this to say about the difference between subjective Zionist intentions in colonizing Palestine and the ensuing objective situation:[7]

I can assure you – you can check up on this, at any point in the

> history of that period (pre-1948) – that the intention of the Jews at that moment was not in any way to drive out Palestinians. You may tell me that this is naive, and that *objectively* it doesn't change anything. *Subjectively*, the intention – admittedly naive – was to live side by side with the Palestinians. You have to admit this about the Jewish pioneers of that time: they certainly had a way of looking at things which we consider naive today. They thought they would arrive in Palestine and be accepted because they were bringing a technical civilization that would benefit everyone who lived in the region. Objectively, the situation was different, and here I will use an almost Marxist method of analysis in emphasizing the difference between subjective will and objective reality. But it must be said, in order to establish the historic truth – in so far as we can speak of truth – that the Zionists had a well-defined subjective will, but that the objective results of their action did not tally with their primary intentions.

In arguing for the uniqueness of Zionism, Friedlander goes on to note the following: (1) The purpose of the exclusivist policies practised by the Histadrut and other institutions was not to deprive the Arabs of any benefits, but to secure favourable conditions for the Jews. (2) While there were those among Jewish settlers who advocated bi-nationalism, a corresponding group among the Palestinians was lacking. In fact, the Arabs rejected even the idea of a Legislative Council proposed by the British in 1922 which would have brought Arabs and Jews within the context of one political framework. (3) It is Zionism, the manifestation of 2,000 years of yearning to return to Jerusalem, and not the Balfour Declaration, which accounts for the Jewish presence in modern Palestine.

Our contention is that although we accept the presence of divergent tendencies in the Zionist movement, our examination of the developments in pre-1948 Palestine leads us to conclude that ultra-nationalistic and fundamentalist Zionism, mediated by the British presence in Palestine, has prevailed in actuality, if not in the rhetoric. The eclipse of the bi-nationalist movement, the nationalist and exclusivist policies of the Histadrut, the policy of Jewish immigration which was pursued at the expense of and contrary to the wishes of the indigenous Arab population, the implicit (and at times explicit) collaboration between the British and the Zionists during the Arab Rebellion, and the eventual dispersal of the Arab population in 1948 – which was dictated in no small measure by the policies of terror employed by the Haganah and the other extremist irregular Zionist forces such as the Irgun – could not all be considered the sole outcome of 'suspended' liberal ideologies, or of the policies of self-restraint.

Zionist claims concerning the metaphysical nature of the Jewish State notwithstanding, had it not been for the political act of the Balfour Declaration of 1917, which stipulated a 'national home for the Jewish people' at a time when the Jews constituted less than 10 per cent of the population, it would have been impossible, in the face of Arab opposition, for the Zionist plan to materialize.[8] When President Wilson established the King-Crane Commission in 1919 to examine the situation in Palestine, it reached the conclusion that[9]

> more than 72 per cent of the petitions received by the Commission in the whole of Syria were against the Zionist programme. The whole non-Jewish population of Palestine was emphatically against the entire Zionist programme. No British officer consulted by the Commission believed that the Zionist programme could be carried out except by force of arms.

Indeed, Weizmann presented the idea of a Jewish State to Britain by arguing that such an entity would further and protect British imperial interests in the area.[10] Similarly, Herzl before him lobbied the British for a concession in Palestine along the lines of British chartered companies in Africa.[11]

As far as the 1922 Legislative Council is concerned, the Arabs rejected it for the same reason that they rejected the Balfour Declaration. In Kirk's words: 'The composition of the proposed Council was indeed weighted against the Arabs, since though Muslims and Christians combined still constituted 89 per cent of the population, their ten elected members could be controlled by the ten official members and the two elected Jewish representatives.'[12] Likewise, the Palestinian reaction to a proposed Arab Agency, which in the view of the Mandatory authorities would be parallel in its functions to the Jewish Agency, was equally emphatic: 'The Arab owners of the country cannot see their way to accept a proposal which tends to place them on an equal footing with the alien Jews. In addition, the name of the Arab Agency would make them feel that they are strangers in their own country.'[13]

What Friedlander does not mention is that the proposal for a Legislative Council was revived in 1935, at a time when the Arabs were amenable to the idea. Zionist pressure against the proposal, in the British Parliament, forced the government to abandon the project. At a time when the Jewish settlers were around 27 per cent of the population they refused to accept less than 50 per cent representation.[14]

In contrast to Friedlander and other Zionist writers like him of non-Marxist persuasion, there are those writers who question the so-called uniqueness of Zionism. Abraham Leon examines the social bases of Zionism from a Marxist perspective, seeking to explain its ideological manifestations in terms of specific class interests:[15]

> In reality, Zionist ideology, like all ideologies, is only the distorted reflection of the interests of a class. It is the ideology of the Jewish petty bourgeoisie, suffocating between feudalism in ruins and capitalism in decay. The refutation of the ideological ruins of Zionism does not naturally refute the real needs which brought them into being. It is modern anti-Semitism, and not mythical 'eternal' anti-Semitism which is the best agitator in favour of Zionism.

For Leon, the persecution of the Jews throughout history is to be understood in terms of their economic location in society. The Jews being a 'people-class', he argues, as long as their preponderance in certain occupational pursuits fulfils a functional role in society they are safe from acts of prejudice and discrimination. However, if as a result of class transformation the new ascending stratum perceives the Jews as posing an economic threat to its position, it resorts to racist ideologies in order to justify the elimination of Jewish economic competition. Therefore the solution to the Jewish problem in the twentieth century is to be sought in the elimination of capitalism, but 'Zionism wishes to resolve the Jewish question without destroying capitalism, which is the principal source of the suffering of the Jews.'[16]

There are problems with this explanation, based as it is solely on economic determinism. While it performs a useful service by highlighting an otherwise neglected aspect in the analysis of Zionism and anti-Semitism, it tends totally to neglect other explanatory factors. For example, nowhere in this analysis is religion, in particular Christianity, accorded a place in sustaining the image of the Jews as the enemies of Christ. Likewise, unless one assumes that the force of nationalism is a distorted reflection of the interests of the ruling class, it too must be incorporated into the analysis as a determining factor in its own right.[17]

Finally, a fourth group of writers[18] argues that Zionism is essentially a Messianic movement, and that the culmination of modern Israel is only one step toward realizing the final goal: the Return to Eretz Israel. Relying on biblical interpretations, non-Jews living in any part of the ancient land of Israel, for example, the Arabs, are viewed by this group as temporary occupants or guardians of the land. It should be apparent that to the advocates of this fundamentalist philosophy, the essence of the problem is the Arabs, their very presence in biblical Eretz Israel. Once the Arabs are removed from Palestine, either through expulsion or through so-called population transfer and/or exchange, the issue will be automatically resolved.

Here lies the predicament of Zionism. Unwittingly the Jewish problem has become increasingly interconnected with that of the Palestinians, the very people whom Zionism ignored and considered peripheral until very recently. It must be stated that this process of recognition of the Palestinian factor is going on within a Zionist ideological strait-jacket. This is particularly true in the West, where the dominance of Zionist propaganda has managed to stifle public dissent from within Zionism's own ranks.[19] Like no other ideological movement, Zionism in the West has secured an immunity for itself by making criticism of Zionism tantamount to anti-Semitism. In direct contrast to the near conspiracy of silence exercised by Western Zionist spokesmen concerning Zionism's historical and contemporary role in the Palestinian question, the range of opinion in Israel concerning the Palestinians is less rigid and monolithic.[20]

Trends in Palestinian scholarship

It would be naive, if not intellectually dishonest, to absolve Arab writers and ideologists from some responsibility for the current predicament of the Palestinians, and the impasse in which Palestinian–Israeli relations find themselves. However, this impasse must be looked at within its historical context. It is accurate to say that whatever studies Arab writers on pre-1948 Palestine carried out during the time of Zionist colonization and British occupation, they were limited in their scope; on the whole they did not match the output of experienced Zionist writers of the time whose skills and orientations were European in origin.[21] Arab writers did not have among them the equivalents of Ruppin,[22] Granott,[23] Bonné[24] and Gruenbaum,[25] not to mention the more influential writers of key Zionist ideology such as Herzl, Weizmann, Gordon, Borochov, Jabotinsky and Ben-Gurion. While among the former group there were those who wrote what became in Western circles standard works on the land-tenure system, the demography, and economics of Palestine, it was another group of writers who focused primarily on the sociological features of the 'Arabs of Eretz Israel'. Among the known writers of this genre, we note Waschitz,[26] Patai[27] and Shimoni.[28]

The fact that most of the former professional writers. in particular Ruppin, Granott and Gruenbaum, were active Zionists – and occupied high positions in the Jewish Agency in charge of colonization in Palestine – mattered little to Western researchers. In all likelihood, and for a very long time, their works were considered to be *the* authentic interpretations of Palestinian society.

It is almost a truism to say that ideas and theories are best understood in their social context. Mannheim's[29] notion of the socially unattached, free-floating intellectuals is of questionable validity, paritcularly when examined in the context of the plethora of Zionist-Western writings on Palestine. We are not implying here that the Arab interpretation of Palestinian history is, *by definition*, more valid than a Zionist account of the Palestinian experience. Our point is that ideas about society flourish when they are presented in a dialectical fashion. This controversial, or oppositionary, interpretation of Palestinian society has been traditionally lacking. The monopoly exercised by Zionist writers is not to be understood solely in terms of their ideological commitments, but also, as we have shown them in Chapter 4, in terms of the frameworks of analysis adopted. Usually these frameworks have relegated the study of the Palestinians to the decoding of their cultural and psychological make-up at the expense of studying objective historical factors which would account for the retarding impact of Zionism and British imperialism on Palestinian social development.

As we have seen throughout this study, key assumptions which underlie the reasoning of Zionist writers on pre-1948 Palestine are many; they range from assumptions on issues of political history to those on demography and land ownership. I have singled out for recapitulation two sociological features of such key assumptions. First to be noted is the nature of the social process surrounding the class transformation of the Palestinians from peasantry to proletariat. A sophisticated elaboration of this social process by some writers runs as follows: the pull of the Palestinian peasants to the city and urban centres of Palestine was due to land tenure and inheritance systems which, coupled with the large size of peasant families, put the economic viability of the land in jeopardy. In this manner, writers such as Carmi and Rosenfeld[30] provide a detailed examination of the process of proletarianization among the Palestinian peasantry, pointing to the important finding that such a process did not bring with it a new socio-economic order to the Arab village, but perpetuated existing traditional social structures. However, what Carmi and Rosenfeld ignore is the role of Zionist colonization in dispossessing Arabs of their land, the role of British tax and concession policies in encouraging intensive agriculture and industrialization, and the general impact of a competitive, well-financed Zionist sector on existing Arab economies.

A second argument, related in part to the one above, is based on the premise of two independent sectors, the Arab and the Jewish, with no functional relationship between them. To the extent that the impact of the Jewish sector on the Arab is acknowledged, it is only to note that the presence of a modern and technologically advanced settler group is likely to have a 'revolutionary' impact upon Arab society in terms of abolishing feudalism, raising living standards and transmitting new technological knowledge; above all, it is implied that the presence of a modern regime will speed up the withering away of the 'Asiatic mode of production', to replace it by a modern-industrial one. In this, class antagonisms will be the main catalyst in a societal transformation which will signal the advent of an egalitarian social order devoid of feudal exploitation.[31]

Before commenting on these claims, we would like to provide a disclaimer to the orthodox position, the converse of our own, which postulates that the Palestinians in pre-1948 were colonized by either the British or the Zionist settlers, or both, in the *classical* sense of colonialism. While it is true that the attitudes and orientations of most Zionists settlers toward the indigenous Arab population in Palestine exhibited a sense of superiority characteristic of white settlers in Africa and elsewhere, the main socio-political structure had other, more important features. The situation in pre-1948 was more like a dual society, with one society, mainly the Zionist, deriving benefits from the sponsoring imperial power at the expense of the other, namely the indigenous Palestinian society.

The fact that the Zionist colonization of Palestine did not exhibit features characteristic of classical colonialism does not necessarily uphold the alternative thesis of separate developments or even the uniqueness of Zionism. As Weinstock remarks:[32]

> But for the Arab peasants, the *fellaheen*, the policy of exclusively Jewish labour had dramatic results. It meant not only that they were evicted from the land they tilled after the Arab landowner had sold it to the Zionist concerns, but also that they were prevented on principle from finding employment on the Jewish farms, or in industry. Likewise, the policy of Jewish produce [i.e., the boycotting of Arab produce] impeded the development of an Arab bourgeoisie and proletariat in Palestine. Thus Arab resentment to Zionist colonization could be channelled into neither bourgeois nationalism nor proletarian socialism, since the social classes that normally convey these policies remained embryonic owing to the Zionist segregationalism which blocked their emergence.

Similarly one cannot endorse Shlomo Avineri's thesis[33] that the main reason behind the stagnation of the Middle East was the 'indirect' form of British imperialism which relied on recruitment of foreign élites, while at the same time perpetuating traditional social systems, in particular the Asiatic mode of production. Accepting this interpretation of the Middle East in general and Palestine in particular leads one to ascribe a positive role to Zionism and, later, to Israel in terms of modernizing the class structure of Arab society. Avineri sees in Israeli society a catalyst in bringing about the sort of change in the Middle East which, because of its peculiar features, British imperialism did not succeed in doing, namely the dismantling of feudalism.

As Turner points out, this type of analysis, which allocates to Zionism the role of a revolutionizing force, is fraught with problems. Both British imperialism and Zionism played a direct role in 'stunting' the development of Arab society. Moreover, Israel's class structure, with the nature of the *Yishuv* during the British Mandate, does not resemble that of European-capitalist societies. Traditionally the means of production in Zionist Palestine were not dominated by a property-owning bourgeoisie. Hence, according to Turner, there is no parallel with Marx's model of capitalism or even with his discussion of British imperialism in India. The situation is closer to Britain's relationship with Ireland.[34]

> For a number of reasons (in terms of colonization, depending on foreign capital and the peculiarities of the class structure) Israel is a society which is very different from Marx's theoretical model of capitalism; therefore the attempt to form an analogy between the Middle East and India or between indirect Chinese rule and Middle East imperialism is not only superficial, but misleading. Just as Marx noted a 'stunting effect' in Britain's relationship with Ireland so one might find a stunted development in the Middle East under the dual impact of British and Israeli colonization.

It should be stated here that in no way do we discount the influence of internal features of Arab village life such as religion, traditional familial and kinship systems, and inheritance and land tenure. What is problematic in the study of pre-1948 Palestine, and what, in our view, has received little attention so far, is the role that political and economic forces play in *maintaining* a traditional social order. Consider the *hamula* as one such institution. Its perpetuation during the Mandate (and later on in the State of Israel) is due in large measure to the manipulative policies which the British and the Israelis directed toward the Arab sector, and the *distorted* form of urbanization and class transformation by which peasants were forced off the land to become rural proletariat. Concerning the latter factor, Arab urbanization in Palestine more closely resembled a process of partial ruralization of the cities – a phenomenon encountered in many Third World cities nowadays – with two noted features: first, the bulk of the proletariat remained in the village;

second, the city-based industries were mostly non-Arab controlled, belonging to either the British, the Zionist settlers, or international concerns.

The war of 1948 had two main consequences. First, it saw the exodus of a large proportion of the Palestinians to become refugees and displaced persons in the Arab countries and other parts of the world. Second, it reduced the status of the Palestinians in their own homeland to that of a minority who, until 1967, lived under Israeli, Jordanian and Egyptian rule. The 1967 war resulted in bringing more than half of the Palestinians under Israeli control.

As for the Palestinians living in pre-1967 Israel, their situation could be characterized by the following: (1) the continuation of the proletarianization process which had begun in pre-1948 Palestine; (2) the institutionalization of effective systems of social, political and economic control legitimated by Zionist ideology; (3) further land expropriation and marginalization of the Arab sector; (4) the ensuring of Jewish dominance in the face of the high Palestinian rate of natural increase, through the passage of both the Law of Return and the Nationality Act, which grant automatic Israeli citizenship to Jews anywhere in the world who would like to settle in Israel on religious grounds; (5) an efficient system of co-option whereby Zionist hegemony is ensured through selective occupational recruitment of Palestinians as long as their allegiance to Zionist political culture is assured; and (6) cultural domination, via the school system and mass media, through state manipulation of Palestinian national and political symbols.

The model of internal colonialism, when applied to the Arabs in Israel, differs from the dual society model, applicable to pre-1948 Palestine. As we noted earlier, in the pre-1948 period the Palestinians did not constitute an internally colonized minority. However, the internal colonialism model also differs significantly from the fashionable models of cultural and social pluralism which are the favourite of most Israeli and Western social scientists. The thrust in Israeli research on the Arabs in Israel is to focus on their cultural and psychological characteristics, and to attribute the economic stagnation of the Arab sector to something akin to Patai's 'Arab mind'.[35] This obsession with cultural traits at the expense of historical factors is symptomatic not only of the treatment of the Arabs, but also of established trends among Western social scientists who write in the tradition of 'modernization' in the Third World. The policy implications of such a theoretical perspective are clear: the resolution of the Palestinian–Israeli conflict is to be sought in 'educating' the Arabs in a modern culture which would appreciate the significance of an advanced Israel and would enable Arabs to adjust better to its modern culture.

In spite of the disadvantaged position of the Arabs in Israel, compared to the Jewish population, typical Zionist writings on the subject do not hesitate to stress that the position of the Arabs in Israel is, relatively speaking, better than that of their Palestinian brethren outside Israel.

Neither of these assumptions is borne out by empirical evidence. As regards the former claim, the converse appears to be true: the higher the level of education among the Arabs in Israel, the more aware and dissatisfied about their status in Israeli society they become. Militancy among Arab intellectuals and university students in Israel provides a case in point.[36] As for the latter claim, that the Palestinian Arabs are better off, recent data available on Palestinians outside Israel, compared to those inside it, produce a different picture. At the university level, the attainment of the Palestinians in the occupied territories, as well as in the Arab world and outside it, far exceeds that shown by the Arabs in Israel. This myth has recently been exposed by two Israeli Arab researchers.[37] They point out that even at the primary school level the percentage of Palestinian youth in the occupied territories attending schools is similar to, if not higher than, that shown by Israeli Arabs. More important, these researchers find that the earning power and occupational attainment of Palestinians living outside Israel surpass those of the Arabs in Israel. As Said and Zahlan point out,[38] it is estimated that of every ten high-level manpower persons in the Arab world one is a Palestinian. If studies of patterns of upward mobility were to be carried out on Palestinians in general, there is no doubt that the results would show Palestinians to have the highest rates of upward mobility in the Middle East as a whole. It is in this context that the isolated cultural and psychological explanations of the disadvantaged position of the Arabs in Israel become of dubious validity.

Unlike the cultural model of pluralism, and other variants of it, the internal colonialism model accounts for possible politicization and reaction against forms of domination. Rather than projecting a static and segmentalized image of a pacified-controlled minority, it leaves the possibility open that a structural transformation in the status of the colonized minority, such as proletarianization, is likely to bring about a change in its level of awareness and consciousness.

It is ironic that in contrast to research on the Arabs in Israel, contemporary research on the Palestinians in the Arab world is rather limited, in spite of an upsurge in Palestinian research facilities. In the view of this author, there are two main reasons for this. First, there is a lack of comprehensive and reliable national statistics provided by the host countries concerned, and, secondly, for a long time the Palestinian problem has been defined first and foremost as a pan-Arab problem. This definition, in turn, defined *ipso facto* the Palestinians in the Arab world as non-problematic. Their political identity has been subsumed for a long time in the all-embracing melting pot of Arab nationalism. Almost every Arab government championed the cause of the Palestinians, not necessarily as perceived by the Palestinians, but as perceived by the Arab governments concerned. Here lies the crux of the research problem faced by the Palestinians until the middle or late 1960s when the Palestine Liberation Organization assumed the role of spokesman for the Palestinians. The rise of the Palestine Liberation Organization signalled the articulation of the Palestinian problem as seen by Palestinians themselves.

Studies on the educational attainments of the Palestinians,[39] case studies of youth politicization,[40] patterns of occupational recruitment,[41] Palestinian camp life,[42] and sociological studies of certain Palestinian communities in the Arab world[43] are few in number but significant nevertheless. This research, conducted mostly by Palestinians, is problem-oriented. It sets out to investigate Palestinians' potential in meeting the needs of a national community. Some of this research has exposed a few popular myths. First it has shown that the treatment of Palestinians in the Arab world has not been benevolent, as popular wisdom has it, but resembles, in terms of class discrimination, and regional and political differentiation, the situation of other oppressed minorities throughout the world.[44] The sooner this fact is recognized, the easier it becomes to acknowledge the pluralist character of Arab society, taking us away from the mythical image of a homogeneous Arab society.

The emphasis on the 'oneness' of Arab society (although it is valid linguistically and culturally) has taken its toll at the expense of the Palestinians. It is precisely this argument which is advanced by Israeli policy-makers and by most Israeli Orientalists. Since the Palestinians are an inseparable part of a homogeneous Arab society, the argument goes, why do not the Arab regimes absorb the Palestinians into what amounts to an extension of their 'natural' environment?

A second false claim, to which we alluded earlier, questions the validity of the notion of traditionalism when applied to the Palestinian case. Neither the Palestinians' level of politicization, nor their sense of motivation, bears witness to a passive and backward social structure, as postulated by conventional writers on the Third World.

Research on the Palestinians is still in its infancy. It is designed to map out the basic historical and demographic features of the Palestinians in order to gather data for future planning. Here too research on the Palestinians has to guard against the fetishism of abstracted empiricism. A research methodology has to be developed in line with the problem at hand. Artificial separation between the researcher and the phenomenon investigated is likely to lead to an imposed definition of and solution to sociological problems. The ultimate objective of such research must be to tap the authentic experience of the Palestinians. Here the Object–Subject dichotomy dissolves. To borrow from Freire's[45] methodology, the existential being, the Subject, becomes the central unit of analysis in a research process designed to unfold and at the same time transform the world one experiences – this is the essence of praxis. The purpose of the research must be neither to mystify nor to overwhelm the masses. Through dialogical training, the usual us–them dichotomy in research is replaced by reciprocal interaction between the researcher and the Subjects. It is, as Paulo Freire remarks, research for and with the people, but not about the people.

Conclusions

It is a fact that in spite of various episodes of large-scale protest and an increasing level of politicization, the Arabs in Israel have not risen *en masse* to protest their situation. Isolated involvement – with guerrilla attacks mounted from the outside into Israel, particularly those which took place in the late 1960s and early 1970s – notwithstanding, the Arabs in Israel have not posed any significant military or political threat to the Zionist State. From the evidence presented in this study, the following factors could be advanced to account for this phenomenon:

(1) The implementation of an effective system of co-option and control which segments an already sectionalized Arab society.

(2) The presence of a distorted form of Arab class structure which did not develop along normal lines characterized by either a militant Arab proletariat or even a bourgeoisie.

(3) The application of a conscious state policy of exclusion by which the Arabs are kept out of the Zionist institutional framework of the state which shapes the dominant ideology and disposes of the states resources.

(4) The operation of various powerful Zionist institutions outside the formal boundaries of the Israeli political system, such as the Jewish Agency and the Jewish National Fund, which give the Zionist movement an extra state immunity. (It is the resources of these institutions which make it possible to colonize Arab land and to actualize the Zionist plan. Owing to the fact that they are cut off from the rest of the Arab world and that they occupy a subordinate position

in the power structure of Israeli society, it is unlikely that the Arabs in Israel will be able to exert a leverage against the concerted efforts of the Zionist movement.)

(5) The military superiority of Israel and the state of disarray in which the so-called 'Arab confrontation states' find themselves, and the dependent position of the Palestine Liberation Organization *vis-à-vis* these Arab regimes. (All this makes it very unlikely that the Arabs in Israel will receive any significant impetus from outside sources in the form of a weakening of the existing Zionist hegemony.)

Implications

These conclusions dictate the following four options, if the situation of the Arabs in Israel is to be resolved:

(1) to continue to work within the Israeli framework by intensifying the demands for civil and political rights, hoping for an eventual alliance with certain strata of Jewish opinion inside Israel;

(2) to demand that international intervention in the form of United Nations as well as superpower pressure be brought to bear in order to effect a change in the Zionist policy toward its Arab population – this pressure must also be directed against the source, namely the numerous Zionist organizations in the West, without whose unquestioning support Israel will not be able to pursue its current policy toward the Arab population;

(3) to hope for a radical change in the structure of political institutions in the Arab world which would resolve the Israeli–Arab conflict in such a way as to settle the entire Palestinian issue once and for all;

(4) to give the Palestinian Arabs in Israel the right of self-determination in terms of whether or not they would want to continue to live under the *status quo*, to be granted regional autonomy, or, if they wish, to secede completely from the existing framework.

There is no doubt that if the *status quo* remains, the Arabs will continue to be dispossessed of their land, even though Zionist policies of dispossession may contribute to further politicization of the Arabs. As a matter of fact, unless international pressure is brought to bear, the Jewish Agency and the Jewish National Fund will continue to work for the 'ingathering of the exiles' at the expense of the Palestinians in Israel. The immediate priority must be to guarantee to the

Arabs in Israel the right to self-determination. Neither liberal Israeli public opinion, nor international pressure, has so far managed to effect a change in the basic Zionist attitude toward the Palestinian question.

Notes

Chapter 1 The problem stated

1 Seymour Martin Lipset, 'Education and equality: Israel and the United States compared', *Society*, March/April 1974, p. 65.

2 Chaim Adler, 'Social stratification and education in Israel', *Comparative Education Review*, vol. 18, no. 1, 1974, p. 12. Similarly Eva Etzioni-Halevy of Tel Aviv University decided to leave the Arabs out of her analysis in a topic dealing with protest and democracy, 'Protest politics in the Israeli democracy', *Political Science Quarterly*, vol. 90, no. 3, 1974, pp. 497–520.

3 The study, *Some Problems of Educating a National Minority* (*A Study of Israeli Education for Arabs*), was funded by the US Department of Health, Education and Welfare for a period from 1 October 1965 to 30 September 1968.

4 Raphael Patai, *On Culture Contact and Its Workings in Modern Palestine*, no. 67, American Anthropological Association Series, vol. 49, 1947; *Israel between East and West*, Philadelphia, The Jewish Publication Society of America, 1953; *The Arab Mind*, New York, Scribner, 1973.

5 Emanuel Marx, *Bedouin of the Negev*, Manchester University Press, 1967.

6 Erik Cohen, 'Arab boys and tourist girls in a mixed Jewish-Arab community', *International Journal of Comparative Sociology*, vol. XII, no. 4, 1971, pp. 217–33; 'Mixed marriage in an Israeli town', *Jewish Journal of Sociology*, vol. XI, no. 1, 1969, pp. 41–50; *Bibliography of Arabs and Other Minorities in Israeli*, Givat Haviva, Israel, Centre for Arab and Afro-Asian Studies, 1974.

7 Yochanan Peres, 'Ethnic relations in Israel', *American Journal of Sociology*, vol. LXXXVI, no. 6, 1971, pp. 1021–47; 'The orientation of Arab students towards Jews as individuals and towards Israel as a state', *Megamot*, vol. 3, 1970, pp. 254–61 (Hebrew); 'Modernization and nationalism in the identity of the Israeli Arabs', *Middle East Journal*, vol. XXLV, no. 4, 1970, pp. 479–92; with Avishai Ehrilick and

Nira Yuval-Davis, 'National education for Arab youth in Israel: a comparative analysis of curricula', *Jewish Journal of Sociology*, vol. XII, no. 2, 1970, pp. 147–63; with Zipporah Levy, 'Ethnic stereotypes in Israel', *Race*, vol. IV, no. 4, 1969, pp. 479–92; with Nira Yuval-Davis, 'Some observations on the national identity of the Israeli Arabs', *Human Relations*, vol. XXII, no. 3, 1969, pp. 219–33.

8 Emmanuel Yalan, Chaim Finkel, Louis Guttman and Chanock Jacobsen, *The Modernization of Traditional Agricultural Villages: Minority Village in Israel*, Publications on Problems of Regional Development, no. 11, Settlement Study Centre, Rehovot, Israel, 1972.

9 Henry Rosenfeld, 'An overview and critique of the literature on rural politics and social change', in Richard Antoun and Iliya Harik (eds.), *Rural Politics and Social Change in the Middle East*, Bloomington, Ind., Indiana University Press, 1972, pp. 45–72; 'Change, barriers to change, and contradictions in the Arab village family', *American Anthropologist*, vol. LXX, no. 4, 1968, pp. 732–52; 'The Arab village proletariat', *New Outlook*, vol. 5, 1962, pp. 7–16; *They Were Peasants*, Hakibbutz Hameuchad, 1964 (Hebrew); 'Non-hierarchical, hierarchical and masked reciprocity in an Arab village', *Social Research Quarterly*, vol. 1, 1972 (Hebrew); with Shulamit Carmi, 'The origins of the process of proletarianization and urbanization of Arab peasants in Palestine', *Annals of the New York Academy of Sciences*, vol. 220, no. 6, 1974, pp. 470–85.

10 Leonard Weller, *Sociology in Israel*, Westport, Conn., Greenwood Press, 1974.

11 Haya Gratch (ed.), *Twenty-Five Years of Social Research in Israel: A Review of the Work of the Israel Institute of Applied Social Research*, Jerusalem, Academic Press, 1973.

12 See Noam Chomsky, *Peace in the Middle East?*, New York, Vintage Books, 1974.

13 S. Eisenstadt, *Israeli Society*, London, Weidenfeld & Nicolson, 1970.

14 S. Eisenstadt, Rivkah Bar Yosef and Chaim Adler, *Integration and Development in Israel*, New York, Praeger, 1970.

15 Two important governmental committees were set up to examine the situation of Oriental Jews. The first, set up in 1971, was headed by D. Horowitz, Governor of the Bank of Israel; the second committee, headed by Professor Israel Katz of the Hebrew University, dealt specifically with Oriental youth. Both committees were appointed by the Prime Minister's office. The findings of the latter committee generated heated debates among social scientists and policy-makers. Its recommendations were summarized in *Davar*, 25 June 1973. It must be pointed out that the Agranat Committee on Juvenile Delinquency also highlighted the position of Oriental youth in Israeli society. The Oriental–European cleavage has been viewed from social, economic, psychological and other facets. Concerning the economic comparisons, see Shaul Zarhi and A. Achiezra, 'Gaps in Israeli society', *Ba-Shaa'r*, January/February 1973, pp. 22–30 (Hebrew); Georges R. Tamarin tackles the psychological aspects in *The Israeli Dilemma: Essays on a Warfare State*, Rotterdam University Press,

1973; Sammy Smooha deals with the social-structural differentiations i n'Pluralism: a study of intergroup relations in Israel', unpublished PhD dissertation, University of California, Los Angeles, 1973.

16 See E. Zureik, 'Arab youth in Israel: their situation and status perceptions', *Journal of Palestine Studies*, vol. III, no. 3, 1974, pp. 97–108.

17 In 1972, S. Toledano, the Prime Minister's Adviser on Arab Affairs, prepared a comprehensive report on the status of the Arab minority living in Israel since 1948; the report dealt extensively with the crisis of Arab intellectuals who are finding it difficult to secure employment that matches their occupational and educational qualifications. For extensive discussions of the report, see the Hebrew dailies *Yediot Aharonot*, 1 September 1972; *Ha-Aretz*, 28 August 1972; *Maariv*, 1 September 1972. In its supplement of 15 December 1975, *Maariv* provides a lengthy article about the dilemmas facing Arab intellectuals in Israel.

18 For a lucid discussion of the various strands of theoretical perspectives in the study of race relations, see John Rex, 'The problem of sociology of race relations', in *Race, Colonialism and the City*, London, Routledge & Kegan Paul, 1973, pp. 193–223. A useful discussion of the issue of conflict versus consensus in American race relations is provided by L. Paul Metzger, 'American sociology and Black assimilation: conflicting perspectives', *American Journal of Sociology*, vol. 76, no. 4, 1971, pp. 627–47.

Chapter 2 The theoretical framework

1 Cited in A. C. Forrest, *The Unholy Land*, Old Greenwich, Conn., The Devin-Adair Company, 1974, p. xiii. Referring to the treatment even a Jew is liable to encounter in the West upon criticizing Israel, Noah Lucas remarks, 'If one dared to criticize any aspect of Israeli policy in a Jewish forum in those years [immediately after 1967], one risked being ostracized from the community' ('Zionism mark III', *New Outlook*, vol. 19, 1976, pp. 7–8). It is common knowledge to anyone familiar with Israeli politics that it is easier to voice such criticism in Israel than it is in the West, particularly where doctrinaire Zionists capitalize upon the sentiments of Jewish communities who are largely informed upon the Middle East conflict through propaganda organizations of the Israeli missions overseas and local Zionist groups.

2 Peter Worsley, *The Third World*, London, Weidenfeld & Nicolson, 1968, p. 268.

3 Peter Berger, *Invitation to Sociology*, New York, Doubleday, 1969.

4 *Ibid.*, pp. 38–9.

5 Maxime Rodinson, *Israel: A Colonial-Settler State?*, New York, Pathfinder Press, 1973, p. 36.

6 See, for example, John Horton, 'Order and conflict theories of social problems', *American Journal of Sociology*, vol. 71, 1966, pp. 283–99.

7 Leading exponents of pluralism in American political science are David Truman, *The Governmental Process*, New York, Knopf, 1975; Robert A. Dahl, *Who Governs?*, New Haven, Conn., Yale University

Press, 1966. An application of these ideas and those of functionalism to the sociology of developing countries is provided by Gabriel A. Almond and James S. Coleman (eds), *The Politics of the Developing Areas*, Princeton University Press, 1966. For a critique of pluralism, see C. Wright Mills, *The Sociological Imagination*, London, Oxford University Press, 1974; Milton Mankoff, 'Power in advanced capitalist society: a review essay on recent Marxist criticism of pluralist theory', in Milton Mankoff (ed.), *The Poverty of Progress*, New York, Holt, Rinehart & Winston, 1972.

8 See Claus Mueller, *The Politics of Communication*, London, Oxford University Press, 1973; Michael Mann, 'The social cohesion of liberal democracy', in Milton Mankoff (ed.), *op. cit.*, pp. 399–419; Ralph Miliband, *The State in Capitalist Society*, London, Weidenfeld & Nicolson, 1969, especially pp. 178–264.

9 Ralf Dahrendorf, *Class and Class Conflict in Industrial Society*, Stanford University Press, 1959.

10 Robert Park, *Race and Culture*, Chicago, Free Press, 1950, p. 150.

11 Quoted in John Rex, *Race, Colonialism and the City*, London, Routledge & Kegan Paul, 1973, p. 260; cf. Sami Zubaida (ed.), *Race and Racialism*, London, Tavistock Publications, 1970. With regard to the debate on pluralism, see the special issue of *Race*, vol. XII, no. 4, 1971.

12 Oliver Cox, 'The question of pluralism', *Race*, vol. XII, no. 4, 1971, pp. 385–400.

13 David Lockwood, 'Race, conflict and plural society', in Zubaida (ed.), *op. cit.*, p. 64.

14 Rex, *op. cit.*, pp. 260–1.

15 *Ibid.*, p. 261.

16 *Ibid.*, p. 204.

17 Michael Banton, *Race Relations*, London, Tavistock Publications, 1967.

18 Rex, *op. cit.*, p. 213.

19 P. L. van den Berghe, 'Towards a sociology of Africa', in *Race and Ethnicity*, New York, Basic Books, 1970, pp. 79–93.

20 *Ibid.*, p. 84.

21 *Ibid.*, p. 81.

22 *Ibid.*, p. 84.

23 *Ibid.*, pp. 89–90.

24 Frantz Fanon, *The Wretched of the Earth*, Harmondsworth, Penguin Books, 1970.

25 Heribert Adam, *Modernizing Racial Domination*, Berkeley, University of California Press, 1972.

26 *Ibid.*, p. 5.

27 *Ibid.*, p. 17.

28 *Ibid.*, p. 31.

29 *Ibid.*, p. 66. We are not implying that class and ethnicity are not salient features of Israeli society. The situation of Oriental *vis-à-vis* European Jews reflects an ethnic as well as a class cleavage. See Raphael Rosenzweig and Georges Tamarin, 'Israel's power élite', *Transaction*, vol. 7, July/August 1970, pp. 26–42; Haim Hanegbi,

Moshe Machover and Akiva Orr, 'The class nature of Israeli society', *New Left Review*, January/February 1971, pp. 3–26.

30 Harold Wolpe, 'The theory of internal colonialism: the South African case', in Ivar Oxaal, Tony Barnett and David Booth (eds), *Beyond the Sociology of Development*, London, Routledge & Kegan Paul, 1975, pp. 229–52.

31 *Ibid.*, p. 240.

32 *Ibid.*, p. 244.

33 *Ibid.*, p. 247.

34 *Ibid.*, p. 249.

35 Dale L. Johnson, 'On oppressed classes', in James D. Cockcroft, André Gunder Frank and Dale L. Johnson (eds), *Dependence and Underdevelopment*, New York, Doubleday, 1972, pp. 269–301.

36 *Ibid.*, p. 285.

37 Sanjaya Lall, 'Is "dependence" a useful concept in analyzing underdevelopment?', *World Development*, vol. 13, 1976, pp. 799–800.

38 *Ibid.*, p. 802.

39 *Ibid.*, p. 800.

40 *Ibid.*, p. 803.

41 David McClelland, *The Achieving Society*, Princeton, Van Nostrand Press, 1961.

42 Daniel Lerner, *The Passing of Traditional Society*, New York, Free Press, 1965; see also Morroe Berger, *The Arab World Today*, New York, Doubleday, 1964.

43 For a critique of the Parsonian scheme, see John Rex, *Race Relations in Sociological Theory*, London, Weidenfeld & Nicolson, 1970.

44 André Gunder Frank, 'Sociology of development and underdevelopment of sociology', in Cockcroft *et al.* (eds), *op. cit.*, pp. 321–97.

45 Caroline Hutton and Robin Cohen, 'African peasants and resistance to change: a reconsideration of sociological approaches', in Oxaal *et al.* (eds), *op. cit.*, pp. 105–30.

46 *Ibid.*, p. 123.

47 Harold Wolpe, 'Industrialism and race in South Africa', in Zubaida, (ed.), *op. cit.*, p. 156.

48 *Ibid.*

49 John Rex, 'The concept of race in sociological theory', in Zubaida (ed.), *op. cit.*, pp. 37–8.

50 Herbert Blumer, 'Race prejudice as a sense of group position', *Pacific Sociological Review*, vol. I, no. 1, 1961, pp. 3–7.

51 A. H. Richmond, 'Sociological and psychological explanations of racial prejudice: some light on the controversy from recent researches in Britain', *Pacific Sociological Review*, vol. 4, no. 2, 1961, pp. 63–8.

52 See my 'Major issues in political socialization research', in Elia Zureik and Robert M. Pike (eds), *Socialization and Values in Canadian Society*, vol. I, Toronto, McClelland and Stewart, Carleton Library Series, 1975, pp. 29–56.

53 Bernard Kutner and Norman B. Gordon, 'Cognitive functioning and prejudice: a nine-year follow-up study', *Sociometry*, vol. 27, 1964, pp. 66–74. The results of the initial study were reported in Kutner,

'Patterns of mental functioning associated with prejudice in children', *Psychological Monographs*, vol. 12, no. 7, 1958.

54 T. W. Adorno *et al.*, *The Authoritarian Personality*, New York, Harper & Row, 1964.

55 Kutner and Gordon, *op. cit.*, pp. 73–4.

56 Henri Tajfel, 'Cognitive aspects of prejudice', *Journal of Social Issues*, vol. XXV, no. 4, 1969, pp. 79–97.

57 Mary Goodman, *Race Awareness in Young Children*, London, Collier-Macmillan, further printing 1970.

58 J. K. A. Morland, 'A comparison of race awareness in northern and southern children', *American Journal of Orthopsychiatry*, vol. 36, 1966, pp. 22–31.

59 Judith Porter, *Black Child, White Child, The Development of Racial Attitudes*, Cambridge, Mass., Harvard University Press, 1971.

60 James W. Prothro and C. M. Grigg, 'Fundamental principles of democracy: bases of agreement and disagreement', *Journal of Politics*, vol. 22, 1960, pp. 276–94.

61 John P. Kirscht and Ronald C. Dillehay, *Dimensions of Authoritarianism: A Review of Research and Theory*, Lexington, University of Kentucky Press, 1967, p. 89.

62 Bruno Bettelheim and Morris Janowitz, *Social Change and Prejudice, Including Dynamics of Prejudice*, London, Collier-Macmillan, 1964, p. 162.

63 Cited in Kirscht and Dillehay, *op. cit.*, p. 88.

64 See Adorno *et al.*, *op. cit.*, pp. 169, 184.

65 W. G. Runciman and C. R. Bagley, 'Status consistency, relative deprivation and attitudes to immigrants', *Sociology*, vol. VI, 1969, pp. 359–75; cf. Derek Birrell, 'Relative deprivation as a factor in conflict in Northern Ireland', *Sociological Review*, vol. 20, 1972, pp. 317–43.

66 Gordon Allport, *The Nature of Prejudice*, Cambridge, Mass., Addison-Wesley, 1964, p. 283.

67 E. G. B. Rose *et al.*, *Colour and Citizenship*, London, Oxford University Press, 1969, p. 739.

68 *Ibid.*, p. 557.

69 Fanon, *op. cit.*, pp. 27–84.

70 *Ibid.*, p. 36.

71 *Ibid.*, p. 48.

72 See Paulo Freire, *Pedagogy of the Oppressed*, New York, The Seabury Press, 1970; M. Carnoy, *Education and Cultural Imperialism*, New York, David McKay, 1974.

73 Fanon, *op. cit.*, pp. 111–12.

74 *Ibid.*, p. 109.

75 *Ibid.*, p. 109.

76 Albert Memmi, *The Colonizer and the Colonized*, Boston, Beacon Press, 1967, p. 10.

77 *Ibid.*, p. 30.

78 *Ibid.*, p. 150.

Chapter 3 Arab social structure in pre-1948 Palestine

1 See Noah Lucas, *The Modern History of Israel*, London, Weidenfeld & Nicolson, 1974, p. 23; Neville Mandel, 'Attempts at an Arab–Zionist entente: 1914–1919', *Middle Eastern Studies*, vol. I, 1965, p. 239; Rafael Rosenzweig and Georges Tamarin, 'Israel's power élite', *Transaction*, vol. 7, July/August 1970, p. 26; Arthur Ruppin gives a somewhat higher figure for the Jewish population (34,000) in *The Jewish Fate and the Future*, Westport, Conn., Greenwood Press, 1972 (originally published in 1940), p. 322. I have adopted the lower estimate because of the wider acceptance of this figure. According to Turkish sources cited by Janet Abu-Lughod, there were close to half a million people living in Palestine in the middle of the nineteenth century, with the Jewish population amounting to 5 to 7 per cent. By 1900 there were 50,000 Jews living in Palestine ('The demographic transformation of Palestine', in Ibrahim Abu-Lughod (ed.), *The Transformation of Palestine*, Evanston, Ill., Northwestern University Press, 1971, p. 140).

2 See Neville Mandel, 'Turks, Arabs and Jewish immigration into Palestine, 1882–1914', *Middle Eastern Affairs*, No. 4, St Anthony's Papers, Albert Hourani (ed.), London, Oxford University Press, 1965, pp. 83–4.

3 Cited in Yaacov Ro'i, 'The Zionist Attitude to the Arabs, 1908–1914', *Middle Eastern Studies*, vol. 4, no. 2, 1968, pp. 216–17. It is worth noting that the 1921 Royal Commission of Inquiry reached a similar conclusion, namely that 'there is no inherent anti-Semitism in the country, racial or religious' (*Palestine Disturbances in May 1921*, London, p. 59).

4 Emile Marmorstein, 'European Jews in Muslim Palestine, a review article', *Middle Eastern Studies*, vol. II, 1975, p. 78.

5 See Mandel, 'Turks, Arabs and Jewish immigration . . .', p. 82.

6 Lucas, *op. cit.*, p. 25.

7 Achad Ha-Am, 'The truth from Eretz-Israel', in *Writings of Achad Ha-Am*, Tel Aviv, 1961 (Hebrew).

8 See Rosenzweig and Tamarin, *op. cit.*, p. 28; J. Abu-Lughod, *op. cit.*, p. 141, notes that in 1914, the Jewish population in Palestine amounted to no more than 60,000 out of a total of 689,272, that is to say, slightly less than 10 per cent.

9 Mandel, 'Attempts at an Arab–Zionist entente . . .', p. 239.

10 This point is made by Shlomo Avineri, 'Political and social aspects of Israeli and Arab nationalism', in Michael Curtis, Joseph Neyer, Chaim L. Waxman and Allen Pollack (eds), *The Palestinians, People, History and Politics*, New Brunswick, N.J., Transaction Books, 1975, p. 107.

11 Ruppin, *op. cit.*, p. 335.

12 See Maxime Rodinson, *Israel, A Colonial Settler State?*, New York, Pathfinder Press, 1973; for an attempted rebuttal, see Bernard Avishai, 'Zionist "colonialism": myth and dilemma', *Dissent*, Spring 1975, pp. 125–34.

13 In the words of Rosenzweig and Tamarin, 'The main opposition to these practices [of labour Zionists] came from Brit Shalom (Peace Association) a loose organization whose principal spokesmen were people like philosopher Martin Buber, Yehuda Magnes, first President of the Hebrew University, and Ernst Simon. . . . But none of these men belonged to the leadership group of the second or third wave and their criticisms went largely unheeded. A pattern of moral astigmatism towards the Arabs had already been established' (*op. cit.*, p. 28).

14 *Ibid.*, p. 28.

15 Cited in Arie Bober (ed.), *The Other Israel*, New York, Doubleday, 1972, p. 12.

16 Cited in Glenn Yago, 'Whatever happened to the "Promised Land"?', paper presented at the annual meeting of the society for the Study of Social Problems, New York, 1976, p. 12.

17 See Ian S. Lustick, 'Institutionalized segmentation: one factor in the control of Israel's Arabs', paper delivered at the Middle East Studies Association Conference, Louisville, Kentucky, 1975, pp. 9–10.

18 Yago, *op. cit.*, pp. 11–12.

19 See Rodinson, *op. cit.*, *passim.*: David Waines, *The Unholy War*, Montreal, Chateau Books, 1971; Richard P. Stevens, 'Smuts and Weizmann', *Journal of Palestine Studies*, vol. III, no. 1, 1973, pp. 35–59.

20 Cited in Rodinson, *op. cit.*, p. 43.

21 Vladimir Jabotinsky, 'Evidence submitted to the Palestine Royal Commission 1937', in Walid Khalidi (ed.), *From Haven to Conquest*, Beirut, Institute for Palestine Studies, 1971, p. 325.

22 Cf. Alan R. Taylor, *The Zionist Mind*, Beirut, Institute for Palestine Studies, 1974; and Lucas, *op. cit.*, pp. 3–66.

23 Cf. J. M. N. Jeffries, 'Analysis of the Balfour Declaration'; and Michael Ionides, 'Zionists and the land', in Khalidi, *op. cit.*, pp. 173–88; pp. 255–71.

24 For a discussion of Herzl's opposing views, see L. M. C. van der Hoeven-Leonhard, 'Shlomo and David in Palestine', in Khalidi, *op. cit.*, pp. 115–24. Cf. Alan R. Taylor, 'The theory and practice of Zionism', paper delivered at the Symposium on Zionism, Baghdad University, 1976.

25 Lucas, *op. cit.*, p. 30.

26 Cited in Rosemary Sayigh, 'The Palestinian experience viewed as socialization', unpublished MA thesis, American University of Beirut, 1976, p. 30.

27 Mandel, 'Turks, Arabs and Jewish immigration . . .', p. 85.

28 Cited in Stephen Vines, 'The Zionization of World Jewry', in Uri Davis, Andrew Mack and Nira Yuval-David (eds), *Israel and the Palestinians*, London, Ithaca Press, 1975, p. 231.

29 Cited in Khalidi (ed.), *op. cit.*, p. 92.

30 Cited in Mandel, 'Turks, Arabs and Jewish immigration . . .', p. 95.

31 Cf. Ro'i, *op. cit.*

32 A similar argument is advanced by John Marlowe in his account of the 1936 Arab Rebellion. His interpretation (which we challenge in the text) is based on the premise that the general strike and rebellion

in 1936–9 were middle-class-inspired, for fear that the Jewish presence might weaken the well-to-do Arabs' economic position; in contrast to the middle class, 'the landlords stood to gain something by selling land to the Jews at a high price; the peasants stood to gain by an increased market for their produce; the labourers stood to gain as a result of a great demand for their services' (John Marlowe, *Rebellion in Palestine*, London, The Cresset Press, 1946, pp. 66–7). But as David Waines notes in 'The failure of the nationalist resistance', in I. Abu-Lughod (ed.), *op. cit.*, pp. 207–35, Marlowe modified his views in his later work, *The Seat of Pilate: An Account of the Palestine Mandate*, London, The Cresset Press, 1959, p. 132.

33 See A. Granott, *The Land System in Palestine*, London, Eyre & Spottiswoode, 1952.

34 According to Granott, 'In its legal aspects *Miri* land is looked on to this day as a kind of gift, the transfer of rights as sort of a favour. On this theory the right of ownership remains with the State, only the right of usage and the right of transfer – apart from the transfer by will – are reserved to the owner of the property as long as he tills the ground' (*ibid.*, p. 90).

35 *Ibid.*, p. 202.

36 *Ibid.*, pp. 174–80.

37 *Ibid.*, pp. 45–65. According to A. N. Poliak, 'The [Jewish] banker family of Farhi, whose members had considerable influence on the commercial and political life of the province of Damascus and Acre in the first half of the nineteenth century, held many villages in Palestine as tax-farmers' (*Feudalism in Egypt, Syria, Palestine and Lebanon, 1250–1900*, London, 1939, p. 52).

38 Raphael Patai, '*Musha'a* tenure and co-operation in Palestine', *American Anthropologist*, vol. 51, 1949, p. 438.

39 Cf. Paula Rayman, 'Kibbutzim: The vanguard of Zionist-socialism', in Uri Davis *et al.* (eds), *op. cit.*, pp. 289–300.

40 R. Sayigh, *op. cit.*, pp. 66–7.

41 See John Russell, 'Aspects of Palestine agriculture', in J. B. Hobman (ed.), *Palestine's Economic Future*, London, Lund Humphries, 1946, pp. 116–29. No distinction is made between Jews and non-Jews regarding the average size of farms cited above. Doreen Warriner in *Land and Poverty in the Middle East*, London, Royal Institute of International Affairs, 1948, quotes official figures showing that the average size of farms declined from 12.5 acres in 1931 to 10.5 in 1944 whereas the rural population increased from 648,330 to 872,090 during this period. Bearing in mind that Arab land was concentrated in the hill regions, Arab agriculture could hardly show economic viability and support the rural population when it was estimated that thirty-two acres are needed for minimum subsistence of non-irrigated land and eight or nine acres of half-irrigated land (*ibid.*, p. 57).

42 Based on an unpublished report by Yusuf Sayigh and cited in R. Sayigh, *op. cit.*, p. 69.

43 M. Aumann, 'Land ownership in Palestine: 1880–1948', in Curtis *et al.* (eds), *op. cit.*, p. 23.

44 *Ibid.*, p. 23.

45 Granott, *op. cit.*, p. 278.
46 Aumann, *op. cit.*, p. 23.
47 Warriner, *op. cit.*, p. 65.
48 Ya'akov Firestone, 'Crop-sharing economics in mandatory Palestine – Part I', *Middle Eastern Studies*, vol. II, no. 1, 1975, pp. 3–23; 'Crop-sharing economics in mandatory Palestine – Part II', *ibid.*, vol. II, no. 2, 1975, pp. 175–94.
49 *Ibid.*, part I, p. 6.
50 Yacov Shimoni, *The Arabs of Eretz Israel*, Tel Aviv, Am-Oved, 1946 (Hebrew) acknowledges this factor too, p. 166.
51 Granott, *op. cit.*, p. 29.
52 See Walter Lehn, 'The Jewish National Fund', *Journal of Palestine Studies*, vol. III, no. 4, 1974, pp. 74–96.
53 *Ibid.*, p. 95.
54 Cited in Haim Hanegbi, Moshe Machover and Akiva Orr, 'The class nature of Israeli society', *New Left Review*, January/February 1971, p. 14.
55 See A. L. Tibawi, *Arab Education in Mandatory Palestine*, London, Luzac, 1956, pp. 120–35.
56 Neville Barbour, *Nisi Dominus*, Beirut, Institute for Palestine Studies, 1959, p. 121.
57 Y. Kolton, *Toward the Jewish Question and Its Solution*, Tel Aviv, 1932, p. 68 (Hebrew).
58 *Ibid.*, p. 69.
59 Tom Bowden, 'The politics of the Arab rebellion in Palestine: 1936–1939', *Middle Eastern Studies*, vol. II, no. 2, 1975, p. 168; George Antonius foresaw what Bowden confirmed almost forty years later. In *The Arab Awakening*, New York, Putnam's, 1946 (originally published in 1938), Antonius remarks: 'One of the most prevalent misconceptions is that the trouble in Palestine is the result of an engineered agitation. It is variously attributed to the intrigues of the *Effendi* class, to the political ambitions of the Grand Mufti. . . . The rebellion today is to a greater extent than ever before, a revolt of villagers, and its immediate cause is the proposed scheme of Partition and, more particularly, that aspect of it which envisages the eventual displacement of a large Arab peasantry to make room for the immigrant citizens of the proposed Jewish state' (pp. 405–6).
60 Barbour, *op. cit.*, p. 123.
61 Warriner, *op. cit.*, p. 63. By 1945, it is estimated, 35 per cent of village families were landless (Sayigh, *op. cit.*, p. 69).
62 Aumann, *op. cit.*, p. 27.
63 Yehoshua Porath, 'The land problem in mandatory Palestine', *Jerusalem Quarterly*, no. 1, 1976, pp. 18–27.
64 See S. N. Eisenstadt, *Israeli Society*, London, Weidenfeld & Nicolson, 1970, p. 11.
65 Data taken from John Chapple, 'Jewish land settlement in Palestine', in Khalidi (ed.), *op. cit.*, Appendix I, pp. 841–3. Cf. J. Abu-Lughod, *op. cit.*

66 Fred Gottheil, 'Arab immigration into pre-state Israel: 1922–1931', in Curtis *et al.* (eds), *op. cit.*, pp. 30–40.
67 J. Abu-Lughod, *op. cit.*, p. 142.
68 See *ibid.*, p. 149.
69 Lister G. Hopkins, 'Population', in S. B. Himadeh (ed.), *The Economic Organization of Palestine*, Beirut, 1938, p. 19.
70 See *ibid.*, Table XIV, p. 30.
71 Fred M. Gottheil, 'On the economic development of the Arab region in Israel', in M. Curtis and M. S. Chertoff (eds), *Israel: Social Structure and Change*, New Brunswick, N.J., Transaction Books, 1973, pp. 237–48.
72 See Edward Hagopian and A. B. Zahlan, 'Palestine's Arab population: the demography of the Palestinians', *Journal of Palestine Studies*, vol. III, no. 4, 1974, Table 2, p. 43; cf. Nathian Weinstock, 'The impact of Zionist colonization on Palestine Arab society before 1948', *Journal of Palestine Studies*, vol. II, no. 2, 1973, p. 56.
73 Hagopian and Zahlan, *op. cit.*, Table 3, p. 43.
74 R. Sayigh, *op. cit.*, pp. 55–6.
75 Hagopian and Zahlan, *op. cit.*, p. 41.
76 Quoted in G. Mansur, *The Arab Worker in the Palestine Mandate*, Jerusalem, The Commercial Press, 1936, p. 25.
77 *Ibid.*, p. 25.
78 *Ibid.*, p. 26.
79 See *ibid.*, pp. 25–6.
80 R. Sayigh, *op. cit.*, p. 32.
81 Shimoni, *op. cit.*, p. 200.
82 It is estimated that between 1920 and 1935, Jewish capital investment in Palestine amounted to £P 80 million, forty times greater than the British Mandate investment. By 1938, $1,000,000,000 were spent to settle 400,000 Jews (Barbour, *op. cit.*, p. 137).
83 James Zogby, 'The Palestinian revolt of the 1930's', in Ibrahim Abu-Lughod and Baha Abu-Laban (eds), *Settler Regimes in Africa and the Arab World*, Wilmette, Ill., Medina University Press, 1974, p. 103.
84 Shimoni, *op. cit.*, pp. 185–90.
85 I. M. Smilianskaya, 'From subsistence to market economy, 1850's', in Charles Issawi (ed.), *The Economic History of the Middle East*, University of Chicago Press, 1966, pp. 227–47.
86 See Shimoni, *op. cit.*, p. 190.
87 Cited in *ibid.*, p. 190.
88 See Mansur, *op. cit.*, p. 42.
89 Henry Rosenfeld, 'The Arab village proletariat', *New Outlook*, vol. 13, no. 5, 1962, p. 8.
90 *Ibid.*, p. 15.
91 See John Ruedy, 'Dynamics of land alienation', in I. Abu-Lughod (ed.), *op. cit.*, pp. 119–36.
92 See Don Peretz, 'Palestinian social stratification – the political implications', *Journal of Palestine Studies*, vol. VII, no. 1, 1977, pp. 48–74.
93 R. Sayigh, *op. cit.*, p. 38.

94 Talal Asad, 'Anthropological texts and ideological problems', *Economy and Society*, vol. 4, 1975, p. 262.
95 William Polk, David Stamler and Edmund Asfour, *Backdrop to Tragedy: The Struggle for Palestine*, Boston, Mass., Beacon Press, 1957, p. 335.
96 Kolton, *op. cit.*, p. 75.
97 *Ibid.*, p. 76.
98 Cited in Fawwaz Trabulsi, 'The Palestine problem: Zionism and imperialism in the Middle East', *New Left Review*, no. 57, September/October 1969, p. 179.
99 Shimoni, *op. cit.*, p. 194.
100 See Trabulsi, *op. cit.*, p. 65.
101 *Ibid.*, p. 65.
102 See Warriner, *op. cit.*, p. 62.
103 Kolton, *op. cit.*, p. 82.
104 Shulamit Carmi and Henry Rosenfeld, 'The origins of the process of proletarianization and urbanization of Arab peasants in Palestine', *Annals of New York Academy of Sciences*, vol. 220, 1974, p. 479. It is worth noting that a similar 'cultural' reasoning was given for the South African 'civilized labour' policy and later the 'cost of living' principle which granted higher wages to unskilled whites performing jobs similar to those carried out by blacks (see Robert Davies, 'The White working-class in South Africa', *New Left Review*, vol. 82, 1973, p. 45).
105 *Ibid.*, p. 478.
106 Warriner, *op. cit.*, p. 69.
107 Russell, in Hobman (ed.), *op. cit.*, p. 118.
108 Moshe Smelansky, 'Citrus growers have learnt to cooperate', in M. Buber, J. L. Magnes and E. S. Simon (eds), *Towards Union in Palestine*, Westport, Conn., Greenwood Press, 1972, pp. 57–65.
109 Asfour, in Polk, Stamler and Asfour, *op. cit.*, p. 325.
110 See Shimoni, *op. cit.*, p. 164.
111 See *ibid.*, p. 164.
112 R. Sayigh, *op. cit.*, p. 58.
113 Cited in Eisenstadt, *op. cit.*, p. 73.
114 Similarly, Patricia Garrett notes that while there had been a general rise in the proportion of goods workers received in wages in Palestine, an overall rise from 37 per cent in 1939 to 45 per cent in 1942, she goes on to say: 'Arab workers, however, received a decreasing share. Their wages dropped from 38 per cent of gross output in 1939 to 29 per cent in 1942. Jewish workers, on the other hand, received an increased share – 41 per cent in 1939 and 49 per cent in 1942. Likewise, employees of the state concessions which were mainly in Zionist hands received a larger share – 25 per cent in 1939 and 37 per cent in 1942' ('Orphans of empires: a case study of the Palestinian refugees', unpublished MS thesis, University of Wisconsin, Madison, 1970, pp. 74–5).
115 Asad, *op. cit.*, p. 262.
116 For the impact of tax policies, see *ibid.*, pp. 262–3.

117 For a discussion of various concessions secured by the Zionists from the British, see Adel Hamed El-Jader, 'The policies of granting concessions to large scale operations in Palestine during the mandate', *Palestine Affairs*, no. 55, 1976, pp. 185–205 (Arabic). In a table reproduced from the British census data, Patricia Garrett lists six major concessions made in 1939 and five in 1942. Only one concession, an importing agency, was in the hands of Arabs. The rest were under Zionist control, including the Palestine Salt Company, Palestine Potash and Sulphur Quarries (*op. cit.*, p. 73).

118 See Mansur, *op. cit.*, p. 19, and Appendix no. 7, p. 54.

119 *Ibid.*, p. 19.

120 See Barbour, *op. cit.*, pp. 160–2. For a critical assessment of the Histadrut's policies, see Mansur, 'Attitudes of the Histadrut towards Arab labour', *op. cit.*, pp. 27–9. Like other Zionist institutions, the Histadrut attempted to improve its image among the Arab workers by calling on them in its Arabic newspaper to unite with Jewish workers who are of the same 'common Semitic origin' against 'the colonizing Western nation'. This call for working-class solidarity, based on racial lines, went unheeded by the Arab workers in view of the racialist practices of the Histadrut and its Jewish, exclusivist character. See Barbour, *op. cit.*, pp. 140–1; Mansur, *op. cit.*, p. 40. Marlowe describes the activities of the Histadrut in a similar fashion (*op. cit.*, p. 87).

121 See Michael F. J. McDonnell and R. J. Manning, 'The "town planning" of Jaffa', in Khalidi (ed.), *op. cit.*, pp. 343–51.

122 Barbour, *op. cit.*, p. 133.

123 Mansur, *op. cit.*, p. 34.

124 See Mansur, *op. cit.*, p. 34.

125 See the accounts of this strike in the diaries of the co-founder of the Palestinian union movement, Husni Saleh Al-Khuffash, *The Arab Palestine Labour Movement: Memoirs*, Beirut, Palestine Liberation Organization Research Centre, 1973, pp. 28–81 (Arabic); cf. Mansur, *op. cit.*, p. 31.

126 Y. Waschitz, *The Arabs in Palestine*, Tel Aviv, Sifriat Poalim, 1947 (Hebrew), p. 175.

127 Kolton, *op. cit.*, pp. 68–82.

128 Barbour, *op. cit.*, p. 196.

129 Quoted in Yago, *op. cit.*, p. 7.

130 David Ben-Gurion, 'Britain's contribution to arming the Hagana', in Khalidi (ed.), *op. cit.*, p. 372. See also, on the illegal involvement of the British commander Orde Wingate in training the Hagana forces, *ibid.*, pp. 375–82; and for Ben-Gurion's praise of Wingate, *ibid.*, pp. 382–7.

131 Concerning the various debates surrounding the Arab exodus in 1948, see Lucas, *op. cit.*, pp. 252–3 and pp. 460–1; also Walid Khalidi, 'Plan Dalet', *Middle East Forum*, November 1961, pp. 22–8.

132 Cited in Asad, *op. cit.*, p. 265.

133 See Tibawi, *op. cit.*, pp. 171–75; p. 227.

134 Trabulsi, *op. cit.*, p. 64.

135 Tibawi, *op. cit.*, pp. 162–6.
136 *Ibid.*, p. 169.
137 Quoted in Barbour, *op. cit.*, p. 95.
138 See Tibawi, *op. cit.*, pp. 175–6.
139 See *ibid.*, pp. 177–8.
140 *Ibid.*, p. 177.
141 Hagopian and Zahlan, *op. cit.*, Table 7, p. 47.
142 See *ibid.*, Table 8, p. 48.

Chapter 4 The Arabs in Israeli social science writings

1 S. N. Eisenstadt, 'Israel before and after the War of Yom Kippur', *Gesher*, vol. XIX, nos. 3–4, 1973, pp. 7–15 (Hebrew).
2 See Sh. Zarhi and A. Achiezra, 'Gaps in Israeli society', *Ba-Sha'ar*, January/February 1973, pp. 22–30 (Hebrew).
3 Georges R. Tamarin, *The Israeli Dilemma: Essays on a Warfare State*, Rotterdam University Press, 1973.
4 Nathan Weinstock, 'The impact of Zionist colonization on Palestine Arab society before 1948', *Journal of Palestine Studies*, vol. II, no. 2, 1973, pp. 50–63.
5 Maxim Ghilan, *How Israel Lost its Soul*, Harmondsworth, Penguin Books, 1974.
6 The same theme appears in other writings, notably Maxime Rodinson, *Israel: A Colonial Settler State?*, New York, Monad Press, 1973; A. Bober (ed.), *The Other Israel*, New York, Doubleday, 1972; and Sabri Jiryis, *The Arabs in Israel*, Beirut, Lebanon, The Institute for Palestine Studies, 1973 (Arabic) (an English translation of this updated version is published by Monthly Review Press, 1976); Fouzi El-Asmar, *To be an Arab in Israel*, London, Frances Pinter, 1975; Felicia Langer, *With My Own Eyes*, London, Ithaca Press, 1975; Uri Davis, Andrew Mack and Nira Yuval-Davis (eds), *Israel and the Palestinians*, London, Ithaca Press, 1975; Noam Chomsky, *Peace in the Middle East?*, New York, Vintage Books, 1974, and 'Israel and the Palestinians', *Socialist Revolution*, vol. 5, 1975, pp. 45–86, and notes pp. 131–41.
7 S. N. Eisenstadt, *Israeli Society*, London, Weidenfeld & Nicolson, 1970.
8 *Ibid.*, p. 5.
9 Eisenstadt, 'Israel before . . .', p. 8.
10 *Ibid.*, p. 13.
11 Eisenstadt, 'Israel before . . .', p. 10.
12 Eisenstadt, *Israeli Society*, p. 675.
13 Eisenstadt, 'The sociological structure of the Jewish community in Palestine', *Jewish Social Studies*, vol. X, no. 2, 1948, pp. 3–18.
14 Eisenstadt, *Israeli Society*, p. 401.
15 *Ibid.*, p. 394.
16 Moshe Lissak, *Social Mobility in Israel*, Jerusalem, Israel Universities Press, 1969.
17 *Ibid.*, p. 4.

18 *Ibid.*, p. 2.
19 *Ibid.*, p. 27.
20 Sammy Smooha, 'Pluralism: a study of intergroup relations in Israel', unpublished PhD dissertation, University of California, Los Angeles, 1973.
21 Yochanan Peres, 'Ethnic relations in Israel', *American Journal of Sociology*, vol. LXXVI, no. 6, 1971, pp. 1021–47.
22 Lissak, *op. cit.*, p. 61.
23 *Ibid.*, p. 62.
24 See *ibid.*, p. 64.
25 Frank Parkin, *Class, Inequality and Political Order*, London, Paladin, 1972.
26 Lissak, *op. cit.*, pp. 64–6.
27 *Ibid.*, p. 68.
28 *Ibid.*, p. 71.
29 *Ibid.*, pp. 99–100.
30 Smooha, *op. cit.*, p. 66.
31 *Ibid.*, pp. 50–1.
32 *Ibid.*, p. 123.
33 *Ibid.*, pp. 79–80.
34 Arieh Tartakower, 'The making of Jewish statehood in Palestine', *Jewish Social Studies*, vol. X, 1948, no. 3, pp. 207–22, and 'The sociology of political life in Israel', *Jewish Social Studies*, vol. 22, no. 1, 1960, pp. 83–96.
35 Albert Memmi, 'Zionism, Israel and the Third World', *Bi-Tefutsot Ha-Golah*, nos. 2, 4, 1972, pp. 22–24 (Hebrew).
36 B. Avishai, 'Zionist "colonialism": myth and dilemma', *Dissent*, Spring 1975, pp. 125–34.
37 Noah Lucas, *The Modern History of Israel*, London, Weidenfeld & Nicolson, 1974.
38 Tartakower, 'The making of Jewish statehood . . .', p. 208.
39 *Ibid.*, p. 201.
40 Cited in William Quandt, Fuad Jabber and Ann Mosely Lesch, *The Politics of Palestinian Nationalism*, Berkeley, University of California Press, 1973, p. 12.
41 Tartakower, 'The sociology of political life . . .', p. 89.
42 Albert Memmi, *The Colonizer and the Colonized*, Boston, Mass., Beacon Press, 1967.
43 *Ibid.*, p. 38.
44 Rodinson, *op. cit.*
45 Memmi, *op. cit.*, p. 27.
46 Avishai, *op. cit.* p. 41.
47 Achad Ha-Am, 'The truth from Eretz Israel', in *Writings of Achad Ha-Am*, Tel Aviv, pp. 25–6 (Hebrew).
48 Avishai, *op. cit.*, p. 127.
49 Alan R. Taylor, *The Zionist Mind*, Beirut, Institute for Palestine Studies, 1974, p. 103. Cf. Lucas, *op. cit.*, p. 141. For a perceptive treatment of the early Zionist attitudes toward the Arabs of Palestine,

see 'The Arab problem', in Jay Gonen, *A Psychohistory of Zionism*, New York, Mason/Charter, 1975, pp. 179–212.

50 Avishai, *op. cit.*, p. 130.

51 Cited in 'Education for Zionism', *Bi-Tefutsot Ha-Golah*, nos. 67, 68, 1973, pp. 54–76 (Hebrew).

52 Avishai, *op. cit.*, p. 133.

53 S. M. Lipset, 'Education and equality: Israel and the United States compared', *Society*, March/April 1974, p. 66.

54 Avishai, *op. cit.*, p. 133.

55 Cited in Yosef Waschitz, 'Commuters and entrepreneurs', *New Outlook*, vol. 18, 1975, p. 46.

56 Lucas, *op. cit.*, p. 119.

57 *Ibid.*, p. 157.

58 Cf. Edward Said, 'Shattered myths', in Naseer H. Aruri (ed.), *Middle East Crucible*, Wilmette, Ill., Medina University Press International, 1975, pp. 408–47.

59 Raphael Patai, *Israel between East and West*, Philadelphia, The Jewish Publication Society of America, 1953.

60 Sol Kugelmass, Amia Lieblich and D. Bossik, 'Patterns of intellectual ability in Jewish and Arab children in Israel', *Journal of Cross-Cultural Psychology*, vol. 5, 1974, pp. 184–98.

61 Amia Lieblich, Sol Kugelmass and Chedva Ehrlich, 'Patterns of intellectual ability in Jewish and Arab children in Israel: II, urban matched samples', *Journal of Cross-Cultural Psychology*, vol. 6, no. 2, 1975, pp. 218–26.

62 Raphael Patai, *The Arab Mind*, New York, Scribner, 1973.

63 *Ibid.*, p. 298.

64 *Ibid.*, pp. 299–300.

65 Raphael Patai, *On Culture Contact and its Workings in Modern Palestine*, American Anthropological Association Monographs, vol. 49, no. 67, 1947.

66 Benjamin Beit-Hallahmi, 'Some psychological and cultural factors in the Arab–Israeli conflict: a review of the literature', *Journal of Conflict Resolution*, vol. XVI, no. 2, p. 272.

67 *Ibid.*, p. 272.

68 Sh. Avineri, 'Political and social aspects of Israeli and Arab nationalism', in Michael Curtis, Joseph Neyer, Chaim L. Waxman and Allen Pollack (eds), *The Palestinians, People, History and Politics*, New Brunswick, N. J., Transaction Books, 1975, pp. 97–111; for a similar argument see also Charles Issawi (ed.), *The Economic History of the Middle East, 1800–1914*, University of Chicago Press, 1966, pp. 3–13.

69 Shlomo Avineri, 'Modernization and Arab society: some reflections', in Irving Howe and Carl Greshman (eds), *Israel, the Arabs and the Middle East*, New York, Bantam Books, 1972, p. 307.

70 Gil Carl Alroy (ed.), 'Patterns of hostility', in *Attitudes toward Jewish Statehood in the Arab World*, New York, American Academic Association for Peace in the Middle East, 1971 (pp. 1–69), pp. 58–9.

71 Said, *op. cit.*

72 Yaacov Ro'i, 'The Zionist attitude to the Arabs: 1908–1914', *Middle*

Eastern Studies, vol. 4, no. 2, 1968, pp. 198–242; Y. Porath, *The Emergence of the Palestinian-Arab National Movement, 1918–1929*, London, Frank Cass, 1974.

73 Abdullah Schleifer, review of William Quandt's *Palestinian Nationalism: Its Political and Military Dimensions* and Gerard Chaliand's *The Palestinian Resistance*, in *Journal of Palestine Studies*, vol. II, no. 2, 1973, pp. 120–31.

74 Alroy, *op. cit.*, p. 48.

75 B. Beit-Hallahmi, 'Some roles of religion in the Arab–Israeli conflict', mimeographed, University of Michigan, n.d. (1972?), pp. 18–19.

76 Jacob M. Landau, *The Arabs in Israel: A Political Study*, London, Oxford University Press, 1969.

77 *Ibid.*, p. 23.

78 *Ibid.*, p. 32.

79 *Ibid.*, pp. 33–4.

80 *Ibid.*, pp. 134.

81 Y. Bar-Gal, 'Changes in the structure of the minority villages in Israel–outline and reasons', *Sociologia Ruralis*, vol. XV, 1975 (pp. 173–87), p. 185.

82 *Ibid.*

83 C. Jacobsen, 'Modernity in traditional villages', *Rural Sociology*, vol. 38, 1973, pp. 283–95. See also the complete study, Emmanuel Yalan, Chaim Finkel, Louis Guttman and Chanock Jacobsen, *The Modernization of Traditional Agricultural Villages: Minority Villages in Israel*, Publications on Problems of Regional Development, no. 11, Settlement Study Centre, Rehovot, Israel, 1972.

84 *Ibid.*, p. 284.

85 *Ibid.*, p. 294.

86 Joseph D. Francis, 'Bookreview', *Rural Sociology*, vol. 38, 1973, pp. 512–15.

87 Fred M. Gottheil, 'On the economic development of the Arab region in Israel', in M. Curtis and M. S. Chertoff (eds), *Israel: Social Structure and Change*, New Brunswick, N. J., Transaction Books, 1973, pp. 237–48.

88 *Ibid.*, p. 241.

89 *Ibid.*, p. 245.

90 Y. Waschitz, *op. cit.*, p. 47.

91 *Ibid.*, p. 52.

92 Henry Rosenfeld, 'The Arab village proletariat', *New Outlook*, vol. 13, no. 5, 1962, p. 8.

93 *Ibid.*, p. 16.

94 Abner Cohen, *Arab Border Villages in Israel*, Manchester University Press, 1965.

95 Henry Rosenfeld, 'An overview and critique of the literature on rural politics and social change', in R. Antoun and I. Harik (eds), *Rural Politics and Social Change in the Middle East*, Bloomington, Ind., Indiana University Press, 1972 (pp. 45–74), pp. 70–1. A more trenchant criticism of Cohen's work is provided by Talal Asad, 'Anthropological texts and ideological problems: an analysis of Cohen on

Arab villages in Israel', *Economy and Society*, vol. 4, 1975, pp. 251–82.

96 See Simha Flapan, 'National inequality in Israel', *New Outlook*, vol. 7, no. 9, 1964, pp. 24–36, and 'Integrating the Arab village', *New Outlook*, vol. 5, 1962, pp. 22–30.

97 Flapan, 'National inequality in Israel', p. 26.

98 The relevant works of Peres and Cohen are listed in Chap. 1, nn. 6 and 7.

99 Tamarin, *op. cit.*

100 John E. Hofman, 'Readiness for social relations between Arabs and Jews in Israel', *Journal of Conflict Resolution*, vol. XVI, no. 2, 1972, pp. 243–351; also in *Maariv*, 31 July 1970.

101 Benjamin Beit-Hallahmi, 'National character and national behaviour in the Middle East conflict: the case of the Arab personality', *International Journal of Group Tension*, vol. II, no. 3, 1972, pp. 19–28.

102 Noam Chomsky, 'Israel and the Palestinians', *Socialist Revolution*, vol. 5, 1975 (pp. 45–86), pp. 61–2. A similar assessment of Jiryis' work is provided by Gabriel Stern, 'Sabri Jiryis from another angle', *New Outlook*, December 1976, pp. 32–4.

103 Landau, *op. cit.*, p. xi. For a critical assessment of Landau's work, see Ian Lustick's review, *Journal of Palestine Studies*, vol. VI, no. 4, 1977, pp. 130–7.

104 Lustick, *op. cit.*

105 K. Nakhleh, 'Cultural determinants of Palestinian collective identity: the case of the Arabs in Israel', *New Outlook*, vol. 18, 1975, pp. 31–40.

106 K. Nakhleh, 'The direction of local-level conflict in two Arab villages in Israel', *American Ethnologists*, vol. 2, no. 3, 1975, p. 498.

107 *Ibid.*, p. 512.

108 *Ibid.*, p. 513.

109 K. Nakhleh, 'Palestinians in Israel: an assessment of the sociological and anthropological literature', *Journal of Palestine Studies*, vol. VI, no. 4, 1977, pp. 41–70.

110 Mustapha Ghanaim, 'Arab youth in Israel', *New Outlook*, vol. 18, 1975, pp. 54–7.

111 Mahmud Bayadsi, 'The Arab local authorities: achievements and problems', *New Outlook*, vol. 18, 1975, pp. 58–61.

112 S. Geraisy, 'Arab village youth in Jewish urban centres: a study of youth from Um El-Fahm working in the Tel Aviv metropolitan area', unpublished PhD thesis, Massachusetts, Brandeis University, 1971.

113 Ghanaim, *op. cit.*, p. 55.

114 *Ibid.*, p. 56.

115 Subhi Abu-Gush, 'The election campaign in the Arab sector', in Alan Arian (ed.), *The Elections in Israel – 1969*, Jerusalem, Academic Press, 1972, p. 242.

116 *Ibid.*, p. 242.

117 Elia Zureik, 'Introduction and overview', in Elia Zureik and Robert N. Pike (eds), *Socialization and Values in Canadian Society*, vol. I, Toronto, McClelland and Stewart, 1975, p. 12.

118 Sharif Kanaana, 'Survival strategies of Arabs in Israel', *Middle East Research and Information Project*, no. 41, October 1975, pp. 3–18.

119 Sami Mar'i and N. Dhahir, *Facts and Levels in the Development of Arab Education in Israel*, University of Haifa Institute for Research and Development of Arab Education, 1976 (Hebrew).
120 Sami Mar'i, 'School and society in Arab villages in Israel', mimeographed, pp. 4–5, originally published in *Studies in Education*, no. 4, 1974 (Hebrew).
121 Sami Mar'i and Muhamad Manna, 'Active coping ability of Arab youth', *Studies in Education*, no. 13, 1976, pp. 111–26 (Hebrew).
122 Daniel Heradstveit, 'Israeli élite perceptions of the Middle East conflict', *Journal of Palestine Studies*, vol. II, no. 3, 1973, pp. 68–93.
123 Edward Said, 'Palestinians and Arabs', *New Outlook*, vol. 19, 1976, pp. 27–30.

Chapter 5 The transformation of Arab class structure in Israel

1 It is difficult to reach a precise assessment of the number of North American Jews immigrating to Israel, since the Israeli census does not separate European from North American immigrants in its data. Overall, the most optimistic claim put the total number of North American Jewish immigrants prior to the 1967 war in the region of 20,000. Leonard Weller estimates that since 1967 the average annual immigration of North American Jews has risen to 6,000–8,000 (*Sociology in Israel*, Westport, Conn., Greenwood Press, 1974, pp. 29–35). These estimates are slightly inflated, compared to those reported in the Israeli press. In 1973, 4,393 American Jews immigrated, compared to 2,693 in 1974. For the same years, 1,300 and 800 French and British Jews immigrated to Israel per year (*Yediot Aharonot*, 6 January 1975, cited in the *Bulletin of the Institute for Palestine Studies*, vol. V, no. 2, 1975, p. 44 (Arabic)). It is also interesting to note that the West, rather than Israel, is becoming an increasingly attractive place for Russian Jewish immigrants. According to Noam Chomsky, 'It is safe to assume that the emigration of Russian Jews, if permitted by the Soviet authorities, will turn towards the West. Already in December 1974, 35 per cent of the Russian Jews reaching Vienna chose to go to the West, as compared to four per cent in 1973' ('Reflections on the Arab–Israeli conflict', *Journal of Contemporary Asia*, vol. 5, no. 3, 1975, p. 341). The General Director of the immigration division of the Jewish Agency cites the figure of 30 per cent of Russian Jews who remained in reception centres in Vienna (see *Davar*, 2 September 1975, cited in the *Bulletin of the Institute for Palestine Studies*, vol. V, no. 18, 1975, p. 500 (Arabic)).
2 See *Al-Hamishmar*, 13 February 1975, cited in the *Bulletin of the Institute for Palestine Studies*, vol. 7, no. 7, 1975, p. 217.
3 N. Chomsky, 'The interim agreement', *New Politics*, vol. XI, 1976, p. 21.
4 *Ibid.*, p. 21, n. 53.
5 D. Elizur, 'Attitudes and intentions of Israelis residing in the US towards returning to Israel', *International Migration*, vol. II, nos. 1–2, 1973, p. 6.

6 Cf. Georges R. Tamarin, *The Israeli Dilemma: Essays on a Warfare State*, Rotterdam University Press, 1973.

7 *Maariv*, 14 June 1973.

8 Nina Toren, 'The effect of economic incentives on return migration', *International Migration*, vol. XIII, 1975, pp. 134–44. According to *The Israel Economist*, June 1976, 40 per cent of Western immigrants return to Israel during the first five years after emigration.

9 See Yachiel Harari, *The Arabs in Israel: Facts and Figures*, no. 4, Givat Haviva, Centre for Arab and Afro-Asian Studies, 1974, p. 10.

10 Ian Lustick, based on my personal communication with the author.

11 The figures up to 1948 were based on data cited by Edward Hagopian and A. B. Zahlan, 'Palestine's Arab population: the demography of the Palestinians', *Journal of Palestine Studies*, vol. III, no. 4, 1974, pp. 32–73; data for 1948 were obtained from *Statistical Abstract of Israel*, Jerusalem, 1971, p. 21.

12 See Don Peretz, *Israel and the Palestine Arabs*, Washington, DC, The Middle East Institute, 1958, p. 99; cf. J. Abu-Lughod, 'The demographic transformation of Palestine', in I. Abu-Lughod (ed.), *The Transformation of Palestine*, Evanston, Ill., Northwestern University Press, 1971, p. 161.

13 Data for 1960–74 were taken from Harari, *op. cit.*, p. 2.

14 See Chomsky, 'The interim agreement', p. 26.

15 M. F. Bustani, 'Population in Israel: analysis and estimates for 1990', *Supplement to the Bulletin of the Institute for Palestine Studies*, vol. III, no. 2, 1973, p. 394 (Arabic).

16 Data for 1948 and 1961 are taken from Sabri Jiryis, *The Arabs in Israel*, Beirut, Institute for Palestine Studies, 1973, p. 17 (Arabic); for 1968 and 1973 data from Harari, *op. cit.*, p. 6.

17 Cf. Joseph Waschitz, 'The plight of the Bedouin', *New Outlook*, vol. 18, 1975, pp. 62–6. Jiryis' discussion of the Bedouin predicament remains the most comprehensive (see chap. 2, 'Liberation of the land', *op. cit.*, pp. 175–230).

18 See Joseph L. Ryan, 'Refugees within Israel: the case of the villages of Kafr Birim and Iqrit', *Journal of Palestine Studies*, vol. II, no. 4, 1973, pp. 55–81. It is worth noting in this context that while Israel 'opened' its frontiers to Southern Maronite Christians during the civil war in Lebanon, the villages of Birim and Iqrit, which were razed to the ground by the Israeli military, were also Maronite villages.

19 Chomsky, 'The interim agreement', p. 26.

20 There is little research on the implications of the legal system for land ownership in Israel. Israel Shahak comments on further confiscation of Arab land recently as follows: '(1) Most of the confiscated land belongs to Arabs. (2) The "displaced owners" cannot choose their compensation; they must take what is offered to them. (3) The cash offered is not "market value", but according to the estimates of a governmental "appraiser", whose valuations are usually 5–20 per cent of the market value. (4) The land which is offered as a compensation, although nominally state land, really belongs to Arab refugees. (5) The

plan for the "Judaisation" of Galilee was strongly opposed in 1966, especially round the town of Carmiel built at that date. Many joint Arab–Jewish demonstrations were held, and broken by stiff prison sentences. . . . Finally for what purpose is the land confiscated, both from Arabs and from Jews? So long as it is private, the owner can discriminate on it or not, as he pleases. Once it becomes "Judaised", it becomes apartheid country, on which Israeli citizens who are not Jews have no right to live' (*The Economist*, 10 April 1976, p. 6). This procedure of unfair land compensation characterized the policy of the Israeli government all along. According to Peretz, *op. cit.*, p. 184, 'In 1950 Arabs were permitted to sell land exclusively to the Jewish National Fund. They received no more than £I 25 per *dunum* and in some places as little as £I 15 per *dunum*, whereas the present price was nearer to £I 250 or £I 350 per *dunum*.' See also n. 117 below.

21 Data for 1955, 1961 and 1971 are taken from Jiryis, *op. cit.*, p. 18; for 1973, from Harari, *op. cit.*, p. 9.

22 Vivian Z. Klaff, 'Ethnic segregation in urban Israel', *Demography*, vol. 10, no. 2, 1973, pp. 161–84.

23 Dov Friedlander and Calvin Goldscheider, 'Peace and the demographic future of Israel', *Journal of Conflict Resolution*, vol. 18, no. 3, 1974, pp. 486–501. A major flaw in the Friedlander-Goldscheider study is that they do not take into account the substantial emigration of Palestinians from the West Bank and Gaza, which has been tacitly encouraged by the Israeli authorities. It is estimated that around 40,000 Palestinians emigrated from the occupied territories between December 1972 and December 1976 (see *Isralefi*, no. 118, 1 December 1977, p. 5).

24 U. O. Schmelz, 'The demographic development in Israel since 1967', *Gesher*, nos. 3–4, 1972, pp. 118–37 (Hebrew).

25 Bustani, *op. cit.*

26 Data for 1951–1970 are taken from *Statistical Abstract of Israel*, Jerusalem, 1971, Tables C/2, C/3, pp. 60–1; data for 1973, from Harari, *op. cit.*, p. 4.

27 Yoram Ben-Porath, 'Short-term fluctuations in fertility and economic activity in Israel', *Demography*, vol. 10, no. 2, 1973, pp. 185–204 (data based on Tables A-1 and A-2, p. 202).

28 See *Statistical Abstract of Israel*, Jerusalem, 1971, p. 84.

29 Emmanuel Yalan, Chaim Finkel, Louis Guttman and Chanock Jacobsen, *The Modernization of Traditional Agricultural Villages: Minority Villages in Israel*, Publications on Problems of Regional Development, no. 11, Settlement Study Centre, Rehovot, Israel, 1972, p. 32.

30 This claim is advanced by S. D. Horowitz, 'Arab economy in Palestine', in J. B. Hobman (ed.), *Palestine Economic Future*, London, Lund Humphries, 1946, p. 55.

31 Data for 1961 on number of persons per family are taken from *Statistical Abstract of Israel*, Jerusalem, 1963, p. 57, and for 1973 from Harari, *op. cit.*, p. 12; data on age distribution for 1972 and 1960 are from *Statistical Abstract of Israel*, Jerusalem, 1973, p. 44.

32 Data for 1955 and 1965 were taken from *Statistical Abstract of Israel*, Jerusalem, 1971, pp. 60–1; for 1972 from I. Lustik, 'Israeli Arabs: built-in inequality', *New Outlook*, vol. 17, no. 6, 1974, Table 5, p. 36; data for 1973 from Harari, *op. cit.*, p. 4.
33 See N. Chomsky, 'Israel and the Palestinians', *Socialist Revolution*, vol. 5, 1975, n. 40, p. 137.
34 Israel Koenig, 'Top Secret: Memorandum-Proposal – Handling the Arabs in Israel', *Journal of Palestine Studies*, vol. VI, no. 1, 1976, pp. 190–200.
35 Leonard J. Singerman, Joel A. Singerman and Janice Singerman, *The Threat Within: Israel and Population Policy*, New York, Vantage Books, 1975.
36 Amal Samed, 'Palestinian women: entering the proletariat', *Journal of Palestine Studies*, vol. VI, no. 1, 1976 (pp. 159–68).
37 A thorough challenge of the Zionist claim that the Palestinian exodus in 1948 was prompted by calls from the neighbouring Arab countries is provided by Erskine Childers, 'The wordless wish: from citizens to refugees', in I. Abu-Lughod (ed.), *The Transformation of Palestine*, Evanston, Ill., Medina University Press, 1971, pp. 165–202.
38 According to Simha Flapan, 'Integrating the Arab village', *New Outlook*, vol. 7, no. 9, 1964, 'there are still nearly 20,000 Arab "absentees" living in Israel, who enjoy all the rights granted to all citizens except one: to regain their former possessions' (p. 25).
39 Peretz, *op. cit.*, p. 142.
40 *Ibid.*, p. 152.
41 *Ibid.*, pp. 143–7.
42 Cited in Jiryis, 'Recent Knesset legislation and the Arabs in Israel', *Journal of Palestine Studies*, vol. I, no. 1, 1971, p. 54.
43 *Ibid.*, p. 61.
44 Chomsky, 'The interim agreement', pp. 24–5. Cf. Amal Samed, *op. cit.*
45 Because of the application of Jewish National Fund principles to state lands, Uzzi Ornan of the Hebrew University estimates that 95 per cent of the land within the pre-1967 borders is classified as state land (cited in Chomsky, 'Israel and the Palestinians', pp. 138–9, n. 49).
46 Cf. Michael Curtis, Joseph Neyer, Chaim L. Waxman and Allen Pollack (eds), *The Palestinians, People, History and Politics*, New Brunswick, N.J., Transaction Books, 1975.
47 Chomsky, 'The interim agreement', p. 24.
48 For a discussion of the implications of this law, see Walter Lehn, 'The Jewish national fund', *Journal of Palestine Studies*, vol. III, no. 4, pp. 74–96, and Noam Chomsky, 'Israel and the Palestinians', pp. 45–86.
49 *Great Britain and Palestine: 1915–1945*, Information Paper No. 20, London, Royal Institute of International Affairs, 1946, p. 36.
50 Peretz, *op. cit.*, p. 126.
51 Cited in Emanuel Dror, 'The emergency regulations', in Arie Bober (ed.), *The Other Israel*, New York, Doubleday, 1972, p. 138.

52 *Ibid*., pp. 138–9.
53 Cited in *ibid*., p. 134.
54 Aharon Cohen, *Israel and the Arab World*, London, W. H. Allen, 1970, p. 494.
55 Tamarin, *op. cit*., pp. 27–49.
56 See S. Jiryis, 'The expropriation of Arab land in Israel', *Journal of Palestine Studies*, vol. II, no. 4, 1973, pp. 94–5.
57 *Ibid*., p. 98.
58 See Jiryis' discussion of this and related laws in 'Recent Knesset legislation . . .'; also Tamarin, *op. cit*.
59 Cited in Jiryis, 'Recent Knesset legislation . . .', p. 66.
60 See Y. Porath, *The Emergence of the Palestinian-Arab National Movement, 1918–1929*, London, Frank Cass, 1974, p. 19.
61 *Statistical Abstract of Israel*, Jerusalem, 1963, p. 25.
62 See Harari, *op. cit*., pp. 9–10.
63 See Arieh Tartakower, *The Jewish Society*, Tel Aviv, Massadah Publishers, 1959 (Hebrew).
64 See Schmelz, *op. cit*., p. 122; Harari, *op. cit*., p. 6.
65 Data for 1931 were obtained from Y. Porath, *op. cit*., p. 19; for 1963, we relied on Y. Ben-Porath, *The Arab Labour Force in Israel*, Jerusalem, Israel Universities Press, 1966, Table 2–1, p. 22; for 1972, see Harari, *op. cit*., p. 21.
66 We are excluding the large proportion of 47 per cent of Palestinian Arabs from the occupied territories who, out of more than 50,000 Arab transient workers in 1972, are employed primarily in construction (see *Journal of Palestine Studies*, vol. III, no. 4, 1974, pp. 171–84).
67 See Y. Waschitz, 'Commuters and entrepreneurs', *New Outlook*, vol. 18, 1975 (pp. 45–53), p. 46.
68 Lustick, *op. cit*., pp. 34–5.
69 See Harari, *op. cit*., p. 20.
70 See Waschitz, *op. cit*., p. 47.
71 Sh. Zarhi and A. Achiezra, *The economic conditions of the Arab minority in Israel*, no. 1, Givat Haviva, Centre for Arab and Afro-Asian Studies, 1966, pp. 4–5.
72 See Waschitz, *op. cit*., p. 47.
73 *Ibid*., p. 47.
74 See Ian Lustick, 'Institutionalized segmentation: one factor in the control of Israeli Arabs', unpublished paper delivered at the Middle East Studies Association Conference, Louisville, Kentucky, 1975, p. 6.
75 *Ibid*., p. 6.
76 Waschitz, *op. cit*., p. 47.
77 Data cited in Harari, *op. cit*., p. 9.
78 S. Geraisy, 'Arab Village Youth in Jewish Urban Centres: A Study of Youth from Um El-Fahm Working in the Tel Aviv Metropolitan Area', unpublished PhD thesis, Brandeis University, 1971, pp. 96–7.
79 Ben-Porath, *op. cit*., 1966, p. 70.

80 See Doreen Warriner, *Land and Poverty in the Middle East*, London, Royal Institute of International Affairs, 1948, pp. 61–2.

81 See Zarhi and Achiezra, *op. cit.*, p. 12.

82 Waschitz, *op. cit.*, p. 48.

83 Evidence to this effect is quoted by Talal Asad: 'Accordingly, real wages of Arab labour in September, 1937 fell by 10 per cent as compared with wages in 1931, while wages of Jewish labour increased by 10 per cent. . . . Actual earnings in 1936 and 1937 decreased more than is shown by the index numbers of daily wage rates, because of periods of unemployment and reduced hours of work' ('Anthropological texts and ideological problems: an analysis of Cohen on Arab villages in Israel', in *Economy and Society*, vol. 4, 1975 (pp. 251–82), p. 279, n. 24).

84 See Lustick, 'Israeli Arabs . . .', pp. 32–40, for a discussion of income difference.

85 Waschitz, *op. cit.*, p. 51.

86 *Statistical Abstract of Israel*, Jerusalem, 1974, p. 272.

87 Ran Kislev, 'Land expropriations: history of oppression', *New Outlook*, September/October 1976, p. 31.

88 Data are taken from Ben-Porath, *op. cit.*, 1973, Tables A-3 and A-4; none of the writers on Israel question the reliability and validity of the Israeli census data. Census data on employment, income and occupational distribution – even in Western industrial societies – are not known for their unquestionable authenticity. The notion of the 'discouraged' worker (that is to say, the worker who gives up hope of securing employment and as such does not appear in the official statistics, since he does not report to the labour exchange, which is the main source for unemployment statistics) has been invoked to account for underestimation of unemployment rates in census data. This is more relevant for Israel, since the Arab workers are not accustomed to report to labour exchanges as a main source of employment. Personal contact is an important method of job-seeking. In commenting on this phenomenon, M. Ghanaim remarks: 'Most of the young men find work through friends or relatives, or by personallylo oking in likely places. Very few find jobs by applying to the labour exchanges or other official agencies' ('Arab youth in Israel', *New Outlook*, vol. 18, 1975, p. 55).

89 Harari, *op. cit.*, pp. 16–17.

90 Sammy Smooha, 'Pluralism: a study of intergroup relations in Israel'' unpublished PhD thesis, University of California, Los Angeles, 1973, p. 159.

91 Lustick, 'Institutionalized segmentation . . .', pp. 10–11.

92 See Ian Lustick, 'Arabs in the Jewish State: a study in the effective control of a national minority', unpublished PhD thesis, University of California, Berkeley, 1976, p. 332.

93 Zarhi and Achiezra, *op. cit.*, p. 16.

94 See *Statistical Abstract of Israel*, Jerusalem, 1973, p. 283.

95 See *ibid.*

96 See Aharon Cohen, *op. cit.*, p. 504. In presenting census data on the size of residential units for Arabs and Jews, Harari, *op. cit.*, cites the following, (p. 25):

Size of dwelling	*1961* Jews	Arabs	*1972* Jews	Arabs
	%	%	%	%
1 room	3.0	12.6	0.5	3.0
2	41.8	59.8	6.3	40.0
3	50.9	17.1	60.0	21.9
4+	4.3	10.1	33.2	35.1
	~100.0	~100.0	100.0	100.0

Earlier in his monograph (p. 15), Harari argues that the recent decline in marriage rates among Arabs, as well as their relatively lower rate compared to the Jewish population, is due to housing shortage. In 1972 the marriage rates (per 1,000 of the average yearly population) for Muslims, Christian and Druze Arabs were 7.0, 6.5 and 7.7, respectively. For the Jewish population, it was 9.9.

97 Ran Kislev, *op. cit.*, p. 31.

98 *Statistical Abstract of Israel*, Jerusalem, 1971, pp. 193–6.

99 See *ibid.*, p. 285. For 1972, the 'official' figure is 52 per cent who work outside their residence (Harari, *op. cit.*, p. 22). However, as Harari remarks, these official figures are based on questionnaire surveys and as such suffer from the usual defects of sampling and survey research. As shown in Harari's monograph, the official figures are at variance with data offered by other researchers, such as Geraisy's case-study of one Arab village. The official figures seem to inflate the number of Arabs who work in their residence.

100 See Ben-Porath, *op. cit.*, 1966, p. 70.

101 See Zarhi and Achiezra, *op. cit.*, p. 19.

102 Jiryis, *The Arabs in Israel*, p. 386.

103 See Jacob M. Landau, *The Arabs in Israel: A Political Study*, London, Oxford University Press, 1969, p. 20. Geraisy reaches similar conclusions: of the respondents living in the city '5.95 per cent (five persons) preferred their city dwelling, 5.95 per cent (five persons) thought that they were equal, while 88.10 per cent (seventy-four persons) preferred their village dwelling' (*op. cit.*, p. 103). Furthermore, Geraisy points out (pp. 89–91) that most of the people who leave the village do so not because village life is dreary, but because of economic necessity. Eighty-eight per cent of his respondents could not find work in the village.

104 See Lustick, 'Israeli Arabs. . . .', p. 33.

105 Cited in Waschitz, *op. cit.*

106 Waschitz, *op. cit.*, p. 46.

107 See *Yediot Aharonot*, 1 September 1972.
108 Kislev, *op. cit.*, p. 25.
109 The main points summarized in the text are taken from press coverage of both studies in *Al-Hamishmar*, 22 March 1970, and *Maariv*, 22 March 1970.
110 Ben-Porath, *op. cit.*, 1966, p. 34.
111 Fred M. Gottheil, 'On the economic development of the Arab region in Israel', in M. Curtis and M. S. Chertoff (eds), *Israel: Social Structure and Change*, New Brunswick, N.J., Transaction Books, 1973, pp. 239–40.
112 See Lustick, 'Institutionalized segmentation . . .'.
113 See also the statement of an Arab Member of Knesset (Mapam Party) who charged that not more than 1 per cent of the funds devoted to local development are spent in the Arab sector (*Davar*, 3 September 1973); Simha Flapan, writing a decade earlier, cites an identical figure of $1\frac{1}{2}$ per cent of the total government expenditure as being channelled to the Arab sector ('National inequality in Israel', *New Outlook*, vol. 7, no. 9, 1964, pp. 24–36).
114 M. Bayadsi, 'The Arab local authorities: achievements and problems', *New Outlook*, vol. 18, 1975 (pp. 58–62), p. 60.
115 Cited in Ran Eddelist and Kassem Zayd, 'Koenig's bite: worse than his bark', *New Outlook*, January/February 1977, p. 60.
116 Data are taken from Jiryis, *The Arabs in Israel*, Table 13, p. 392. It is also worth noting that the majority of Arab rural settlements are characterized by their small size which renders them unviable economically, especially when they have to compete against more efficient Jewish agriculture. In 1961, the proportion of 'large' Arab rural settlements was about 20 per cent; in 1970 it rose to 42 per cent. In the Jewish sector in 1961, out of 708 settlements, only 57, that is, slightly more than 10 per cent, were classified as 'small' settlements; in 1971, the figure declined to fifty (*Statistical Abstract of Israel*, Jerusalem, 1971, pp. 30–1). Flapan, 'Integrating the Arab village', 1964, says with regard to Jewish settlements: 'these settlements are only called rural because their main occupation is farming. In all other respects they can hardly be called rural in the usual sense' (p. 32). When placed in a historical context it can be seen that the initial Zionist pattern of settlements has eventually led to a more viable agricultural sector. By 1943, 'only 19.7 per cent of the Jews lived in the hill districts (as opposed to the fertile plains) . . ., compared to 56.7 per cent of the Arabs' (Nathan Weinstock, 'The impact of Zionist colonization on Palestine-Arab society before 1948', *Journal of Palestine Studies*, vol. II, no. 2, 1977, p. 57).
117 Peretz, *op. cit.*, p. 143. A detailed study by Jiryis shows that of 1,080,984 *dunums* belonging to Arabs in 1945, more than 1,000,000 were confiscated, seized or declared 'state land' by the Zionist authorities (*The Arabs in Israel*, p. 225). Cf. the systematic accounting by Israel Shahak of the names and locations of villages in pre-1948 Israel and those remaining now. Out of 475 villages, 385 could not be accounted for ('Arab villages destroyed in Israel', in Uri Davis and

Norton Mezvinsky (eds), *Documents from Israel, 1967–1973*, London, Ithaca Press, 1975, pp. 43–54).

118 Abner Cohen, *Arab Border Villages in Israel*, Manchester University Press, 1965.

119 Lustick, 'Israeli Arabs. . .', p. 38.

120 Jiryis, *The Arabs in Israel*, pp. 396–7.

121 *Ibid.*, see p. 397, n. 121.

122 Bayadsi, *op. cit.*

123 Lustick, '*Arabs in the Jewish State. . .*', p. 329.

124 Cf. *ibid.*, pp. 343–4.

125 *Al-Hamishmar*, 1 September 1972.

126 Jiryis, *The Arabs in Israel*, Table 12, p. 337. According to Rosenfeld, while there are 2.5 tractors for every thousand *dunums* in the Jewish sector, there is only 0.5 in the Arab sector ('Change, barriers to change and contradictions in the Arab village family', *New Outlook*, vol. 13, no. 2, 1970, p. 29).

127 See Jiryis, *The Arabs in Israel*, p. 370.

128 *Statistical Abstract of Israel*, Jerusalem, 1971, p. 354.

129 Weinstock, *op. cit.*

130 Borochovism is named after Ben Borochov (1881–1917), a Russian Jew who tried to apply Marxist theory to stress the need to build the Zionist movement on a base of 'proletarian Zionism'. For this brand of Zionist socialism to succeed, Borochov argued, the Jews should realize their own territory, for the latter is the only means to ensure that a Jewish labour force will eventually develop in a normal manner with its large base of proletarian strata involved in the production of primary economies. As long as the Jews continue to be extra-territorial, Borochov claimed, they will always remain marginal and absorbed in the secondary sector of the economy, with the continuous threat of fierce competition from the host society. For a critique of Borochovism, see M. Machover, 'Borochovism', in Bober (ed.), *op. cit.*, pp. 145–58.

A. D. Gordon (1856–1922) was a Polish Jew who settled in Palestine in 1904. He tackled the problem of the unnatural Jewish occupational life by popularizing the theme of the return to the land. Only through labouring the soil and coming in contact with the land, Gordon claimed, will it be possible for the Jews to solve their dilemmas and revive their 'national civilization'. See A. Taylor, *The Zionist Mind*, Beirut, Institute for Palestine Studies, 1974, for a treatment of Gordon's philosophy; according to Taylor, Gordon's views were a 'manifestation of the contemporary interest in exploration and involvement in political objects overseas, and not in any sense an expression of messianic fervour' (p. 52).

131 In commenting on the pockets of Zionist settlement in Palestine, Warriner had this to say: 'Yet there seems something very unreal about a socialism so heavily subsidized, which does not contribute directly to raise the level of surrounding poverty' (*op. cit.*, p. 71).

132 J. Talmon, *Israel among the Nations*, London, Weidenfeld & Nicolson, 1970.

Chapter 6 Prejudice, education and social disorganization

1 Georges R. Tamarin, *The Israeli Dilemma: Essays on a Warfare State*, Rotterdam University Press, 1973.
2 *Ibid.*, pp. 27–49.
3 Cf. Mary E. Goodman's classic study, *Race Awareness in Young Children*, London, Collier-Macmillan, further printing 1970.
4 J. Cohen, 'Colonialism and racism in Algeria', in Anthony H. Richmond (ed.), *Readings in Racial and Ethnic Relations*, Oxford, Pergamon Press, 1972, p. 65.
5 Herbert Blumer, 'Race prejudice as a sense of group position', *Pacific Sociological Review*, vol. I, no. 2, 1958, p. 4.
6 See David Pratt, 'The social role of school textbooks in Canada', in Elia T. Zureik and Robert M. Pike (eds), *Socialization and Social Values in Contemporary Canada*, vol. I, Toronto, McClelland and Stewart, Carlton Library Series, 1975, pp. 99–126.
7 Tamar Maroz, 'The adventures of Oz Ya'oz, Tzuptik and Danidin', in Uri Davis and Norton Mezvinsky (eds), *Documents from Israel, 1967–1973*, London, Ithaca Press, 1975, pp. 102–11.
8 J. B. Segal, 'The Arab image in Israeli fiction', *The Jewish Quarterly*, vol. 21, nos. 1–2, 1973, pp. 45–54.
9 *Ibid.*, p. 52. In referring to Smilansky and other writers of Hebrew who immigrated to Palestine at the turn of the century, Segal notes that 'The stories of Moshe Smilansky (born 1874) have a mawkish, paternalistic flavour, not far removed from the writings of white settlers in southern Africa or the plantation-owners in the deep south of the United States' (p. 46). Segal singles out Brenner as the main 'left-wing' Zionist writer of this period who addressed himself to 'mutual understanding between Arabs and Jews'.
10 Yona Bachur, 'The Arabs in modern Hebrew literature', *New Outlook*, vol. VII, no. 3, 1964, pp. 40–64.
11 Leon I. Yudkin, *Escape into Siege*, London, Routledge & Kegan Paul, 1974.
12 See Ibrahim El-Bahrawi, 'Stories of despair and isolation in Israeli literature after the [October] war', *El-Jadid*, no. 2, January 1974, pp. 38–42 (Arabic publication of the Israeli Communist Party). This article is reprinted from the Egyptian periodical *El-Majalah*.
13 Yochanan Peres, 'Ethnic relations in Israel', *American Journal of Sociology*, vol. LXXVI, no. 6, 1971, pp. 1021–47, cf. Tables 11, 12, 14.
14 *Ibid.*, Table 14.
15 See 'The test hour of the Israeli Arabs', *Yediot Aharonot*, 28 November 1969. Tamarin makes the following remark which is highly relevant in explaining the Jewish attitude towards the Arabs: 'On the other hand, the knowledge that their Arab fellow-citizen is discriminated against and in some aspects defenseless has a corrupting effect on the Jewish population. This is primarily true for those primitive elements who are in everyday contact with them, since their attitude is based not only on the feeling of *strength* of the majority, but also on feelings of

superiority towards the 'inferior' and defenseless. . . . [This leads to the feeling]: "I know the Arabs well; they are all cowards and treacherous. A kick in the teeth is the only language they understand" ' (*op. cit.*, p. 43).

16 Abel Jacob, 'Trends in Israeli public opinion on issues related to the Arab–Israeli conflict, 1967–1972', *Jewish Journal of Sociology*, vol. XVI, no. 2, 1974, pp. 187–208.
17 *Ibid.*, p. 205.
18 Cited in Ronald Segal, *Whose Jerusalem?*, London, Jonathan Cape, 1973, p. 15.
19 Emmanuel Yalan, Chaim Finkel, Louis Guttman and Chanock Jacobsen, *The Modernization of Traditional Agricultural Villages: Minority Villages in Israel*, Publications on Problems of Regional Development, no. 11, Settlement Study Centre, Rehovot, Israel, 1972, p. 31.
20 John E. Hofman, 'Readiness for social relations between Arabs and Jews in Israel', *Journal of Conflict Resolution*, vol. XVI, no. 2, 1972, p. 248.
21 Erik Cohen, 'Mixed marriage in an Israeli town', *Jewish Journal of Sociology*, vol. XI, no. 1, 1969, pp. 41–50.
22 Fouzi El-Asmar, *To Be an Arab in Israel*, London, Frances Pinter, 1975, p. 77; see also Fouzi El-Asmar, 'Israel revisited, 1976', *Journal of Palestine Studies*, vol. VI, no. 3, 1977, pp. 66–76.
23 Yochanan Peres and Zipporah Levy, 'Jews and Arabs: Ethnic stereotypes in Israel', *Race*, vol. 10, no. 4, 1969, pp. 479–92.
24 *Ibid.*, p. 487–8.
25 *Ibid.*, p. 490.
26 Tamarin, *op. cit.*, pp. 149–68.
27 *Ibid.*, p. 163.
28 Erik Cohen, 'Arab boys and tourist girls in a mixed Jewish–Arab community', *International Journal of Comparative Sociology*, vol. XII, no. 4, 1971, pp. 217–33.
29 *Ibid.*, p. 21.
30 Yochanan Peres, 'Modernization and nationalism in the identity of the Israeli Arab', *Middle East Journal*, vol. XXIV, no. 4, 1970, pp. 479–92.
31 See *Statistical Abstract of Israel*, Jerusalem, 1974, p. 633.
32 Cf. N. Shaath, 'High level Palestinian manpower', *Journal of Palestine Studies*, vol. I, no. 2, 1972, pp. 80–95; and I. Abu-Lughod, 'Educating a community in exile: the Palestinian experience', *Journal of Palestine Studies*, vol. II, no. 3, 1973, pp. 94–111.
33 See Peres, 'Modernization and nationalism . . .', Table VII, p. 489.
34 Yochanan Peres and Nira Yuval-Davis, 'The orientation of Arab students towards Jews as individuals and towards Israel as a State', *Megamot*, vol. 3, 1970, p. 256 (Hebrew).
35 See Sami Mar'i, 'School and society in Arab villages in Israel', mimeographed, p. 14, originally published in *Studies in Education*, no. 2, 1974 (Hebrew).
36 Cited in S. Smooha, 'Pluralism: a study of inter-group relations in Israel', unpublished PhD dissertation, University of California, Los

Angeles, 1973, p. 158.

37 Cited in Sami Mar'i and N. Dhahir, *Facts and Levels in the Development of Arab Education in Israel*, Haifa, Institute for Research and Development of Arab Education, University of Haifa, 1976, p. 55 (Hebrew).
38 Cited in Smooha, *op. cit.*, p. 158.
39 *Statistical Abstract of Israel*, Jerusalem, 1974, p. 608.
40 Sabri Jiryis, *The Arabs in Israel*, Beirut, Institute for Palestine Studies, 1973, pp. 340–7 (Arabic).
41 See *Statistical Abstract of Israel*, 1963, Table 8, p. 635, and *Statistical Abstract of Israel*, 1974, Tables 12 and 13, pp. 618–19.
42 Mar'i and Dhahir, *op. cit.*, pp. 52–3.
43 *Idib.*, p. 58.
44 Up to 1970–1, data taken from Jiryis, *op. cit.*, p. 356. Data for 1972–3 are calculated from *Statistical Abstract of Israel*, 1974, pp. 43 and 628.
45 *al-Itihad*, 16 October 1971 (Arabic).
46 See Elie Rekhness, 'Study of Arab university students in Israel', mimeographed, Tel Aviv University, n.d.
47 See *ibid.*
48 See *Statistical Abstract of Israel*, 1974, p. 633.
49 *Ibid.*, p. 633.
50 Data cited in Frank H. Epp, *The Palestinians*, Toronto, McClelland and Stewart, 1976, p. 66.
51 See Rekhness, *op. cit.*
52 Yachiel Harari, *The Arabs in Israel*, Givat Haviva, Israel, 1974, p. 30.
53 See Mar'i and Dhahir, *op. cit.*, pp. 67–8.
54 *Ibid.*, p. 67.
55 Harari, *op. cit.*, p. 30.
56 Data calculated on the basis of census figures in *Statistical Abstract of Israel*, 1974, p. 620.
57 See Rekhness, *op. cit.*
58 Cited in Epp, *op. cit.*, p. 66.
59 See Rekhness, *op. cit.*
60 Mar'i and Dhahir, *op. cit.*, p. 67.
61 Rekhness, *op. cit.*, p. 31.
62 *Yediot Aharonot*, 5 March 1970 (Hebrew).
63 Yochanan Peres and Nira Yuval-Davis, 'Some observations on the national identity of the Israeli Arab', *Human Relations*, vol. XXII, no. 3, 1969, pp. 219–33.
64 The data are based on Yochanan Peres, Avishai Ehrilik and Nira Yuval-Davis, 'National education for Arab youth in Israel: a comparative analysis of curriculum', *The Jewish Journal of Sociology*, vol. XII, no. 2, 1970, pp. 147–63.
65 *Ibid.*
66 For supporting evidence concerning the positive impact of the 1973 October War on the Arabs, see P. O. Starr, 'How the Arabs see themselves after the war', *New Society*, January 1975, pp. 186–7. For related findings inside Israel see Erik Cohen's research on Israeli Arab youth in Acre in *Yediot Aharonot*, 5 December 1974. John Hofman replicated a 1972 study on the identity of Israeli Arab youth in 1975

and discovered a greater sense of polarization as measured along the semantic differential scale. Christian and Muslim youth in Israel set themselves apart from Jews in general. This increase in social distance is attributed by Hofman to the 1973 war. However, the Lebanese civil war seems to have negatively affected the perception by Christian Arab youth in Israel of Lebanese Muslims. It is striking that Hofman did not include in the national groups the category of 'Palestinian', in order to find out whether or not the events in Lebanon reduced the gap between Muslim and Christian Palestinians (*Stereotypes of Arab Youth in Israel*, Haifa, The Institute for Research and Development of Arab Education, 1977 (Hebrew)).

67 Y. Peres, 'Ethnic relations in Israel', Table 23.

68 See for example, E. S. Greenberg, 'Children and the political community: a comparison across racial lines', *Canadian Journal of Political Science*, vol. II, no. 4, 1969, pp. 471–92; Schiley R. Lyons, 'The political socialization of ghetto children: efficacy and cynicism', *Journal of Politics*, vol. XXXVII, no. 2, 1960, pp. 288–304; and Dean Jaros *et al.*, 'The malevolent leader: political socialization in an American sub-culture', *American Political Science Review*, vol. LXII, 1968, pp. 564–75.

69 A report on Hofman's preliminary findings appeared in *Maariv* 21 July 1970.

70 Wallace E. Lambert, Moshe Anisfeld and Grace Yeni-Komshian, 'Evaluational reactions of Jewish and Arab adolescents to dialects and language variations', *Journal of Personality and Social Psychology*, vol. II, no. 1, 1965, p. 88.

71 See Ronald Segal, *op. cit.*, p. 15.

72 See Henri Tajfel, Gustav Jahoda, Charlem Nemith, Y. Rim and N. B. Johnson, 'The devaluation by children of their own national and other ethnic groups', mimeographed, University of Bristol, 1971.

73 Tamarin, *op. cit.*, p. 154.

74 See *Encyclopedia of Zionism*, Table 8, p. 224. Adjusting the 1970 data to all persons who are aged twenty or over, Smooha notes that the rates of Arab to Jewish convicted adult offenders stand at the ratio of 4:1 (*op. cit.*, p. 294).

75 The 1969 data are taken from *Statistical Abstract of Israel*, Jerusalem, 1971; the rates for 1969 are based on the absolute number of offenders per 1,000 in the population aged nine and above; the remaining figures are taken from R. Patai (ed.), *Encyclopedia of Zionism*, vol. 1, 1971, Table 1, p. 221, and Table 3, p. 222.

76 David Reifen, *Patterns and Motivations of Juvenile Delinquency among Israeli Arabs*, Jerusalem, Ministry of Social Welfare, 1964.

77 *Ibid.*, pp. 27–8.

78 *Ibid.*, p. 31.

79 P. Palgi and Y. Fuchs, 'The Israeli Moslem rural family – continuity and change', in Arie Jarus, Joseph Marcus, Joseph Oren and Chanan Rapaport (eds), *Children and Families in Israel, Some Mental Health Perspectives*, New York, Gordon and Breach, 1970, pp. 137–50.

80 Cf. Shlomo Shoham, 'The application of the "culture-conflict" hypothesis to the criminality of immigrants in Israel', *Journal of Criminal Law*, 1962, vol. 53, pp. 207–14.
81 S. Giora Shoham, Esther Segal and Giora Rahav, 'Secularization, deviance and delinquency among Israeli Arab villagers', *Human Relations*, vol. 28, no. 7, p. 672.
82 See Khalil Nakhleh, 'Multiplicity of legal systems in Israel: the case for legal heterogeneity', *The Third World Review*, vol. 1, no. 1, 1974, pp. 28–38.
83 Cf. Frantz Fanon, *The Wretched of the Earth*, Harmondsworth, Penguin Books, 1970.
84 Israel Drapkin and Simha F. Landau, 'Drug offenders in Israel: a survey', *British Journal of Criminology*, vol. 6, 1966, pp. 376–90.
85 Simha F. Landau, Israel Drapkin and Shlomo Arad, 'Homicide victims and offenders: an Israeli study', *Criminology*, vol. 65, no. 3, 1974, pp. 390–6.
86 Heribert Adam, *Modernizing Racial Domination*, Oxford University Press, 1971, p. 102.
87 *Prison Service: Yearly Report*, 1972 (Hebrew); see tables pp. 90–3 for adults; pp. 122–5 for juveniles. It is significant to note that for Arab adults, out of 313 cases listed under the 'public order' category for adults, more than half, 193, refer to 'hostile sabotage violations'. For juveniles, 11 out of 69 cases in the 'public order' category are 'hostile sabotage violations', while another 22 are classified as border 'infiltrations'. These figures do not include non-Israeli Arabs, e.g. Palestinian guerrillas who were jailed in Israel. According to Ze'ev Schiff and Raphael Rothstein, 'As of November, 1970, Israel's nine jails held approximately 3,000 fedayeen. Of this total, 1,500, including sixty-five women, had been convicted by Israeli courts; 1000 were awaiting trial and 500 had been detained temporarily by administrative order' (*Fedayeen: Guerrillas against Israel*, New York, David McKay, 1972). According to Toledano, 305 Israeli Arabs have been sentenced in Israeli courts for participating in guerrilla activities (see *Ha-tsofe*, 7 July 1974 (Hebrew)). For a more recent statement concerning the treatment of Arab prisoners in Israeli jails, see 'Israel tortures Arab prisoners', *Sunday Times*, 19 June 1977.
88 M. Brewster Smith, 'Competence and socialization', in John A. Clausen (ed.), *Socialization and Society*, Boston, Little, Brown, 1968, p. 313.
89 Judith Porter, *Black Child, White Child*, Cambridge, Mass., Harvard University Press, 1971.

Chapter 7 The Politicization of Israeli Arabs

1 See Joel Beinen, 'The Palestinian communist party', *Middle East Research and Information Project*, no. 55, 1975, pp. 3–17.
2 For a discussion of the 1965 split in the Israeli Communist Party, see Dunia Nahas, *The Israeli Communist Party*, London, Croom Helm, 1976.

3 Martin W. Slann, 'Ideology and ethnicity in Israel's two communist parties: the conflict between Maki and Rakah', *Studies in Comparative Communism*, vol. 7, no. 4, 1974 (pp. 354–74), Table 2, p. 374.
4 *Ibid.*, Table 1, p. 373. To all intents and purposes Maqi ceased to exist as a political force, if not as a political party, in Israeli politics.
5 To be precise, 62 per cent of the Arab vote went to the Alignment and Mapam in 1965, compared to 46 per cent in 1973 (see Yachiel Harari, *The Arabs in Israel*, Givat Havina, Israel, Centre for Arab and Afro-Asian Studies, 1974, Tables EL/5 and EL/8).
6 Data taken from 'Analysis of the elections to the eighth Knesset', *Supplement No. 2 of the Bulletin of the Institute for Palestine Studies*, January 1974, p. 60 (Arabic).
7 Yachiel Harari, *Elections in the Arab Sector*, 1973, Givat Haviva, Israel, 1974, Table 5, p. 44 (Hebrew).
8 See Alan Arian, *The Choosing People*, Cleveland, Ohio, Case Western University Press, 1973, pp. 167–73.
9 It is important to point out here that by the rural dimension in the Jewish sector, we are not implying what is traditionally meant by 'rural' in the context of developing societies. As Arian notes (*ibid.*, pp. 152–67), the left-of-centre nature of the Jewish rural sector is due to the fact that the Kibbutzim and Moshavim have been dominated since pre-1948 Palestine by Mapai, Ahadut ha-Avoda and Mapam; these settlements usually vote with 'their' parties.
10 See *Supplement No. 2 of the Bulletin of the Institute for Palestine Studies*, p. 61.
11 See Harari, *The Arabs in Israel*, Tables E10, p. 35, and EL/14, p. 38.
12 See Harari, *Elections in the Arab Sector*, p. 3, and Table 1, p. 12.
13 *Ibid.*, Tables 1 and 2, pp. 24–5, and Tables 6–8, pp. 45–7.
14 Jacob M. Landau, 'The Arab vote', in Alan Arian (ed.), *The Elections in Israel – 1969*, Jerusalem, Academic Press, 1972, pp. 253–63.
15 Harari, *Elections in the Arab Sector*, Table 12, p. 20.
16 Figures for 1960 and 1965 are taken from Jacob M. Landau, *The Arabs in Israel: A Political Study*, London, Oxford University Press, 1969, p. 179; data for 1973 from Harari, *Elections in the Arab Sector*, p. 12.
17 See Arian, *The Choosing People*, p. 78.
18 Harari, *The Arabs in Israel*, p. 38.
19 See *ibid.*, p. 38.
20 *Ibid.*, p. 39.
21 Sabri Jiryis, *The Arabs in Israel*, Beirut, Institute for Palestine Studies, 1973, p. 314 (Arabic).
22 See John K. Cooley, *Green March, Black September*, London, Frank Cass 1973, pp. 51–2.
23 Ian Lustick, 'Institutionalized segmentation: one factor in the control of Israeli Arabs', unpublished paper delivered at the Middle East Studies Association Meeting, Louisville, Kentucky, 1975, p. 25.
24 Cited in *ibid.*, p. 25.
25 *Ibid.*, p. 25.

26 Landau, *The Arabs in Israel*, p. 94.
27 See Sabri Jiryis, 'The legal structure for the expropriation and absorption of Arab lands in Israel', *Journal of Palestine Studies*, vol. II, no. 4, 1973, pp. 82–104.
28 See Don Peretz, *Israel and the Palestine Arabs*, Washington, DC, The Middle East Institute, 1958, pp. 103–5.
29 See Jiryis, *The Arabs in Israel*, pp. 240–61.
30 Cited in *ibid.*, p. 319.
31 See Landau, *The Arabs in Israel*, p. 99.
32 See Jiryis, *The Arabs in Israel*, p. 325.
33 *Ibid.*, p. 327.
34 Landau, *The Arabs in Israel*, p. 103.
35 *Ibid.*, p. 100.
36 Jiryis, *The Arabs in Israel*, p. 332.
37 Fouzi El-Asmar, *To be an Arab in Israel*, London, Frances Pinter, 1975, pp. 73–4.
38 See Jiryis's article in *Al-Nahar*, 15 May 1975 (Arabic Daily in Beirut).
39 See Larry L. Fabian and Ze'ev Schiff (eds), *Israelis Speak*, New York and Washington DC, Carnegie Endowment for International Peace, 1977.
40 See Jiryis, *The Arabs in Israel*, p. 332.
41 There has been a remarkable consistency in the demands of Arab students in the last two decades. Contrast these earlier demands with those advocated by Arab students in the mid-1970s (see Khalil Nakhleh, 'Nationalistic Consciousness and University Education: The Dilemma of Palestinians in Israel', unpublished study, Haifa, The Institute for Research and Development of Arab Education, Haifa University, 1976, p. 101).
42 See *Al-Itihad*, 7 December 1971.
43 See *Davar*, 7 May 1975.
44 *Davar*, 13 March 1975.
45 *Yediot Aharonot*, 23 April 1975.
46 *Ibid.*
47 *Bulletin of the Institute for Palestine Studies*, April 1972, pp. 178–89 (Arabic).
48 See R. Shapira and E. Etzioni-Halevy, *Who is the Israeli Student?* Tel Aviv, Am Oved, 1973 (Hebrew).
49 See Yaffa-Nicole Reich, 'Arabs on campus', *Israel Magazine*, vol. IV, no. 1, 1977, pp. 16–24.
50 Elie Rekhness, 'Study of Arab university students in Israel', mimeographed, Tel Aviv University, n.d., p. 29.
51 Quoted in Reich, *op. cit.*, p. 24.
52 Sami Mar'i 'School and society in Arab villages in Israel', mimeographed n.d., p. 17; originally published in *Studies in Education*, no. 2, 1974 (Hebrew).
53 Quoted in Reich, *op. cit.*, p. 24.
54 Reprinted in *Journal of Palestine Studies*, vol. VII, no. 1, 1976, p. 154.
55 See Kokhavi Shemesh, 'The destroyers and ravagers out of ye will come', in Uri Davis and Morton Mezvinsky (eds), *Documents from*

Israel, 1967–1973, London, Ithaca Press, 1975, pp. 123–6.
56 Joseph Waxmann, 'The Panthers dream to fight together with the Arabs against the establishment', in Davis and Mezvinsky (eds), *op. cit.*, pp. 120–2.
57 See note 41 above.
58 Cited in Landau, *The Arabs in Israel*, p. 45.
59 *Ibid.*, p. 47.
60 Pro-government writings are most evident in the Zionist-sponsored Arabic press; See Ellen Joyce Kubersky Geffner, 'Attitudes of Arab editorialists in Israel, 1947–1967: an analysis of *al-Itihad*, *al-Mirsad* and *al-Yawm*', unpublished PhD thesis, University of Michigan, Ann Arbor, 1973.
61 Cooley, *op. cit.*, p. 83.
62 Landau, *The Arabs in Israel*, p. 58.
63 Ghassan Kanafani, *Palestinian Resistance Literature under Occupation*, Beirut, Institute for Palestine Studies, 1968, p. 54 (Arabic).
64 Frantz Fanon, *The Wretched of the Earth*, Harmondsworth, Penguin Books, 1970, p. 192.
65 Cooley, *op. cit.*, p. 49.
66 See Emile Marmorstein, 'Rashid Husain: portrait of an angry young Arab', *Middle Eastern Studies*, vol. 1, no. 1, 1964, pp. 3–20. Another Israeli Arab writing in Hebrew is A. Mansour, who works as a correspondent for the Hebrew daily *Ha-Aretz*.
67 El-Asmar, *op. cit.*, p. 61.
68 See Emile A. Nakhleh, 'Wells of bitterness: a survey of Israeli-Arab political poetry', in Naseer Aruri (ed.), *The Palestinian Resistance to Israeli Occupation*, Wilmette, Ill., Medina University Press, 1970, pp. 110–11.
69 *Ibid.*, pp. 123–4.
70 Cited by Marmorstein, *op. cit.*, pp. 11–12.
71 See Husain's statement in 'How to speak to the Arabs: a *Maariv* round table', *The Middle East Journal*, vol. 18, 1964, pp. 154–7.
72 Nakhleh, *op. cit.*, pp. 112–13.
73 *Ibid.*, pp. 113–14.
74 Cooley, *op. cit.*, pp. 55–6.
75 *Ibid.*, p. 49.

Chapter 8 Toward a sociology of the Palestinians

1 An exception to this is Enzo Sereni and R. F. Ashery (eds), *Jews and Arabs in Palestine*, New York, Hechzlutz Press, 1936.
2 See Susan Lee Hattis, *The Bi-National Idea in Palestine During Mandatory Times*, Haifa, Shikmona Publishing Company, 1970.
3 Teodor Shanin, 'The price of suspension', in Uri Davis, Andrew Mack and Nira Yuval-Davis (eds), *Israel and the Palestinians*, London, Ithaca Press, 1975, pp. 24–56.
4 *Ibid.*, p. 30.
5 Maxime Rodinson, *Israel: A Colonial Settler State?*, New York, Pathfinder Press, 1973; Arie Bober (ed.) *The Other Israel*, New York,

Doubleday, 1972; Noam Chomsky, 'Israel and the Palestinians', *Socialist Revolution*, vol. 5, 1975, pp. 45–86; Glen Yago, 'Whatever happened to the promised land?', *Berkeley Journal of Sociology*, vol. XXI, 1976, pp. 117–46.

6 Saul Friedlander articulates this point very succinctly in Saul Friedlander and Mahmoud Hussain, *Arabs and Israelis*, New York, Holmes and Meir, 1975; See also Bernard Avishai, 'Zionist "Colonialism": myth and dilemma', *Dissent*, Spring 1975, pp. 125–34.

7 Friedlander and Hussain, *op. cit.*, pp. 151–2.

8 It is significant that after the Arab riots of 1929 Ben-Gurion declared 'The Arabs demand the abolition of the Mandate and the establishment of a national government; we must insist on the Mandate and deny the claim of the present inhabitants to sovereignty over the land. The rights of the Jewish people to Palestine are not inferior to the rights of its present Arab inhabitants. The present Arab population is in possession only of a small [sic] portion of the land and does not need more. Their ownership does not extend over the entire land. But we recognize without any reservations or conditions the full citizenship of all inhabitants of the land, both Arabs and Jews' (David Ben-Gurion, 'Planning Zionist policy', pp. 152–3 in Sereni and Ashery (eds), *op. cit.*, pp. 125–53). A few years earlier, in 1924, Ben-Gurion had already dismissed the bi-nationalist idea by noting that 'Zionism is the desire for a Jewish state, a desire for a country and territorial government'. Likewise, in 1925, he submitted a proposal to the Histadrut calling for Arab–Jewish co-operation based on 'autonomous national blocs', and with the recognition of the positive value and rights of the Jewish immigration to the country (Hattis, *op. cit.*, pp. 76–7). These words were uttered at a time when the Jewish settlers amounted to around 15–18 per cent of the population, and Jewish-owned land amounted to less than 5 per cent of the total area of Palestine. After examining primary sources pertaining to the attitude of 'Zionist socialists' to the Arab issue, Yosef Gorni noted that 'the Ahdut ha-Avoda leaders [the socialist wing of the Zionist movement] . . . were unanimous in their belief in the Jewish national right to Palestine and spoke of the need to define the rights of the Arabs in Palestine as a national minority within a large and expanding Jewish community. This view was expressed at a time when the Jewish community constituted less than ten per cent of the total population of the country!' ('Zionist socialism and the Arab question, 1918–1930', *Middle Eastern Studies*, vol. 13, no. 1, 1977, p. 51).

9 George E. Kirk, *A Short History of the Middle East*, London, Methuen, 1964, pp. 152–3.

10 See *ibid.*, p. 150.

11 See Nathan Weinstock's Introduction in Abram Leon, *The Jewish Question*, New York, Pathfinder Press, 1970, p. 55.

12 Kirk, *op. cit.*, p. 158.

13 *Ibid.*, pp. 324–5.

14 See *ibid.*, pp. 320–1.

15 Leon, *op. cit.*, p. 248.

16 *Ibid.*, p. 249.

17 See Werner J. Cahnman, 'Socio-economic sources of anti-semitism', *Social Problems*, vol. 5, no. 1, July 1957, pp. 21–9; Oscar Handlin, 'Does economics explain racism?', *Commentary*, vol. 6, no. 1, July 1948, pp. 79–85; Maxime Rodinson, in Davis *et al.* (eds), *op. cit.*, pp. 57–68.

18 See the articles by Eldad and Shraga Gafni in Uri Davis and Norton Mezvinsky (eds), *Documents from Israel*, London, Ithaca Press, 1975, pp. 183–99. Gush Emunim, the ultra-right-wing religious movement in Israel which calls for the annexation of the occupied territories, is a concrete example of this thinking. The ruling coalition, Likud, contains within its ranks many adherents to this principle. It is important to note, as Beit-Hallahmi demonstrates, that the influence of religious ideas on the Israeli political culture is not confined to religious fanatics and fundamentalists but is also found to permeate the rhetoric and ideologies of the secular and socialist leadership in Israel ('Some roles of religion in the Arab-Israeli conflict', mimeographed, University of Michigan, n.d.).

19 Among the most recent writings on this debate see Elmer Berger, 'Memoirs of an anti-Zionist Jew', *Journal of Palestine Studies*, vol. V, nos. 1–2, 1975/1976, pp. 3–55; Joseph Shattan, 'Why Breira?', *Commentary*, vol. 63, no. 4, 1977, pp. 60–6; cf. letters to the editor in *Commentary*, vol. 63, no. 6, 1977.

20 See Larry L. Fabian and Ze'ev Schiff (eds), *Israelis Speak*, New York and Washington, DC, Carnegie Endowment for International Peace, 1977. Similarly, Michael Benazon, a Canadian Jew and Zionist, remarked, 'For too long a conspiracy of silence has prevailed among Diaspora Jews on anything touching the blunders, lapses and faults committed by Israel' ('Second thoughts, Israel 1977', *Canadian Forum*, May 1977, pp. 9–15). In contrast, for the diversity of Israeli points of view, see Rael Jean Isaac, *Israel Divided*, Baltimore, Johns Hopkins University Press, 1976; Charles Glass, 'Jews against Zion: Israeli Jewish anti-Zionism', *Journal of Palestine Studies*, vol. V, nos. 1–2, 1975–1976, pp. 56–81.

21 This is not to say that there are no pre-1948 Arab writings on Palestine; See the extensive annotated bibliography in Walid Khalidi and Jill Khadduri (eds), *Palestine and the Arab–Israel Conflict*, Beirut, Institute for Palestine Studies, 1974.

22 Arthur Ruppin, *Three Decades of Palestine: Speeches and Papers on the Upbuilding of the Jewish National Home*, Jerusalem, Schoken, 1936.

23 A. Granott, *The Land System in Palestine*, London, Eyre & Spottiswoode, 1952.

24 Alfred Bonné, *State and Economics in the Middle East*, London, Routledge & Kegan Paul, 1955.

25 Ludwig Gruenbaum, *National Income and Outlay in Palestine*, Jerusalem, Economic Research Institute, Jewish Agency, 1941; *Outlines of a Development for Jewish Palestine*, Jerusalem, Economic Research Institute, Jewish Agency, 1946.

26 Y. Waschitz, *The Arabs in Palestine*, Tel Aviv, Sifriat Poalim, 1947 (Hebrew).

27 Raphael Patai, *On Culture Contact and its Workings in Modern Palestine*, American Anthropological Association Monograph, vol. 49, no. 67, 1947.

28 Y. Shimoni, *The Arabs of Eretz Israel*, Tel Aviv, Am Oved, 1946 (Hebrew).

29 Karl Mannheim, *Ideology and Utopia*, London, Routledge & Kegan Paul, 1968, pp. 136–46.

30 Shulamit Carmi and Henry Rosenfeld, 'The origins of the process of proletarianization and urbanization of Arab peasants in Palestine', *Annals of New York Academy of Sciences*, vol. 220, 1974, pp. 470–85.

31 As noted in Chapter 3, this has become a standard argument in Zionist writings on pre-1948 Palestine. See M. Aumann, 'Land ownership in Palestine: 1880–1948', in M. Curtis *et al.* (eds), *The Palestinians: People, History, Politics*, New Brunswick, N.J., Transaction Books, 1975, pp. 21–9. A more sophisticated route, via Marxism, but leading to a similar end, is that adopted by Shlomo Avineri, 'Modernization and Arab society: some reflections', in Irving Howe and Carl Gresham (eds), *Israel, the Arabs and the Middle East*, New York, Bantam Books, 1973, pp. 300–11; cf. Bryan Turner's criticism of Avineri, 'Avineri's view of Marx's theory of colonialism: Israel', *Science and Society*, vol. XL, no. 4, 1976–7, pp. 385–409.

32 Weinstock, *op. cit.*, pp. 55–6.

33 Avineri, *op. cit.*

34 Turner, *op. cit.*, p. 406.

35 See Raphel Patai, *The Arab Mind*, New York, Scribner, 1973. See also the critical review of Patai's book by Malcolm Kerr, *Muslim World*, vol. LXVI, no. 4, 1976, pp. 300–2.

36 See Fouzi El-Asmar, 'Israel revisited', *Journal of Palestine Studies*, vol. VI, no. 3, 1977, pp. 66–76.

37 Sami Mar'i and N. Dhahir, *Facts and Levels in the Development of Arab Education in Israel*, Haifa Institute for Research and Development of Arab Education, Haifa University, 1976 (Hebrew).

38 Rosemary Said and A. B. Zahlan, 'The cultural and educational needs of the Palestinians', *Journal of Palestine Studies*, vol. VI, no. 4, 1977, pp. 103–12.

39 Ibrahim Abu-Lughod, 'Educating a community in exile: the Palestine experience', *Journal of Palestine Studies*, vol. 2, no. 2, 1973, pp. 94–111.

40 Tawfic Farah, 'Political socialization of Palestinian children', *Journal of Palestine Studies*, vol. VI, no. 4, 1977, pp. 90–102.

41 A comprehensive analytical study of the Palestinian occupational structure in the Arab world is lacking. A start is provided by the statistical compilation of Jacqueline Farhood Jerisati, 'The Palestinian people: figures and pointers', *Palestine Affairs*, January/February 1975, pp. 399–431 (Arabic).

42 Rosemary Sayigh, 'The Palestinian experience viewed as socialization', unpublished MA thesis, American University at Beirut, 1976; Bassem

Sirhan, 'Palestinian refugee life in Lebanon', *Journal of Palestine Studies*, vol. IV, no. 2, 1975, pp. 91–107.

43 Bassem Sirhan, 'Family and kinship among Palestinians in Kuwait', unpublished manuscript, Kuwait University, 1976.

44 See Fawaz Turki, 'The Palestinian estranged', *Journal of Palestine Studies*, vol. V, nos. 1 and 2, 1975, pp. 82–96.

45 Paulo Freire, *Pedagogy of the Oppressed*, New York, The Seabury Press, 1970.

Index

Routledge Social Science Series

Routledge & Kegan Paul London, Henley and Boston

39 Store Street, London WC1E 7DD
Broadway House, Newtown Road, Henley-on-Thames, Oxon RG9 1EN
9 Park Street, Boston, Mass. 02108

Contents

Authors wishing to submit manuscripts for any series in this catalogue should send them to the Social Science Editor, Routledge & Kegan Paul Ltd, 39 Store Street, London WC1E 7DD

●*Books so marked are available in paperback*
All books are in Metric Demy 8vo format (216×138mm approx.)

International Library of Sociology

General Editor John Rex

GENERAL SOCIOLOGY

Barnsley, J. H. The Social Reality of Ethics. *464 pp.*
Belshaw, Cyril. The Conditions of Social Performance. *An Exploratory Theory. 144 pp.*
Brown, Robert. Explanation in Social Science. *208 pp.*
● Rules and Laws in Sociology. *192 pp.*
Bruford, W. H. Chekhov and His Russia. *A Sociological Study. 244 pp.*
Cain, Maureen E. Society and the Policeman's Role. *326 pp.*
●**Fletcher, Colin.** Beneath the Surface. *An Account of Three Styles of Sociological Research. 221 pp.*
Gibson, Quentin. The Logic of Social Enquiry. *240 pp.*
Glucksmann, M. Structuralist Analysis in Contemporary Social Thought. *212 pp.*
Gurvitch, Georges. Sociology of Law. *Preface by Roscoe Pound. 264 pp.*
Hodge, H. A. Wilhelm Dilthey. *An Introduction. 184 pp.*
Homans, George C. Sentiments and Activities. *336 pp.*
Johnson, Harry M. Sociology: *a Systematic Introduction. Foreword by Robert K. Merton. 710 pp.*
●**Keat, Russell,** and **Urry, John.** Social Theory as Science. *278 pp.*
Mannheim, Karl. Essays on Sociology and Social Psychology. *Edited by Paul Keckskemeti. With Editorial Note by Adolph Lowe. 344 pp.*
Systematic Sociology: *An Introduction to the Study of Society. Edited by J. S. Erös and Professor W. A. C. Stewart. 220 pp.*
Martindale, Don. The Nature and Types of Sociological Theory. *292 pp.*
●**Maus, Heinz.** A Short History of Sociology. *234 pp.*
Mey, Harald. Field-Theory. *A Study of its Application in the Social Sciences. 352 pp.*
Myrdal, Gunnar. Value in Social Theory: *A Collection of Essays on Methodology. Edited by Paul Streeten. 332 pp.*
Ogburn, William F., and **Nimkoff, Meyer F.** A Handbook of Sociology. *Preface by Karl Mannheim. 656 pp. 46 figures. 35 tables.*
Parsons, Talcott, and **Smelser, Neil J.** Economy and Society: *A Study in the Integration of Economic and Social Theory. 362 pp.*
Podgórecki, Adam. Practical Social Sciences. *About 200 pp.*
●**Rex, John.** Key Problems of Sociological Theory. *220 pp.*
Sociology and the Demystification of the Modern World. *282 pp.*
●**Rex, John** (Ed.) Approaches to Sociology. *Contributions by Peter Abell, Frank Bechhofer, Basil Bernstein, Ronald Fletcher, David Frisby, Miriam Glucksmann, Peter Lassman, Herminio Martins, John Rex, Roland Robertson, John Westergaard and Jock Young. 302 pp.*
Rigby, A. Alternative Realities. *352 pp.*
Roche, M. Phenomenology, Language and the Social Sciences. *374 pp.*

Sahay, A. Sociological Analysis. *220 pp.*

Simirenko, Alex (Ed.) Soviet Sociology. *Historical Antecedents and Current Appraisals. Introduction by Alex Simirenko. 376 pp.*

Strasser, Hermann. The Normative Structure of Sociology. *Conservative and Emancipatory Themes in Social Thought. About 340 pp.*

Urry, John. Reference Groups and the Theory of Revolution. *244 pp.*

Weinberg, E. Development of Sociology in the Soviet Union. *173 pp.*

FOREIGN CLASSICS OF SOCIOLOGY

● **Durkheim, Emile.** Suicide. *A Study in Sociology. Edited and with an Introduction by George Simpson. 404 pp.*

● **Gerth, H. H.,** and **Mills, C. Wright.** From Max Weber: *Essays in Sociology. 502 pp.*

● **Tönnies, Ferdinand.** Community and Association. (*Gemeinschaft und Gesellschaft.*) *Translated and Supplemented by Charles P. Loomis. Foreword by Pitirim A. Sorokin. 334 pp.*

SOCIAL STRUCTURE

Andreski, Stanislav. Military Organization and Society. *Foreword by Professor A. R. Radcliffe-Brown. 226 pp. 1 folder.*

Carlton, Eric. Ideology and Social Order. *Preface by Professor Philip Abrahams. About 320 pp.*

Coontz, Sydney H. Population Theories and the Economic Interpretation. *202 pp.*

Coser, Lewis. The Functions of Social Conflict. *204 pp.*

Dickie-Clark, H. F. Marginal Situation: *A Sociological Study of a Coloured Group. 240 pp. 11 tables.*

Glaser, Barney, and **Strauss, Anselm L.** Status Passage. *A Formal Theory. 208 pp.*

Glass, D. V. (Ed.) Social Mobility in Britain. *Contributions by J. Berent, T. Bottomore, R. C. Chambers, J. Floud, D. V. Glass, J. R. Hall, H. T. Himmelweit, R. K. Kelsall, F. M. Martin, C. A. Moser, R. Mukherjee, and W. Ziegel. 420 pp.*

Johnstone, Frederick A. Class, Race and Gold. *A Study of Class Relations and Racial Discrimination in South Africa. 312 pp.*

Jones, Garth N. Planned Organizational Change: *An Exploratory Study Using an Empirical Approach. 268 pp.*

Kelsall, R. K. Higher Civil Servants in Britain: *From 1870 to the Present Day. 268 pp. 31 tables.*

König, René. The Community. *232 pp. Illustrated.*

● **Lawton, Denis.** Social Class, Language and Education. *192 pp.*

McLeish, John. The Theory of Social Change: *Four Views Considered. 128 pp.*

Marsh, David C. The Changing Social Structure of England and Wales, 1871-1961. *288 pp.*

Menzies, Ken. Talcott Parsons and the Social Image of Man. *About 208 pp.*

●**Mouzelis, Nicos.** Organization and Bureaucracy. *An Analysis of Modern Theories. 240 pp.*

Mulkay, M. J. Functionalism, Exchange and Theoretical Strategy. *272 pp.*

Ossowski, Stanislaw. Class Structure in the Social Consciousness. *210 pp.*

●**Podgórecki, Adam.** Law and Society. *302 pp.*

Renner, Karl. Institutions of Private Law and Their Social Functions. *Edited, with an Introduction and Notes, by O. Kahn-Freud. Translated by Agnes Schwarzschild. 316 pp.*

SOCIOLOGY AND POLITICS

Acton, T. A. Gypsy Politics and Social Change. *316 pp.*

Clegg, Stuart. Power, Rule and Domination. *A Critical and Empirical Understanding of Power in Sociological Theory and Organisational Life. About 300 pp.*

Hechter, Michael. Internal Colonialism. *The Celtic Fringe in British National Development, 1536–1966. 361 pp.*

Hertz, Frederick. Nationality in History and Politics: *A Psychology and Sociology of National Sentiment and Nationalism. 432 pp.*

Kornhauser, William. The Politics of Mass Society. *272 pp. 20 tables.*

●**Kroes, R.** Soldiers and Students. *A Study of Right- and Left-wing Students. 174 pp.*

Laidler, Harry W. History of Socialism. *Social-Economic Movements: An Historical and Comparative Survey of Socialism, Communism, Co-operation, Utopianism; and other Systems of Reform and Reconstruction. 992 pp.*

Lasswell, H. D. Analysis of Political Behaviour. *324 pp.*

Martin, David A. Pacifism: *an Historical and Sociological Study. 262 pp.*

Martin, Roderick. Sociology of Power. *About 272 pp.*

Myrdal, Gunnar. The Political Element in the Development of Economic Theory. *Translated from the German by Paul Streeten. 282 pp.*

Wilson, H. T. The American Ideology. *Science, Technology and Organization of Modes of Rationality. About 280 pp.*

Wootton, Graham. Workers, Unions and the State. *188 pp.*

CRIMINOLOGY

Ancel, Marc. Social Defence: *A Modern Approach to Criminal Problems. Foreword by Leon Radzinowicz. 240 pp.*

Cain, Maureen E. Society and the Policeman's Role. *326 pp.*

Cloward, Richard A., and **Ohlin, Lloyd E.** Delinquency and Opportunity: *A Theory of Delinquent Gangs. 248 pp.*

Downes, David M. The Delinquent Solution. *A Study in Subcultural Theory. 296 pp.*

Dunlop, A. B., and **McCabe, S.** Young Men in Detention Centres. *192 pp.*

Friedlander, Kate. The Psycho-Analytical Approach to Juvenile Delinquency: *Theory, Case Studies, Treatment. 320 pp.*

Glueck, Sheldon, and **Eleanor.** Family Environment and Delinquency. *With the statistical assistance of Rose W. Kneznek. 340 pp.*

Lopez-Rey, Manuel. Crime. *An Analytical Appraisal. 288 pp.*

Mannheim, Hermann. Comparative Criminology: *a Text Book. Two volumes. 442 pp. and 380 pp.*

Morris, Terence. The Criminal Area: *A Study in Social Ecology. Foreword by Hermann Mannheim. 232 pp. 25 tables. 4 maps.*

Rock, Paul. Making People Pay. *338 pp.*

●**Taylor, Ian, Walton, Paul,** and **Young, Jock.** The New Criminology. *For a Social Theory of Deviance. 325 pp.*

●**Taylor, Ian, Walton, Paul,** and **Young, Jock** (Eds). Critical Criminology. *268 pp.*

SOCIAL PSYCHOLOGY

Bagley, Christopher. The Social Psychology of the Epileptic Child. *320 pp.*

Barbu, Zevedei. Problems of Historical Psychology. *248 pp.*

Blackburn, Julian. Psychology and the Social Pattern. *184 pp.*

●**Brittan, Arthur.** Meanings and Situations. *224 pp.*

Carroll, J. Break-Out from the Crystal Palace. *200 pp.*

●**Fleming, C. M.** Adolescence: Its Social Psychology. *With an Introduction to recent findings from the fields of Anthropology, Physiology, Medicine, Psychometrics and Sociometry. 288 pp.*

● The Social Psychology of Education: *An Introduction and Guide to Its Study. 136 pp.*

●**Homans, George C.** The Human Group. *Foreword by Bernard DeVoto. Introduction by Robert K. Merton. 526 pp.*

● Social Behaviour: *its Elementary Forms. 416 pp.*

●**Klein, Josephine.** The Study of Groups. *226 pp. 31 figures. 5 tables.*

Linton, Ralph. The Cultural Background of Personality. *132 pp.*

●**Mayo, Elton.** The Social Problems of an Industrial Civilization. *With an appendix on the Political Problem. 180 pp.*

Ottaway, A. K. C. Learning Through Group Experience. *176 pp.*

Plummer, Ken. Sexual Stigma. *An Interactionist Account. 254 pp.*

●**Rose, Arnold M.** (Ed.) Human Behaviour and Social Processes: *an Interactionist Approach. Contributions by Arnold M. Rose, Ralph H. Turner, Anselm Strauss, Everett C. Hughes, E. Franklin Frazier, Howard S. Becker, et al. 696 pp.*

Smelser, Neil J. Theory of Collective Behaviour. *448 pp.*

Stephenson, Geoffrey M. The Development of Conscience. *128 pp.*

Young, Kimball. Handbook of Social Psychology. *658 pp. 16 figures. 10 tables.*

SOCIOLOGY OF THE FAMILY

Banks, J. A. Prosperity and Parenthood: *A Study of Family Planning among The Victorian Middle Classes. 262 pp.*

Bell, Colin R. Middle Class Families: *Social and Geographical Mobility. 224 pp.*

Burton, Lindy. Vulnerable Children. *272 pp.*

Gavron, Hannah. The Captive Wife: *Conflicts of Household Mothers. 190 pp.*

George, Victor, and **Wilding, Paul.** Motherless Families. *248 pp.*

Klein, Josephine. Samples from English Cultures.

1. Three Preliminary Studies and Aspects of Adult Life in England. *447 pp.*
2. Child-Rearing Practices and Index. *247 pp.*

Klein, Viola. The Feminine Character. *History of an Ideology. 244 pp.*

McWhinnie, Alexina M. Adopted Children. *How They Grow Up. 304 pp.*

● **Morgan, D. H. J.** Social Theory and the Family. *About 320 pp.*

● **Myrdal, Alva,** and **Klein, Viola.** Women's Two Roles: *Home and Work. 238 pp. 27 tables.*

Parsons, Talcott, and **Bales, Robert F.** Family: Socialization and Interaction Process. *In collaboration with James Olds, Morris Zelditch and Philip E. Slater. 456 pp. 50 figures and tables.*

SOCIAL SERVICES

Bastide, Roger. The Sociology of Mental Disorder. *Translated from the French by Jean McNeil. 260 pp.*

Carlebach, Julius. Caring For Children in Trouble. *266 pp.*

George, Victor. Foster Care. *Theory and Practice. 234 pp.*

Social Security: *Beveridge and After. 258 pp.*

George, V., and **Wilding, P.** Motherless Families. *248 pp.*

● **Goetschius, George W.** Working with Community Groups. *256 pp.*

Goetschius, George W., and **Tash, Joan.** Working with Unattached Youth. *416 pp.*

Hall, M. P., and **Howes, I. V.** The Church in Social Work. *A Study of Moral Welfare Work undertaken by the Church of England. 320 pp.*

Heywood, Jean S. Children in Care: *the Development of the Service for the Deprived Child. 264 pp.*

Hoenig, J., and **Hamilton, Marian W.** The De-Segregation of the Mentally Ill. *284 pp.*

Jones, Kathleen. Mental Health and Social Policy, 1845-1959. *264 pp.*

King, Roy D., Raynes, Norma V., and **Tizard, Jack.** Patterns of Residential Care. *356 pp.*

Leigh, John. Young People and Leisure. *256 pp.*

● **Mays, John.** (Ed.) Penelope Hall's Social Services of England and Wales. *About 324 pp.*

Morris, Mary. Voluntary Work and the Welfare State. *300 pp.*

Nokes, P. L. The Professional Task in Welfare Practice. *152 pp.*

Timms, Noel. Psychiatric Social Work in Great Britain (1939-1962). *280 pp.*

● Social Casework: *Principles and Practice. 256 pp.*

Young, A. F. Social Services in British Industry. *272 pp.*

SOCIOLOGY OF EDUCATION

Banks, Olive. Parity and Prestige in English Secondary Education: a Study in Educational Sociology. *272 pp.*

Bentwich, Joseph. Education in Israel. *224 pp. 8 pp. plates.*

●**Blyth, W. A. L.** English Primary Education. *A Sociological Description.*
1. Schools. *232 pp.*
2. Background. *168 pp.*

Collier, K. G. The Social Purposes of Education: *Personal and Social Values in Education. 268 pp.*

Dale, R. R., and **Griffith, S.** Down Stream: *Failure in the Grammar School. 108 pp.*

Evans, K. M. Sociometry and Education. *158 pp.*

●**Ford, Julienne.** Social Class and the Comprehensive School. *192 pp.*

Foster, P. J. Education and Social Change in Ghana. *336 pp. 3 maps.*

Fraser, W. R. Education and Society in Modern France. *150 pp.*

Grace, Gerald R. Role Conflict and the Teacher. *150 pp.*

Hans, Nicholas. New Trends in Education in the Eighteenth Century. *278 pp. 19 tables.*

● Comparative Education: *A Study of Educational Factors and Traditions. 360 pp.*

●**Hargreaves, David.** Interpersonal Relations and Education. *432 pp.*

● Social Relations in a Secondary School. *240 pp.*

Holmes, Brian. Problems in Education. *A Comparative Approach. 336 pp.*

King, Ronald. Values and Involvement in a Grammar School. *164 pp.*

School Organization and Pupil Involvement. *A Study of Secondary Schools.*

●**Mannheim, Karl,** and **Stewart, W. A. C.** An Introduction to the Sociology of Education. *206 pp.*

Morris, Raymond N. The Sixth Form and College Entrance. *231 pp.*

●**Musgrove, F.** Youth and the Social Order. *176 pp.*

●**Ottaway, A. K. C.** Education and Society: An Introduction to the Sociology of Education. *With an Introduction by W. O. Lester Smith. 212 pp.*

Peers, Robert. Adult Education: *A Comparative Study. 398 pp.*

Pritchard, D. G. Education and the Handicapped: *1760 to 1960. 258 pp.*

Stratta, Erica. The Education of Borstal Boys. *A Study of their Educational Experiences prior to, and during, Borstal Training. 256 pp.*

Taylor, P. H., Reid, W. A., and **Holley, B. J.** The English Sixth Form. *A Case Study in Curriculum Research. 200 pp.*

SOCIOLOGY OF CULTURE

Eppel, E. M., and **M.** Adolescents and Morality: *A Study of some Moral Values and Dilemmas of Working Adolescents in the Context of a changing Climate of Opinion. Foreword by W. J. H. Sprott. 268 pp. 39 tables.*

●**Fromm, Erich.** The Fear of Freedom. *286 pp.*

● The Sane Society. *400 pp.*

Mannheim, Karl. Essays on the Sociology of Culture. *Edited by Ernst Mannheim in co-operation with Paul Kecskemeti. Editorial Note by Adolph Lowe. 280 pp.*

Weber, Alfred. Farewell to European History: *or The Conquest of Nihilism. Translated from the German by R. F. C. Hull. 224 pp.*

SOCIOLOGY OF RELIGION

Argyle, Michael and **Beit-Hallahmi, Benjamin.** The Social Psychology of Religion. *About 256 pp.*

Glasner, Peter E. The Sociology of Secularisation. *A Critique of a Concept. About 180 pp.*

Nelson, G. K. Spiritualism and Society. *313 pp.*

Stark, Werner. The Sociology of Religion. *A Study of Christendom.*
- Volume I. *Established Religion. 248 pp.*
- Volume II. *Sectarian Religion. 368 pp.*
- Volume III. *The Universal Church. 464 pp.*
- Volume IV. *Types of Religious Man. 352 pp.*
- Volume V. *Types of Religious Culture. 464 pp.*

Turner, B. S. Weber and Islam. *216 pp.*

Watt, W. Montgomery. Islam and the Integration of Society. *320 pp.*

SOCIOLOGY OF ART AND LITERATURE

Jarvie, Ian C. Towards a Sociology of the Cinema. *A Comparative Essay on the Structure and Functioning of a Major Entertainment Industry. 405 pp.*

Rust, Frances S. Dance in Society. *An Analysis of the Relationships between the Social Dance and Society in England from the Middle Ages to the Present Day. 256 pp. 8 pp. of plates.*

Schücking, L. L. The Sociology of Literary Taste. *112 pp.*

Wolff, Janet. Hermeneutic Philosophy and the Sociology of Art. *150 pp.*

SOCIOLOGY OF KNOWLEDGE

Diesing, P. Patterns of Discovery in the Social Sciences. *262 pp.*

●**Douglas, J. D.** (Ed.) Understanding Everyday Life. *370 pp.*

●**Hamilton, P.** Knowledge and Social Structure. *174 pp.*

Jarvie, I. C. Concepts and Society. *232 pp.*

Mannheim, Karl. Essays on the Sociology of Knowledge. *Edited by Paul Kecskemeti. Editorial Note by Adolph Lowe. 353 pp.*

Remmling, Gunter W. The Sociology cf Karl Mannheim. *With a Bibliographical Guide to the Sociology of Knowledge, Ideological Analysis, and Social Planning. 255 pp.*

Remmling, Gunter W. (Ed.) Towards the Sociology of Knowledge. *Origin and Development of a Sociological Thought Style. 463 pp.*

Stark, Werner. The Sociology of Knowledge: *An Essay in Aid of a Deeper Understanding of the History of Ideas. 384 pp.*

URBAN SOCIOLOGY

Ashworth, William. The Genesis of Modern British Town Planning: *A Study in Economic and Social History of the Nineteenth and Twentieth Centuries. 288 pp.*

Cullingworth, J. B. Housing Needs and Planning Policy: *A Restatement of the Problems of Housing Need and 'Overspill' in England and Wales. 232 pp. 44 tables. 8 maps.*

Dickinson, Robert E. City and Region: *A Geographical Interpretation 608 pp. 125 figures.*

The West European City: *A Geographical Interpretation. 600 pp. 129 maps. 29 plates.*

● The City Region in Western Europe. *320 pp. Maps.*

Humphreys, Alexander J. New Dubliners: *Urbanization and the Irish Family. Foreword by George C. Homans. 304 pp.*

Jackson, Brian. Working Class Community: *Some General Notions raised by a Series of Studies in Northern England. 192 pp.*

Jennings, Hilda. Societies in the Making: *a Study of Development and Redevelopment within a County Borough. Foreword by D. A. Clark. 286 pp.*

●**Mann, P. H.** An Approach to Urban Sociology. *240 pp.*

Morris, R. N., and **Mogey, J.** The Sociology of Housing. *Studies at Berinsfield. 232 pp. 4 pp. plates.*

Rosser, C., and **Harris, C.** The Family and Social Change. *A Study of Family and Kinship in a South Wales Town. 352 pp. 8 maps.*

●**Stacey, Margaret, Batsone, Eric, Bell, Colin,** and **Thurcott, Anne.** Power, Persistence and Change. *A Second Study of Banbury. 196 pp.*

RURAL SOCIOLOGY

Haswell, M. R. The Economics of Development in Village India. *120 pp.*

Littlejohn, James. Westrigg: *the Sociology of a Cheviot Parish. 172 pp. 5 figures.*

Mayer, Adrian C. Peasants in the Pacific. *A Study of Fiji Indian Rural Society. 248 pp. 20 plates.*

Williams, W. M. The Sociology of an English Village: *Gosforth. 272 pp. 12 figures. 13 tables.*

SOCIOLOGY OF INDUSTRY AND DISTRIBUTION

Anderson, Nels. Work and Leisure. *280 pp.*

●**Blau, Peter M.**, and **Scott, W. Richard.** Formal Organizations: *a Comparative approach. Introduction and Additional Bibliography by J. H. Smith. 326 pp.*

Dunkerley, David. The Foreman. *Aspects of Task and Structure. 192 pp.*

Eldridge, J. E. T. Industrial Disputes. *Essays in the Sociology of Industrial Relations. 288 pp.*

Hetzler, Stanley. Applied Measures for Promoting Technological Growth. *352 pp.*

Technological Growth and Social Change. *Achieving Modernization. 269 pp.*

Hollowell, Peter G. The Lorry Driver. *272 pp.*

●**Oxaal, I., Barnett, T.,** and **Booth, D.** (Eds). Beyond the Sociology of Development. *Economy and Society in Latin America and Africa. 295 pp.*

Smelser, Neil J. Social Change in the Industrial Revolution: *An Application of Theory to the Lancashire Cotton Industry, 1770–1840. 468 pp. 12 figures. 14 tables.*

ANTHROPOLOGY

Ammar, Hamed. Growing up in an Egyptian Village: *Silwa, Province of Aswan. 336 pp.*

Brandel-Syrier, Mia. Reeftown Elite. *A Study of Social Mobility in a Modern African Community on the Reef. 376 pp.*

Dickie-Clark, H. F. The Marginal Situation. *A Sociological Study of a Coloured Group. 236 pp.*

Dube, S. C. Indian Village. *Foreword by Morris Edward Opler. 276 pp. 4 plates.*

India's Changing Villages: *Human Factors in Community Development. 260 pp. 8 plates. 1 map.*

Firth, Raymond. Malay Fishermen. *Their Peasant Economy. 420 pp. 17 pp. plates.*

Gulliver, P. H. Social Control in an African Society: a Study of the Arusha, Agricultural Masai of Northern Tanganyika. *320 pp. 8 plates. 10 figures.*

Family Herds. *288 pp.*

Ishwaran, K. Tradition and Economy in Village India: *An Interactionist Approach.*
Foreword by Conrad Arensburg. 176 pp.

Jarvie, Ian C. The Revolution in Anthropology. *268 pp.*

Little, Kenneth L. Mende of Sierra Leone. *308 pp. and folder.*

Negroes in Britain. *With a New Introduction and Contemporary Study by Leonard Bloom. 320 pp.*

Lowie, Robert H. Social Organization. *494 pp.*

Mayer, A. C. Peasants in the Pacific. *A Study of Fiji Indian Rural Society. 248 pp.*

Meer, Fatima. Race and Suicide in South Africa. *325 pp.*

Smith, Raymond T. The Negro Family in British Guiana: *Family Structure and Social Status in the Villages. With a Foreword by Meyer Fortes. 314 pp. 8 plates. 1 figure. 4 maps.*

Smooha, Sammy. Israel: Pluralism and Conflict. *About 320 pp.*

SOCIOLOGY AND PHILOSOPHY

Barnsley, John H. The Social Reality of Ethics. *A Comparative Analysis of Moral Codes. 448 pp.*

Diesing, Paul. Patterns of Discovery in the Social Sciences. *362 pp.*

●**Douglas, Jack D.** (Ed.) Understanding Everyday Life. *Toward the Reconstruction of Sociological Knowledge. Contributions by Alan F. Blum. Aaron W. Cicourel, Norman K. Denzin, Jack D. Douglas, John Heeren, Peter McHugh, Peter K. Manning, Melvin Power, Matthew Speier, Roy Turner, D. Lawrence Wieder, Thomas P. Wilson and Don H. Zimmerman. 370 pp.*

Gorman, Robert A. The Dual Vision. *Alfred Schutz and the Myth of Phenomenological Social Science. About 300 pp.*

Jarvie, Ian C. Concepts and Society. *216 pp.*

●**Pelz, Werner.** The Scope of Understanding in Sociology. *Towards a more radical reorientation in the social humanistic sciences. 283 pp.*

Roche, Maurice. Phenomenology, Language and the Social Sciences. *371 pp.*

Sahay, Arun. Sociological Analysis. *212 pp.*

Sklair, Leslie. The Sociology of Progress. *320 pp.*

Slater, P. Origin and Significance of the Frankfurt School. *A Marxist Perspective. About 192 pp.*

Smart, Barry. Sociology, Phenomenology and Marxian Analysis. *A Critical Discussion of the Theory and Practice of a Science of Society. 220 pp.*

International Library of Anthropology

General Editor Adam Kuper

Ahmed, A. S. Millenium and Charisma Among Pathans. *A Critical Essay in Social Anthropology. 192 pp.*

Brown, Paula. The Chimbu. *A Study of Change in the New Guinea Highlands. 151 pp.*

Gudeman, Stephen. Relationships, Residence and the Individual. *A Rural Panamanian Community. 288 pp. 11 Plates, 5 Figures, 2 Maps, 10 Tables.*

Hamnett, Ian. Chieftainship and Legitimacy. *An Anthropological Study of Executive Law in Lesotho. 163 pp.*

Hanson, F. Allan. Meaning in Culture. *127 pp.*

Lloyd, P. C. Power and Independence. *Urban Africans' Perception of Social Inequality. 264 pp.*

Pettigrew, Joyce. Robber Noblemen. *A Study of the Political System of the Sikh Jats. 284 pp.*
Street, Brian V. The Savage in Literature. *Representations of 'Primitive' Society in English Fiction, 1858–1920. 207 pp.*
Van Den Berghe, Pierre L. Power and Privilege at an African University. *278 pp.*

International Library of Social Policy

General Editor Kathleen Jones

Bayley, M. Mental Handicap and Community Care. *426 pp.*
Bottoms, A. E., and **McClean, J. D.** Defendants in the Criminal Process. *284 pp.*
Butler, J. R. Family Doctors and Public Policy. *208 pp.*
Davies, Martin. Prisoners of Society. *Attitudes and Aftercare. 204 pp.*
Gittus, Elizabeth. Flats, Families and the Under-Fives. *285 pp.*
Holman, Robert. Trading in Children. *A Study of Private Fostering. 355 pp.*
Jones, Howard, and **Cornes, Paul.** Open Prisons. *About 248 pp.*
Jones, Kathleen. History of the Mental Health Service. *428 pp.*
Jones, Kathleen, with **Brown, John, Cunningham, W. J., Roberts, Julian,** and **Williams, Peter.** Opening the Door. *A Study of New Policies for the Mentally Handicapped. 278 pp.*
Karn, Valerie. Retiring to the Seaside. *About 280 pp. 2 maps. Numerous tables.*
Thomas, J. E. The English Prison Officer since 1850: *A Study in Conflict. 258 pp.*
Walton, R. G. Women in Social Work. *303 pp.*
Woodward, J. To Do the Sick No Harm. *A Study of the British Voluntary Hospital System to 1875. 221 pp.*

International Library of Welfare and Philosophy

General Editors Noel Timms and David Watson

● **Plant, Raymond.** Community and Ideology. *104 pp.*

● **McDermott, F. E.** (Ed.) Self-Determination in Social Work. *A Collection of Essays on Self-determination and Related Concepts by Philosophers and Social Work Theorists. Contributors: F. P. Biestek, S. Bernstein, A. Keith-Lucas, D. Sayer, H. H. Perelman, C. Whittington, R. F. Stalley, F. E. McDermott, I. Berlin, H. J. McCloskey, H. L. A. Hart, J. Wilson, A. I. Melden, S. I. Benn. 254 pp.*
Ragg, Nicholas M. People Not Cases. *A Philosophical Approach to Social Work. About 250 pp.*

● **Timms, Noel,** and **Watson, David** (Eds). Talking About Welfare. *Readings in Philosophy and Social Policy. Contributors: T. H. Marshall, R. B. Brandt, G. H. von Wright, K. Nielsen, M. Cranston, R. M. Titmuss, R. S. Downie, E. Telfer, D. Donnison, J. Benson, P. Leonard, A. Keith-Lucas, D. Walsh, I. T. Ramsey. 320 pp.*

Primary Socialization, Language and Education

General Editor Basil Bernstein

Adlam, Diana S., *with the assistance of Geoffrey Turner and Lesley Lineker.* Code in Context. *About 272 pp.*

Bernstein, Basil. Class, Codes and Control. *3 volumes.*
1. *Theoretical Studies Towards a Sociology of Language. 254 pp.*
2. *Applied Studies Towards a Sociology of Language. 377 pp.*
● 3. *Towards a Theory of Educatiomal Transmission. 167 pp.*

Brandis, W., and **Bernstein, B.** Selection and Control. *176 pp.*

Brandis, Walter, and **Henderson, Dorothy.** Social Class, Language and Communication. *288 pp.*

Cook-Gumperz, Jenny. Social Control and Socialization. *A Study of Class Differences in the Language of Maternal Control. 290 pp.*

● **Gahagan, D. M.,** and **G. A.** Talk Reform. *Exploration in Language for Infant School Children. 160 pp.*

Hawkins, P. R. Social Class, the Nominal Group and Verbal Strategies. *About 220 pp.*

Robinson, W. P., and **Rackstraw, Susan D. A.** A Question of Answers. *2 volumes. 192 pp. and 180 pp.*

Turner, Geoffrey J., and **Mohan, Bernard A.** A Linguistic Description and Computer Programme for Children's Speech. *208 pp.*

Reports of the Institute of Community Studies

● **Cartwright, Ann.** Parents and Family Planning Services. *306 pp.*
Patients and their Doctors. *A Study of General Practice. 304 pp.*

Dench, Geoff. Maltese in London. *A Case-study in the Erosion of Ethnic Consciousness. 302 pp.*

● **Jackson, Brian.** Streaming: *an Education System in Miniature. 168 pp.*

Jackson, Brian, and **Marsden, Dennis.** Education and the Working Class: *Some General Themes raised by a Study of 88 Working-class Children in a Northern Industrial City. 268 pp. 2 folders.*

Marris, Peter. The Experience of Higher Education. *232 pp. 27 tables.*
Loss and Change. *192 pp.*

Marris, Peter, and **Rein, Martin.** Dilemmas of Social Reform. *Poverty and Community Action in the United States. 256 pp.*

Marris, Peter, and **Somerset, Anthony.** African Businessmen. *A Study of Entrepreneurship and Development in Kenya. 256 pp.*

Mills, Richard. Young Outsiders: *a Study in Alternative Communities. 216 pp.*

Runciman, W. G. Relative Deprivation and Social Justice. *A Study of Attitudes to Social Inequality in Twentieth-Century England. 352 pp.*

Willmott, Peter. Adolescent Boys in East London. *230 pp.*

Willmott, Peter, and **Young, Michael.** Family and Class in a London Suburb. *202 pp. 47 tables.*

Young, Michael. Innovation and Research in Education. *192 pp.*

●**Young, Michael,** and **McGeeney, Patrick.** Learning Begins at Home. *A Study of a Junior School and its Parents. 128 pp.*

Young, Michael, and **Willmott, Peter.** Family and Kinship in East London. *Foreword by Richard M. Titmuss. 252 pp. 39 tables.*

The Symmetrical Family. *410 pp.*

Reports of the Institute for Social Studies in Medical Care

Cartwright, Ann, Hockey, Lisbeth, and **Anderson, John L.** Life Before Death. *310 pp.*

Dunnell, Karen, and **Cartwright, Ann.** Medicine Takers, Prescribers and Hoarders. *190 pp.*

Medicine, Illness and Society

General Editor W. M. Williams

Robinson, David. The Process of Becoming Ill. *142 pp.*

Stacey, Margaret, *et al.* Hospitals, Children and Their Families. *The Report of a Pilot Study. 202 pp.*

Stimson, G. V., and **Webb, B.** Going to See the Doctor. *The Consultation Process in General Practice. 155 pp.*

Monographs in Social Theory

General Editor Arthur Brittan

●**Barnes, B.** Scientific Knowledge and Sociological Theory. *192 pp.*

Bauman, Zygmunt. Culture as Praxis. *204 pp.*

●**Dixon, Keith.** Sociological Theory. *Pretence and Possibility. 142 pp.*

Meltzer, B. N., Petras, J. W., and **Reynolds, L. T.** Symbolic Interactionism. *Genesis, Varieties and Criticisms. 144 pp.*

●**Smith, Anthony D.** The Concept of Social Change. *A Critique of the Functionalist Theory of Social Change. 208 pp.*

Routledge Social Science Journals

The British Journal of Sociology. *Editor – Angus Stewart; Associate Editor – Leslie Sklair. Vol. 1, No. 1 – March 1950 and Quarterly. Roy. 8vo. All back issues available. An international journal publishing original papers in the field of sociology and related areas.*

Community Work. *Edited by David Jones and Marjorie Mayo. 1973. Published annually.*

Economy and Society. *Vol. 1, No. 1. February 1972 and Quarterly. Metric Roy. 8vo. A journal for all social scientists covering sociology, philosophy, anthropology, economics and history. All back numbers available.*

Religion. Journal of Religion and Religions. *Chairman of Editorial Board, Ninian Smart. Vol. 1, No. 1, Spring 1971. A journal with an interdisciplinary approach to the study of the phenomena of religion. All back numbers available.*

Year Book of Social Policy in Britain, The. *Edited by Kathleen Jones. 1971. Published annually.*

Social and Psychological Aspects of Medical Practice

Editor Trevor Silverstone

Lader, Malcolm. Psychophysiology of Mental Illness. *280 pp.*

● **Silverstone, Trevor,** and **Turner, Paul.** Drug Treatment in Psychiatry. *232 pp.*

Printed in Great Britain by
Lowe & Brydone Printers Limited, Thetford, Norfolk